Ophelia's Moms Speak–In Their Own Words

"The pastel glow drained from Manju's face, leaving the dark pallor of mistrust. For the first time in her life, she screamed at us. 'You used to be my friends.' She paused before delivering the next salvo. 'You've turned into *PARENTS*.' I had betrayed her without warning. For twelve years, I had reasoned with Manju. I discussed options. I gave advice. I listened. I didn't dictate rules. I never acted like a *parent*. Suddenly, I changed. That day she had walked through the door with a boy, a symbol of her new maturity. For the first time in her life, I didn't trust her judgment."

"Now Jamie's fourteen, nearly fifteen. She calls me her probation officer. All the little boys, they're scared to death of me. Other little girls have fewer rules. I try to plant small moral messages in her head. I hope she'll hear a little voice when she needs it."

"At the end of the session, the counselor pulled me aside and said, 'You have two options. Either you let her go, or she'll go.' I had raised Shauna to be strong. Now she was using that strength to salvage her own life, something I was unable to do at her age. I knew I had to do it another way, but I didn't know how to let her go."

"She needed a pair of shoes with a heel of sorts, so that, she said to me, her calf muscles would appear more 'defined.' While your kid is working on showing off her legs, you'll be bemoaning the force of gravity as you hope each morning that your breast doesn't get caught in your jeans zipper. This irony is not lost on me; the more beautiful your kid gets, the less young you look. And if age were really just a state of mind, you'd look even older. Trust me."

"Some days maybe I was better off being numb. At least then I didn't realize the magnitude of my problems or of my daughter's pain. I was numb until the ton of bricks fell on my head. My child wanted to kill herself. She had decided today was the day."

"She walks out of her room in a tight tank top with her midriff showing. I do a double take and rein her in: 'Where do you think you're going in that hoochy wear?' She says, 'Mom. There's nothing else in the stores.' So I take her shopping. She's right. She's absolutely right. There's nothing else. Why are we dressing our girls like whores?"

"I was obsessed with getting rid of my hot flashes. I was stirring all these estrogenic ingredients into my food processor, the magical medicinal mixer, when my fifteen-year-old bounced into the kitchen and announced, 'I've made an appointment with Family Planning: Friday at four. I'd like you to go with me. But if you won't, Josh will take me.' Her long, streaked hair flowed down her back. I had an epiphany: The witch in *Rapunzel* is my hero. That fang-toothed captor is the good guy. I'll rush right up those stairs, push her into her room, lock the door, install a doggy door for food, sit on the balcony, and cast evil spells on any big scruffy male who wants inside."

"Then I noticed the diary. Callie always left it wide open on her bed. But I never read it out of respect for her privacy. To hell with her privacy, I thought. I sat on the edge of the bed, picked up the notebook, and started reading."

"My mom's delusional. Having seven kids lobotomized her. We ask her about our adolescence. Her voice goes all high-pitched and dreamy. She says, 'You were all good all the time.' Discipline? Forget it. I was a whoopee/I'm outta here/later, baby kind of teenager. My sister got pregnant at nineteen. I got pregnant at twenty. But my mom keeps saying, 'No problems, you were good girls.' Shelley, my daughter, asks me about my adolescence. I say, 'Let's ask Grandma.'"

"The sight of the affection between me and Shirlene throws my husband into a paranoid state. He attacks, starts mocking me, pointing to his chest then to me, and obsessively repeats, 'Bad parent. Good parent.' Later I bring up the fight. I confess, 'I'm still so angry.' Robert nods. 'Yeah, Shirlene was so outrageous.' I tell him, 'No. It's not Shirlene. It's your behavior I'm angry about.' So I've made three rules: No hostility. No insults. No generalizations. Trouble is, all three rules apply to both my husband and my daughter."

"When both girls were still at home, I felt trapped in an 'I love you both equally, just differently' quagmire."

"Mya hitting adolescence was like the divorce. It hurt. I couldn't say anything right. Expressing affection was like loading her gun. She aimed it straight at my heart. The rejection. The losing her. It was like losing my husband all over again."

"At fifteen, you are still quiet, especially for a teenager. Once you locked yourself up, you swallowed the key I forged for you. And I am ashamed. And you are still far too silent."

"In your letter, the one you did not write to me, you told me you felt as though you'd been abandoned when I moved. You said that phone calls, cards, and e-mails weren't the same as hugging your mom good night. You said there were times like when you went to the prom last year that you weren't sure what kind of bra to wear with the dress, and you couldn't ask your dad about it. In the letter you didn't write, you let me know that you miss me and love me just as I miss and love you."

"I was the mom who was there for everything: swim practice, swim meets, lacrosse games, school dances, school functions, carpooling, birthday parties, making cookies, shopping for everything, knowing everything. I remember lying with her on her bedroom floor while she went through her yearbook, telling me every girl's name. I loved it. I was living my teenage years again. Now I'm back to being an adult overnight."

Ophelia's Mom

Also by Nina Shandler

Estrogen the Natural Way

Ophelia's Mom

women speak out about loving and letting go of their adolescent daughters

Nina Shandler, ED.D.

foreword by Sara Shandler,
author of *Ophelia Speaks*

 CROWN PUBLISHERS ~ NEW YORK

To my daughters:

MANJU,

*who transforms everything she touches
into a completely unique work of art,
and* **SARA**,
*whose great talent is the intelligence
of her emotions.*

℮∼

Love you so much.

Copyright © 2001 by Nina Shandler
Foreword copyright © 2001 by Sara Shandler

Published by Crown Publishers, New York, New York.
Member of The Crown Publishing Group.

Random House, Inc.
New York, Toronto, London, Sydney, Auckland
www.randomhouse.com

Crown is a trademark and the Crown colophon is a registered trademark of
Random House, Inc.

Printed in the United States of America

DESIGN BY BARBARA STURMAN

Library of Congress Cataloging-in-Publication Data
Shandler, Nina.
    Ophelia's mom : women speak out about loving and letting go of their adolescent
daughters / by Nina Shandler ; with a foreword by Sara Shandler.—1st ed.
      p. cm.
    1. Parent and teenager. 2. Mothers and daughters. 3. Mothers—Psychology.
4. Teenage girls—Family relationships. I. Title.
HQ799.15.S53   2001
306.874'3—dc21   2001028955

ISBN 0-609-60886-X

10 9 8 7 6 5 4 3 2 1

First Edition

acknowledgments

THE CREATIVE INFLUENCE of Betsy Rapoport, my editor at The Crown Publishing Group, is invisibly embossed on every page of *Ophelia's Mom*. From cover to cover, she imprinted affection, enthusiasm, and craftsmanship. Without Betsy, gaping holes would have been left in the portrait of *Ophelia's Mom*. With uncompromising standards and perfectly timed humor, she coached and coaxed me, enabling me to move with ease through my multiple roles: psychologist, mom, storyteller, and host. I could not be more appreciative.

Before Betsy and I could give *Ophelia's Mom* its final shape, mothers of adolescent girls gave the book its substance. My debt extends to every woman who wrote or spoke to me. Each made an impression on *Ophelia's Mom*. Many wished to remain anonymous or to appear in disguise. Others, the women on this page, felt comfortable receiving my thanks in public.

Mary Bernstein
Sande Boritz Berger
Felicia Blasi
Monica Breen
Meryl H. Brownstein
Sandra K. Carter
Denise Crumrine
Gerry Rita DiGesu
Wendy Elliot
Vicki Elson
Marianne Peel
    Forman
Jean L. French
Ellen Furnari
Debbie Gaffney

Theresa Henderson
    Gilstad
Lynda Garner
    Goldstein
Veronica Golos
Parvati Grais
Karen Margulies
    Green
Janis Greve
Nancy J. Hamel
Catherine Hellmann
Char Hogan
Maureen A.
    Humpage
Pamela Jeffreys

Roberta Jones
Cynthia Peel Knight
Peggy F. Kurtz
Remi Beth Langum
Stephanie Large
Carolyn J. Lewis
Susan K. Lutz
Theresa L. Marney
Jan Schmitz Mathew
Jean L. McGroarty
Lisa Pack Miller
Jill C. Morris
Rhonda Morton
Sandra Moulton
Sarena Neyman

Stephanie B. Palladino

Gail Parker

Connie J. Petersen

Judy Pohl

Patricia Nickens Raglin

Monique Rider

Jinny Savolainen

Riki Schneyer

Gail Seligson

Karilee Halo Shames

Pat L. Shuter

Maryann Siebert

Karen Tate

Janice Marin Tramontano

Jan E. Tymorek

Barbara Weinberg

Allana Charise Williams

Among the many women who generously tell their stories in *Ophelia's Mom*, Karen Tate and Monique Rider are especially devoted. Over and over, Karen voiced her willingness to speak with and support other mothers whose daughters have suffered from trauma. Monique Rider expressed the same generosity toward mothers dealing with their daughters' psychological complexities.

I owe a special debt to Pat Schneider, a fine poet and director of Amherst Writers and Artists. Pat is an extraordinary mentor to women writers. She extended her generous spirit to me. She responded warmly to a cold call in the middle of winter. She put me in touch with Tanyss Rhea Martula, Diane Mercier, Renee Schultz, Gene Zeiger, and Stephanie Palladino, women who enabled me to define the scope and purpose of *Ophelia's Mom*.

More heartfelt gratitude goes to women who have provided help and encouragement along the way. Barbara Weinberg and Susan Davis founded Pachamama, a much-needed project designed to support mothers of adolescent girls. Inspired by my daughter's book, *Ophelia Speaks*, Barbara and Susan intended to compile their own anthology. When they learned about *Ophelia's Mom*, they contacted me and, with pure selflessness, channeled women in my direction. Now their interest has turned toward finding out what women are doing, personally and/or as groups, to stay connected with adolescent daughters. Pachamama (PO Box 421, Leverett, MA 01054) is being transformed into a wonderful collecting place for answers. Barbara, a woman of transparent empathy, leads support groups for mothers of adolescent girls. Along with Barbara, Susan brings her great spiritual strength to their new endeavor, Girls' Day— regular events for "girls of all ages: eight to eighty."

Diana Ott has offered her own special form of support to mothers. Diana, a wonderful writer, created a website, opheliasmother.com, giving mothers an opportunity to share their stories on-line. She offered her kindness and honesty as I gathered stories for *Ophelia's Mom*.

Other women who encouraged mothers to be in touch with me include Kathy Dunn (who leads writers' workshops in Amherst, Massachusetts), Susan Forester and Elizabeth Barg (of the Central California Women's Conference), and the NOW net of Florida.

Transforming a manuscript into a book requires a team. The Crown Publishing Group (a division of Random House) devoted themselves to that transformation with unfaltering professionalism. Stephanie Higgs watched carefully to make certain nothing fell through the cracks. Cindy Berman kept her eye on the big picture, ensuring that the entire process proceeded smoothly. Beth Thomas made certain every sentence flowed with perfect punctuation, word use, and meaning. Katherine Beitner skillfully turned the spotlight on *Ophelia's Mom*. I know this book is going to press before I've met all the Crown people to whom I will owe a debt. I'm sorry those names are missing from these acknowledgments.

A cadre of colleagues, friends, and family have steadied my course during the creation of *Ophelia's Mom*. I am, as always, grateful to Philip, Gabrielle, and Sathya Gosselin, and to Margaret, whose infectious joy lives on, Martin and Melly Bock, Jinny and Jamie Elkin, Mary and Herb Bernstein, Joyce Duncan and Sam Gladstone, Jeffrey and Robin Kassis, Parvati Grais and Cory Greenberg, Jack Rosenblum and Corinne Dugas, Vicki and Barry Elson, Rob and Joan Brandt, Sandy Wyner, Laurie Pearlman and Ervin Staub, Ann Berliner, Agnes Birnbaum of Bleecker Street Associates, Jonathan Souweine, and my mother-in-law, Fritzie Fuchs, who has bequeathed the indomitable spirit of the survivor to my daughters.

Working on *Ophelia's Mom* has given me new appreciation for the trials that I inflicted on my own parents. I once looked at my dad and announced, "I was an easy teenager." He stared back in utter disbelief. *"YOU?* You were *THE WORST."* In a flash, I recollected my social activism and my hippie life. I had to admit it. "I was. I was the worst." My poor mom.

My own daughters, Manju and Sara, were not, like me, *THE WORST*. Each traveled through adolescence repeatedly reassuring me, "Mom. Don't worry. I'm a good kid." Now, they're no longer kids. They've grown into loving and accomplished young women. In the summer of 2001, Manju married Stephen Estrin, my son-in-law, a calming influence with a twinkling sense of humor. Sara has begun her senior year at Wesleyan University. In *Ophelia's Mom*, Manju and Sara have allowed me to look back and open the door on their adolescence. Throughout this sometimes worrisome work, my daughters have unwaveringly nurtured and encouraged me. I owe them a tremendous debt.

Finally, my great gratitude goes to my husband, Michael. Thirty years of marriage has done nothing but strengthen my appreciation for him. He has given me the self-confidence and the fortitude to pursue my own path without compromise. Every day and every word of *Ophelia's Mom* has been saturated with his loving attention.

contents

FOREWORD BY SARA SHANDLER ~ xiii

Introduction ~ 1

Backstage Moms ~ 13

A Supporting Role ~ 14

In the Wings ~ 16

part one
Into Adolescent Territory ~ 27

Blood and Tears ~ 28

Mirror Images: Hormones, Body Shapes, and
    Skin Conditions ~ 39

Frozen Affections ~ 49

Passing Storms ~ 59

Limits of Power ~ 71

part two
Disarmed Bodyguards ~ 87

The Culture of School ~ 88

The Influence of Friends ~ 100

The Quest for Love ~ 116

Sex: The Carnal Consequences ~ 123

The Lure of Intoxication: Alcohol and Drugs ~ 142

The Edges of Emotion: Depression and
    Eating Disorders ~ 161

Minding the Body: Illness and Disease ~ 179

part three
Tied in Family Knots ~ 193

Fathers and Husbands ~ 195

Daughters and Sisters ~ 209

Broken Homes ~ 222

Legacies: From Generation to Generation ~ 240

part four
Transitions and Transformations ~ 251

Holding On to Values ~ 253

Pushed into Self-discovery ~ 267

Into the Limelight ~ 281

On to a New Stage ~ 282

RESOURCES FOR MOTHERS OF ADOLESCENT GIRLS ~ 286

foreword

CHRISTMAS MORNING, 1999: I slowly lumbered out of bed and down-stairs. Even at nineteen years old, the prospect of presents was enough to wake me before nine A.M. I found my pajama-clad parents in the family room drinking tea. I collapsed on one end of the couch; my mom sa at the other, bright-eyed despite the hour. Our toes touched. I yawned and mumbled, "I forgot to tell you guys—my book's back on the list this week."

I meant *The New York Times* best-seller list.

My parents looked at me with pride. The success of *Ophelia Speaks* still amazed them.

And my nonchalance drove them crazy. I have to admit that six months earlier, it had also been a big deal to me. I was thrilled when *Ophelia Speaks* debuted at number nine on the *Times* list. When my editor broke the news to me in California at seven P.M., I woke Mom and Dad up at three A.M., London time, to tell them.

And while making it in publishing big-time had been a blessing, it hadn't changed my life. By December, I was back to my real life, recovering from finals and ready to open presents.

My dad congratulated me on the book's return to the best-seller list. My mom pulled her legs to her chest, seemingly self-conscious. Nervously, she looked at my dad, then at me. Fidgeting, she stumbled into a confession. "Sara, I woke up at five this morning with a book idea. But, sweetie, really . . . I won't do it if it makes you uncomfortable in any way."

I looked at her, waiting. I beckoned impatiently with my hand. "Tell already."

She blurted out her predawn brainstorm. "I'd like to do a book telling the mother's side of the Ophelia story."

I sat still as she went on. "Every adolescent girl has a mom who needs support."

It was true. I had received more than a few e-mails from readers of my book with the subject heading "Your Mom." They thanked me for helping them to better understand their daughters, but more important, they asked me how my mom had survived me.

It was a reasonable question.

At thirteen, my best girlfriends and I had sat knee to knee in my back-yard smoking pot, trying to get our first high. We chose my house because we were pretty sure my parents didn't know, or just didn't care, if we tried dope. Sure, my parents had talked to me about drugs. They'd made me promise to stay away from cocaine and heroin and told me again and again of the '60s slogan "Speed Kills." But they were also real-istic about my trying pot: My mom spent more time trying to convince me not to get high and drive with other friends than trying to keep me from getting high at all. So instead of smoking in the graveyard by the high school like everyone else, my friends and I did it in the safety of my own backyard. After our secretive smoking session, my mom found us in the kitchen making waffles at two in the morning. With little idea that we were satisfying our marijuana-induced munchies, she kissed each of our foreheads and went back to bed. I don't know when or whether she caught on to my experimentation, how much she worried about it, or if she simply trusted me not to go too far with it.

Two years later I bopped into that same kitchen and calmly and unself-consciously told my mom that I had made an appointment to go to Family Planning the next day, and if she didn't want to take me to get birth-control pills, my then-boyfriend would. Ironically, I wasn't old enough to drive myself. She sighed and asked me what time we should leave. And while my friends asked me, "How did you ever get the nerve to talk to your mom about sex?," it never really occurred to me that it was harder for my mom to say "yes" than it was for me to ask.

The next year, when that same boyfriend left for college, I filled my time with studying hard enough to get straight As, working out, and polishing my image as the perfect girl. Without any conscious effort, I dropped almost twenty pounds off my already petite frame—oddly, it wasn't until after I had lost all that weight that I became overly concerned with my body image. I knew my mom worried that I put too much pres-sure on myself, but I was more concerned with getting into the best col-lege and maintaining my new size-two body than with how my stress was stressing her. Only much later did I realize how hard it must have been for her to see me run myself ragged, yet feel powerless to help me.

Although both my parents had warned me to take it easy on myself, I didn't heed their advice until after I'd made myself sick enough to go to the emergency room. In the fall of my senior year in high school, I missed two weeks of school because of a mysteriously inflamed stomach lining. My mom made me baby bottles of ginger ale (so I could drink lying down) and Japanese pickled plum soup to help with my nausea. She massaged my head and brought home armfuls of videos for us to watch together while I recovered.

While I was periodically capable of showing gratitude to my mom, those times were relatively few and far between. Like most teenagers, I was almost completely focused on my own problem; I didn't think my parents were terribly clued in to my world, anyway. In truth, my mom often knew much more than I thought she did. (Only after I left for college did she admit that she suspected my boyfriend had sometimes spent the night.) But in my own self-absorption, I had failed to see that my mom could still see me, that she was always in the background waiting to help me.

I never gave much thought to what my own teenage life meant to my mom, or whether anyone was helping her deal with it. It must have taken a lot out of her to take me to get birth control, deal with my self-imposed academic pressure, and nurse my emaciated body back to health. She was certainly always there to support me, but it never occurred to me to wonder who was supporting her.

My experience with my own book has given me much more insight into what the mothers of teen girls go through. At every book signing I've done, mothers and daughters come together. Holding proudly on to their easily embarrassed daughters, mothers ask me what they could do to make this time easier on their daughters . . . and when could they expect it to end? The other mothers in the audience laugh and nod their heads, sharing an obvious bond. At the end of each signing, I often write a similar message on the front page of my book for both daughters and mothers: "It gets better . . . I promise."

That Christmas morning, I knew my mom was right; mothers of teen girls need a book of their own. Looking at her, I smiled and said, "It's a great idea. You're a psychologist and you're my mom. It's perfect."

Throughout my childhood I'd seen how empathetically she'd counseled girls and families in distress. As a psychologist in my elementary school, she proudly called all the troubled ones, even those seriously prone to classroom fits and lunchroom brawls, her "kids"; they were nice to me because they loved my mom. And after getting to the other side of adolescence, I finally realized what she'd gone through raising me and my sister Manju, and gained enough insight to realize that we weren't always particularly easy to raise. Mom says we were always "great," but I know better than that.

Feigning celebrity attitude, I mischievously added, "Besides, reporters always ask me about you."

She looked at me through "I love you so much" tears, and I understood her self-consciousness. She worried then, as I know she still does, that she'd be piggybacking on my success in some way. What she's never fully understood through her motherly selflessness is that *Ophelia Speaks* never would have come to fruition without her.

She encouraged my grandiose seventeen-year-old's plans as only a mother would. We had lunch "meetings" at my favorite restaurants, she helped me organize my time as well as my thoughts, and even stuffed envelopes and licked stamps (thousands!) while I went off to my senior prom. She edited almost every word I wrote and expected nothing in return. At the time, dedicating my book to my mom and dad seemed the best I could do to thank them. If my blessing for her book could be an adequate thank-you, I'd give it a thousand times over.

Over the last year and a half, I've watched my mom write her book. When she finished, she brought the manuscript to me at school, every page that mentioned me tagged with little blue stickies; she wanted to make sure I was okay with everything she wrote. And, while I wasn't always crazy about everything I'd done at fourteen or sixteen, or how I made her feel (I'm downright embarrassed . . .), I now see that being an Ophelia is not a solitary experience: Our moms need a place to speak and to be heard, too. *Ophelia's Mom* is a book every good mother deserves. I just wish my mom had had a similar book to lend her support during my own adolescence.

SARA SHANDLER
April 2001

introduction

THAT CHRISTMAS MORNING IN 1999, WHEN SARA GAVE ME permission to follow in her footsteps, I didn't know how hard it would be to fill her shoes. I had not envisioned how complex it would be to create *Ophelia's Mom.*

It started, of course, with *being* Ophelia's mom.

I had lain in bed, remembering the days when my daughters, Manju and Sara, awoke at dawn mobilized by an irrepressible desire to discover what Santa Claus had deposited under the tree. Visions of them as little girls gave way to memories of their more challenging teenage years.

Manju, with the spirit of an artist, was made vulnerable by her own creative impulses. As a teenager, my older daughter could not find her place in the center of the social scene. Searching on the fringes, she counseled troubled companions. I worried, "How can my daughter stay whole while she nurtures such fragmented souls?" But she did. She came through her adolescence, strong and sure, with an announcement: "I don't apologize for my self-confidence. I worked really hard to get it." This morning, as the horizon began to glow with morning light, I realized that Manju, a twenty-six-year-old woman, had found her place. In New York she had become the rarest of artists— one who makes a living through her talent. Now she slept in the next room with Stephen, her calmly secure partner.

As a teenager, Sara, my younger child, had looked so normal, so good, so much at the center of the "best and the brightest." Yet underneath the polish, she had ached. Literally ached. Sometimes she actually doubled over in pain. The emotional throbbing in her stomach causing involuntary tears. Was it the pressure of keeping the facade perfectly shined? The pull and tug of too many people to please? Teachers to be smart for. Boys to be beautiful for. Friends to be cool for. Parents to be good for. Underneath it all, the soft heart of a girl who confessed, "Mom, I'm so much like you it's scary. All I really want is to love and be settled." That morning Sara, too, had found her strength, comfortably ensconced in her college life.

Lying awake, I remembered other nights. I'd sat in the dark alone, curled into a ball, feeling the panic of not knowing how to protect my daughters or how to let them go. During those oppressive times, I wished for an all-seeing friend and a soothing voice. I wanted my muffled sobs to burst into cathartic wails. I wanted to talk out loud, on and on and on, telling every detail of my daughter-driven story. And I wanted my imaginary friend to return the self-disclosure, to speak of her own angst, to take me step by step into her confidence. I imagined arriving at relief, finding reassurance, and rediscovering laughter. But at three o'clock in the morning, I had whispered my deep secrets to no one.

I looked back and realized my daughters' adolescence had changed me. I saw myself as a woman in the process of being remade. I had not expected the convulsions that reverberated through my identity when my daughters left home.

I had always thought of myself as a woman in balance—a licensed psychologist and a mother/wife—neither too distant nor too close to my daughters. I had no idea how much of me was bound to being their mother, to being needed.

For the first time since my daughters were born, I was free to go where I wanted to go and do what I wanted to do. And I had no idea.

As I pondered my empty nest, visions of other mothers—women I had counseled professionally and known personally—joined the pre-dawn parade through my mind. I recalled conversation after conversation about the universal dance of mothers and daughters and recognized the obvious. While our daughters are swept up in their hormonally propelled roller-coaster ride through adolescence, we mothers are thrust into our own cataclysms. Guilt, mother-love, and approaching menopause spin us around by our apron strings. I knew without doubt that nearly every mother struggles to keep her footing as she guides her daughter through the rugged terrain of adolescence. Yet mothers receive little support.

Not so for adolescent girls. Mary Pipher's book *Reviving Ophelia* had opened the door on their world and offered them nonjudgmental warmth. My daughter Sara, reading that book, made it her mission to give those girls their own voice. In collecting and printing their words, Sara's book, *Ophelia Speaks*, invited girls into a sisterhood of honesty and acceptance.

Girls wrote to Sara from across the United States, but only a few contributions bubbled with youthful humor. Most were burdened confessions about dark and difficult times. Sara resolved to expose her own soul-threatening crisis. She warned me, "Mom, I have to be as honest as I'm asking them to be." As she introduced each section of her book, she confessed her struggles with depression, self-judgment, broken relationships, the pressures of friendship, and the stress of school. She talked about her temptations: eating disorders, alcohol, drugs.

Sara had told the truth, and in so doing, she had outed me. I was no longer the perfect mother who had reared two perfect young women. The veneer had been cracked. Everyone now knew that Sara hadn't followed a rose-strewn path through a charmed adolescence. She had suffered. With the myth of my unerringly high-functioning daughters dispelled, I felt exposed but also freed. As other mothers spoke with me, I knew I wasn't alone.

Then it dawned on me. Now, with both my daughters launched, I could drum up a chorus of support for mothers. I could do for mothers what Sara's book had done for adolescent girls. I was inspired to write the book I most wanted as a companion—a reassuring book steeped in empathy.

No such book existed. I had scoured the bookshelves. Certainly there were how-to books for mothers of adolescent girls, books that dispensed solid advice. Too often these manuals were tinged with a message: "Mother: You're doing it wrong." Of course I had a library of psychological treatises designed to fix the scarring behaviors of mothers toward their daughters. But books to soothe mothers with an empathetic touch? None.

A few hours later, on Christmas morning, I confessed my desire to my daughter. Sara gave me what a mother never expects to receive from her own daughter: a professional purpose. My newborn project, *Ophelia's Mom*, was timed perfectly to relieve my midlife labor pains.

This project would be so simple, so straightforward. After all, I had played secretary to Sara's vision. She was the genius and I was the envelope stuffer for *Ophelia Speaks*. I saw how she sent out invitations to nearly seven thousand school principals, psychologists, English teachers, and clergy. Before she came home from school, I retrieved the contributions that were packed into our family mailbox. I counted them. Over eight hundred. I watched her read, and soul-search, and choose, and write, and construct a gift that broke through the loneliness of other girls. Now I was ready to do the same for their mothers.

But creating *Ophelia's Mom* turned out to be neither simple nor straightforward.

I began as Sara had begun. I contacted women, mothers of adolescent girls.

The ball had not yet dropped on the new millennium when I started collecting stories and thoughts from mothers of adolescent girls. I realized immediately that to gather a rich sample of experience, I needed to give women a choice of writing or being interviewed.

To test the waters, I encouraged friends and friends of friends to write or talk about their daughter-driven challenges. My invitations brought a nearly universal response: "Who has time to write? Give me a call."

Few mothers sit for hours capturing the scenes of their lives on paper and polishing words until they shine in meticulous detail. Unlike adolescent girls, many women tend to shy away from the self-absorption required to write. Instead, women turn to conversation. We're inclined to find intimacy in dialogue. This was my first clue to how much women need to bond over the experience of motherhood, to create a sense of community, and to banish the loneliness and the solitariness of writing about it.

Some women do find that sense of community on the written page. They join writers' groups where they can share their passion for the written word and an intimate connection to one another's experience. I contacted Pat Schneider, founder of Amherst Writers & Artists. Pat, kind and wise mentor, gave me the names of eight women writers. Immediately, they sent their fine work.

The snow was still falling in New England when I set my sights on a voluminous goal: to distribute an invitation to twenty thousand women. I set the number higher than Sara's, anticipating greater difficulty in reaching women. Adolescents have a universal gathering place: school. Adults disperse into a multitude of environments for work and play and are inundated with solicitations for many valuable projects. All mail and e-mail from unknown sources becomes junk mail. How could I make sure my request would speak to them?

The invitation I ultimately distributed read:

An Invitation to Mothers of Adolescent Girls

When adolescence takes possession of our daughters, we, their mothers, find ourselves in alien territory. Our familiar mother/daughter bond is banished. Daily life swerves in unpredictable directions. We careen from emotion to emotion: confusion, laughter, hurt, relief, despair, hope. Still, the mothers' side of the Ophelia saga is seldom told.

An unspoken heritage pressures mothers to remain silent. In *Hamlet,* Ophelia's mother has no part. In our youth-obsessed culture, a bittersweet limelight focuses on our daughters, while we fade in their shadow. *Ophelia's Mom* is an opportunity for mothers to emerge from backstage, to dispel a silence that keeps us feeling alone.

I'd love to receive your thoughts, stories, or interview requests.

Written Contributions   Please see *Ophelia's Mom* as an opportunity to talk to other mothers about your own journey through your daughter's adolescence. Don't worry about spelling or grammar or style. Just dive into your experience and write honestly. Feel free to be funny or sad, angry or ashamed, worried or relieved, uplifted or grief-stricken. Drop me a line or send me ten pages. Focus on any topic that sheds light on your daughter-driven challenges: Separation, Rejection, Discipline, Intimacy, Independence, Aging, Eating Disorders, Menopause, Menstruation, New Meanings and Purposes, Feminism, Girl Power, Racism, Classism, Bigotry, Homophobia, Your Husband/Her Father, Your Children/Her Brothers and Sisters, Your Parents/Her Grandparents, Divorce, Death, Friends, Boyfriends, Love, Sex, Work, School, Alcohol, Drugs, Good Fun, Spirit, Mind, the Mother/Daughter Bond.

Interview Requests   Many of us are most comfortable talking over a cup of coffee, or on the phone, or even chatting on-line. If you'd rather have a conversation, please send me your name (or pen name), your e-mail address, telephone number, and home address. In a few informal sentences, tell me what you'd like to talk about and describe yourself.

NINA SHANDLER

I purposefully designed this invitation to attract a broad participation and spectrum of experience. Over and over, I had listened to the grocery-store critique of Mary Pipher's *Reviving Ophelia* and even Sara's *Ophelia Speaks*. I heard women tell one another, "Those books are skewed toward the abnormal. Most girls just aren't like *that*." On closer scrutiny, I had to admit that the grocery-store analysis held water.

Mary Pipher is, like me, a psychologist. By definition, the girls we encounter endure greater emotional pain than the norm. Some critics had contended that the invitation to participate in *Ophelia Speaks* encouraged girls to focus on the burdensome aspects of their adolescence. I hoped that by distributing an expansively worded invitation, *Ophelia's Mom* would unlock the parallel passage that reshapes the lives of adolescents' mothers while avoiding any sense of an exclusive focus on the dark and the dramatic.

I stepped into the World Wide Web and found myself knee-deep in a tangle of incomprehensible jargon. Fortunately, a sweet young man at Verio, my web-hosting service, beckoned me to take one baby step at a time. "Nina. You can do this." Fueled by that nurturing cheerleader's enthusiasm, this computerphobic woman designed a website, opheliasmom.com.

With my website on-line, I began dropping invitations all over cyberspace. I sent messages to leaders of several hundred writers' groups; several thousand churches and synagogues; dozens of on-line women's chat rooms, e-lists, and e-journals; every chapter of NOW (National Organization for Women) with an e-mail address; every website that appeared when I plugged in the keywords "women," "adolescence," "mothers," "psychologists," "family therapists," or any other relevant word that came to mind. My index finger hit the send icon on my keyboard for three weeks, ten hours a day. By the end that finger was numb, and the glow of the computer screen had imprinted itself on the back of my closed eyelids. I figured I'd sent out roughly four thousand e-mails.

Next I reverted to paper and print, pamphlets and envelopes: six thousand sent to approximately one hundred writers' workshops and women's conferences, three thousand to a random sample of psychologists in all fifty states. Finally, I sent out an invitation in the form of a press release, guaranteed to reach ten thousand journalists who write about women's issues and parental concerns.

By the time this phase was complete, I had distributed approximately twenty-three thousand invitations to a diverse geographical, cultural, and racial population.

Given Sara's experience, I expected an immediate flood of enthusiastic responses. Instead, I got a slow, steady stream. The total count of contributions (thoughts, stories, and interviews) numbered approximately three hundred and fifty—a much smaller response from a far greater number of invites. Why the relative silence? I'd heard anguished conversations from clients and friends, and I didn't believe that women weren't interested in the topic. I supposed that time constraints—jobs, children, aging parents—kept many women from allowing themselves the time to provide thoughtful responses. However, I suspect there's much more going on than that.

I believe that chiefly three pressures—the protective instinct, ageism, and guilt—conspire to keep mothers silent as their daughters pass through adolescence. Instinctually, mothers do everything within their power to shield their daughters from pain. Culturally, mothers are expected to fade into the background when daughters bloom. Psychologically, mothers are expected to absorb the shame for their daughters' emotional distress.

Mothers who did break the taboo of silence did so carefully. Most contributions began with thoughtful inquiries. Women carefully tested my sincerity, hesitant to trust me without making personal contact. Nearly all were wary of public scrutiny. While the idea of reaching out to other women attracted these mothers, they wanted assurances that I wouldn't expose them or their daughters to blame or shame. I believe that my being Sara's mother, unmasked as the parent of a struggling teen, gave these women more confidence that I would understand their own challenges; I was one of them.

In the end, 55 percent of the contributions to *Ophelia's Mom* appear with the names and identifying details disguised. Out of respect for contributors' privacy concerns and to guard against discovery of actual identities, I have not indicated which are disguised and which are not.

Just over half of the contributions grew out of my conversations with women. We talked, always for at least an hour, sometimes for two or three. As we spoke, most mothers became more and more comfortable, willing to be totally honest, to confide their closely held feelings, to admit their insecurities, fears, anxieties, frustrations, hopes, and beliefs. By the end of our time together, I had seen into their lives. They had told me stories so familiar they could have been my own. The communication invariably brought empathy. Often it brought a sigh of relief. After we talked, a mother wrote: "I found myself feeling hopeful and blessed. I began to realize that every time my daughters seemed to be at the edge of an abyss and I was beginning to lose hope, something miraculously and unpredictably shifted. They ended up being okay." The women who spoke for *Ophelia's Mom* hoped to bring warmth and reassurance to other mothers. All contributions based on these interviews use the words "A Story from" or "Thoughts from," as well as quotation marks to indicate conversation.

The other half came to me in writing. There are wonderful writers in these pages. Talented poets. Humorists. Narrators. Women with serious gifts that allow them to express a broad emotional range. For all written contributions, the word "by" appears before the author's name.

In total, *Ophelia's Mom* brings together one hundred and twenty-one contributions. They represent a collage of America. Thirty-three contributions come from cities, thirty-four from suburbs, another thirty-two from small to midsize towns, and a final twenty-two from rural areas. The largest number, sixty-five, originated in the Northeast, fifteen from mid-Atlantic states, ten from the South, nineteen from the Midwest, and twelve from the West Coast. These were culled from a broad range of organizations and individuals. There are contributions from the International Women's Writers' Guild, Sisters Across America (a crosscultural organization for women writers), NOW, the YWCA, the PTA, the clergy, Hadassah, Lilith, the Writer Page, Women Writers' Network, Parents Without Partners, Christian Women, the Central California Women's Conference, Pachamama, and a national sampling of psychologists, to name a very few.

Though I began my project with an inclusive invitation, I did hold a number of expectations. Reality sometimes conformed and sometimes held surprises.

Women took my lead in responding to the long list of topics I proposed in my invitation. The common theme that ran through these topics was the paradoxical challenge of motherhood: to love daughters and to let them go. Surprisingly, aging, eating disorders, menopause, racism, classism, bigotry, death, and simply having good fun with daughters were rarely, if ever, voluntarily addressed.

I was particularly taken aback by the lack of attention given to the tribulations of aging and coping with menopause. After all, we're dealing with our feelings about wrinkles and body parts flowing in a southerly direction at the exact time our daughters are blooming like roses. Only one woman voluntarily broached the topic of her daughter's body developing while hers declines. Having written about and worked with menopausal women, I had anticipated many contributions focused on that cosmic scheduling blunder: adolescence and menopause under the same roof at the same time. So many of us are buying pads and tampons for our daughters even as we're figuring out hot flashes and being revisited by the same hormonal mayhem we thought we left behind in our own adolescence. Why were women being so quiet here?

Given my experiences as a psychologist and mother of former teen daughters, I can only speculate. Mothers talked easily about their daughters beginning to menstruate, but seldom about their developing bodies. I expect this reflects a self-conscious avoidance of their own bodies' decline and a respect for daughters who are often equally self-conscious about impending sexuality. I could not settle on a plausible further explanation but felt the topic was too important not to explore: I interviewed women on this topic to create the chapter "Mirror Images: Hormones, Body Shapes, and Skin Conditions."

In her research for *Ophelia Speaks*, Sara had received more contributions about eating disorders than any other single topic. Yet for *Ophelia's Mom*, only two mothers wrote about their daughters' eating disorders. Two likely explanations account for this discrepancy: First, anorexic and bulimic girls are skillful at hiding their problem; many mothers may simply be unaware of a daughter's pain, especially since many are classically high-achieving "good" girls. Mothers may tend toward denial, focusing with pride on their daughters' accomplishments. Second, mothers may tend toward shamed silence, believing they brought on the illness through poor parenting or neglect.

Beyond specific topics, I had other expectations. Foremost among them: I had thought mothers would overflow with stories about receiving support from other women. They didn't. After months of hearing nothing about the warmth and reassurance mothers offer to one another, I began asking every woman I interviewed, "Where did you get support?"

The answers followed a strikingly similar pattern.

"Not from the women in my family. My sister loved to tell me how I had spoiled my daughter from the beginning. She'd say, 'So. What did you expect?' I couldn't tell my mother. She grew up in another century."

"Not from other mothers in my church. Lord knows, they had no compassion. They just told me I should force my daughter to come to services."

"Not from the teachers at school. I work in a school. I hear the teachers'-room talk: 'I met her parents. Well. What can I say? Now I understand why the girl has problems.' I wasn't about to subject myself to that kind of judgment."

"Not from my friends. I stopped telling my best friends about the really hard moments. Their kids seemed so normal. When I talked honestly, they looked at me with such pity. They didn't mean to, but they made me feel so ashamed of my daughter and myself. I couldn't stand it."

"I felt I had no place to turn."

"I spent a lot of time alone."

"I talked to God."

"I pounded walls."

Our generation grew up talking about everything. We spoke the unspeakable. We brought one taboo topic after another—from sex to childbirth to abortion to abuse to sexual orientation to menopause— into public discourse. Why not talk to one another about our teenage daughters?

When I stopped to ponder that question, my surprise gave way to recognition. The psychological predilection to blame the mother infiltrates even to mother-to-mother relationships. Protection of daughters fuses with protection of self. That fusion doubles the intensity of pride and shame. When our daughters excel, we mothers shamelessly boast— more than we ever would about our own successes. When our daughters stumble, we mothers hide beneath shrouds of guilt—feeling more shame than we ever do about our own missteps. Mothers hide, even from one another, hoping to escape an enmeshed tangle of pride, guilt, and blame.

While the contributors often felt unsupported, they wanted to offer support. The desire to lighten other mothers' burdens was the primary impetus for women who spoke or wrote for *Ophelia's Mom.*

This motivation explains why the majority of women wrote or spoke when their daughters were out of emotional danger. The preponderance of contributions came from mothers whose daughters were either beginning or ending their adolescent journey. Women with young teenage girls looked forward with a mixture of questions and confidence. Women with older daughters looked back with relief and renewed strength.

Still, some mothers did reach out during difficult times. They found compassion for the loneliness of other mothers, even while feeling isolated themselves.

In these pages, mothers of adolescent girls express a colorful array of emotion. Unlike the girls who wrote for *Ophelia Speaks*, mothers didn't limit themselves to serious hues. I cried and I laughed when I read their contributions. Mothers laughed and cried when they spoke with me.

When they cried, most often their tears came from feeling powerless to help their daughters. The topic might have been depression, school failure, boyfriends, social exclusion, sexual molestation, bad-news friends, or menstruation. The specific subject didn't matter. Feeling unable to protect daughters from pain unlocked mothers' tears.

In contrast, mothers who encountered the big fears—the life-threatening foursome: drugs, sex, eating disorders, and suicide—seldom cried when reflecting on those terrors. They were more likely to speak with focused attention. They did not indulge in melodrama. Instead, they resolved to find meaning in near-tragedy.

And laughter. The mothers here never found glee or schadenfreude in their daughters' troubles. Not once. Rather, they laughed with wisdom. They poked affectionate fun at transient adolescent behaviors—eye rolling, moody outbursts, passing embarrassments. They chuckled with self-effacing style at their own equally short-lived lapses of maturity. They found humor when they stepped back to observe the awkward dance between mother and daughter.

Finally, *Ophelia's Mom* is colored with optimism. Hope prevails. The book is not a parade of grim stories. The stories in these pages move through a palette of experience—humor, pathos, insight, rage, sadness, and joy—while holding to the faith that in the end, all comes 'round right.

Ophelia's Mom begins with a short section entitled "Backstage Moms." These two chapters set a welcoming tone and spotlight the place mothers find themselves in as their daughters journey through adolescence.

Part One, "Into Adolescent Territory," speaks to universal adolescent issues and a mother's parallel universe—menstruation, aging, separation, rejection, letting go.

Part Two, "Disarmed Bodyguards," addresses those areas where mothers' ability to protect daughters begins to wane during adolescence: the twin cultures of school and friends, the endless worries about love and sex; the lure of the illicit with drugs and drinking; the fears about the emotional abyss of depression and eating disorders; and every mother's worst fear—the heartbreak of illness and disease.

Part Three, "Tied in Family Knots," is devoted to the complexities of family relationships during daughters' adolescence. How do we cope with the men who are both husbands and fathers? With sibling rivalry and the challenge of rearing more than one daughter? With the pain of divorce? Or with how we've translated wanted and unwanted legacies from one generation to the next?

Part Four, "Transitions and Transformations," highlights the changes that adolescence brings to mothers, daughters, and their enduring relationship. Ultimately, both we and our daughters are pushed toward re-creation and self-discovery.

Together, the mothers who created *Ophelia's Mom* add a new act to the unfolding drama of womanhood. We emerge from backstage not to compete for our daughters' spotlight but to move on, with dignity and gentleness, to our own stage. In these pages, Ophelia's moms—women who live in rural areas, small towns, and cities—overcome a heritage of culturally imposed stage fright, play their roles with pride, and offer other women shelter from the swirling insecurities of living through a daughter's adolescence.

I just wrote the final word in *Ophelia's Mom*. I feel as if I've sewn the last contribution onto a community quilt. For over a year, I gathered thoughts and stories from mothers of adolescent daughters. My task has been to arrange these poems, letters, personal essays, and conversations, then stitch them together with a few words, every once in a while adding a story of my own. Now it's time to wrap up this collective creation and send it along with this wish: May *Ophelia's Mom* bring you warmth, reassurance, hope—and, occasionally, a laugh of recognition.

Backstage Moms

DAUGHTER MUSIC
by Marianne Peel Forman

Most near, most dear, most loved, and most far,
Standing near the piano where I seldom find her
stamping as loud as an orchestra, stubborn with rhythm
Violin and bow determined in her playground hands
Irritated as syncopation but most tender for
The eighth notes and the Baroque tune that inspires her
She is a rhythm no one can deny
Poised like a small melody wanting a finished song.

She will not turn away from the music
Or threaten to discard her instrument
And retreat to her room
But eases into the music stand, a symphony
That only she can create
And so I hide all my urging and all my love
And tell her that she will move
from silence to song.

a supporting role

AS I'VE HEARD FROM MOTHERS, I'VE BEEN AMAZED BY HOW different, yet how alike, we are. *Ophelia's Mom* brings together women who would never meet, who have almost nothing in common. From women who are politically conservative to women who are flaming liberals. From women who believe in the right to life to women who support the right to choose. From women who gave birth at seventeen to women who delayed having children until forty. From women who were stay-at-home moms to women who devoted every day to professional advancement. From women who burned their bras to women who never wore a two-piece bathing suit. From women who live in million-dollar apartments to women who can't afford a modest mortgage. From women who go to Pentecostal churches to women who subscribe to a personal spirituality. Women from every part of the country.

No matter how extreme our differences, mothers share the same struggle: to love our daughters and let them go. This contradictory challenge—to embrace our children while losing control of them—leaves us vulnerable to anxiety, self-doubt, and guilt. Yet we get little support. It's as though when our daughters make their debut as Ophelia on the stage, we're left alone behind the curtains in their shadow, soul-searching.

It's not like our generation to keep our concerns quietly locked away. We came of age during the birth of feminism and the advent of women's support groups. Still, even with our commitment to speaking the unspeakable, we tend to keep a silent watch during our daughters' adolescence.

Let's talk more about judgment, because we've all felt it. Now that we have become mothers of adolescents, fear of that judgment shrouds us in lonely silence. Our protective instinct pushes us into a guarded stance. After all, the real world is full of condemnation. Are we good mothers? Have we raised good daughters? We've heard confidences turned into gossip: "Did you know?" "Drugs." "That bad-news boyfriend." "Her grades." "Poor woman." "Poor child." "Well, something must be going on in that house." "These problems don't come from nowhere." No need to tell. No need to subject ourselves and our daughters to shame. No reason to make a passing problem into an indelible image. No point in scratching the veneer of a decent reputation. When problems become visible, daughters and mothers are indicted. When difficulties stay hidden beneath a charming facade, we and our girls escape incrimination. So why talk? Why risk disgrace?

Because by staying trapped behind walls built of pretense, we make ourselves more vulnerable to self-recrimination. We lose perspective. The normal feels abnormal. The typical feels shameful. The transitory feels everlasting. The secrets keep us lonelier than we need to be, feeling more unstable than we really are. By stepping over the threshold of privacy, by telling stories, crying and laughing at our dilemmas, we're released from self-imposed solitary confinement. We connect. We bring one another comfort.

All of the women who speak in *Ophelia's Mom* left their silent role for one purpose. Like the closest of friends, each and every one wanted to bring empathy, hope, and laughter to other mothers. We support our daughters; this book is here to support you. These stories, so generously told, reassure us: You're not alone, and you're not crazy.

in the wings

I REMEMBER HOW MY MOTHER'S GENERATION REASSURED ONE another. Her friends, her confidantes since childhood, gathered in our living room for Sewing Club. While embroidering, knitting, or mending socks, they consoled one another: "Your daughter, she's a teenager. She's just going through a stage."

That message seeped into my psyche. When my own two daughters reached adolescence, I was prepared for them to enter a stage. But I didn't know my girls were slated to play Ophelia, a motherless adolescent drowning in a Shakespearean tragedy.

This generation of girls entered puberty at the center of public attention. When Mary Pipher wrote *Reviving Ophelia*, she resurrected an archetype, a defining image for female adolescence. By gathering the voices of teenage girls in her book, *Ophelia Speaks*, my daughter Sara Shandler empowered that image with evidence. Now girls leave childhood behind and walk onto a stage where floodlights expose their vulnerabilities and the script reveals threats both old and new. While a bittersweet limelight unmasks daughters, mothers keep vigil without breathing an audible line.

In *Hamlet*, Ophelia's mother has no part. Ophelia blossoms, withers, and dies. But the woman who gave birth to her stays off that stage.

Most of us are backstage moms. We spend twelve years, more or less, preparing our daughters for adolescent stardom. Then we begin to let go. We watch from behind the scenes. Sometimes our view is obstructed. We bite our nails, and pace, and hold our breath, waiting for them to come back into sight. Other times we see more than anyone else. We're privy to the offstage costume changes, the bursting in and out of many-faceted characters, the backstage tantrums, rages and rivalries, tears of joy, and confessions of stage fright.

Mothers know daughters' adolescence can't be contained in a simple tragedy. It's more an epic journey—a hormonally activated, hang-on-tight ride, sometimes exhilarating, sometimes exhausting. Adolescent girls plunge and soar. They delve into dark places, but usually they rise up to burst through the surface.

And mothers: We're catapulted into a parallel universe searching our own souls, oscillating between pride and guilt, independent yet inextricably bound to our daughters and their journey. Yet the mothers' side of the Ophelia saga has seldom been told. Traditionally, we women fade as our girls emerge into womanhood.

Banished to Backstage

Our daughters push us off their stage. It's developmental. Every daughter needs to shine without her mother interfering.

Manju, my older daughter, must have been twelve. I had assumed the role of chauffeur. We were about to leave the house on our way to pick up one of her friends. I stood in front of her, insecurely asking, "Manju, am I dressed okay?" She glanced in my direction, gave me a quick once-over, and issued her instructions: "You look fine. Just don't speak."

I stiffened my quivering lower lip and obeyed.

The time had come for me to be an embarrassment to my daughter. Nearly every mother faces this universal admonition, delivered with obligatory eye-rolling by a newly socially aware teenager. It's a developmental milestone, timed to coincide with the acquisition of sanitary napkins.

For Riki Schneyer, the stage is more than a metaphor. Riki belongs to a semiprofessional theater troupe in an art-loving community in the mid-Atlantic. She loves to act. In full makeup with the spotlight shining, she allows her irrepressible enthusiasm to burst out in song. Riki can't help being herself, but that doesn't stop her from feeling guilty. She described her dilemma:

A STAGE FOR ONE
Thoughts from Riki Schneyer

"I was at this cast party with my husband and daughter. I was laughing and singing. My daughter stood back with a friend, watching me. She told her friend, 'I hate it when my mother has a good time.'

"It's hard for Rene, having a mother who does things, who's good at things. I act. I make art. I shrink heads. I have this tremendous anxiety that I'm too much, that I overwhelm her. She compares herself to me.

"Like with our artwork. When my friend, a talented actress, died from breast cancer, I told myself: 'It's time for you to live your life.' I had painted when I was young. I began painting again. Rene was eleven. I was still the center of her universe. We painted together.

"Then she turned twelve. Anything I did, she didn't want to do. She won't paint or draw at home. At school, the teachers emphasize her talent. She makes prints and draws sketches. But she never shows me any of her work. It's fine. I understand. She's struggling with becoming separate from me. It's a private torment for her, and for me." ⚯

Our daughters push us off their stage and try on new identities. Our girls are adolescents; by definition they're self-centered. They're completely unaware that their role changes affect us in any way. They don't have a clue that we're struggling with our own identities—trying to hold on to who we were, understand who we've become, and grasp who we're turning into.

Sande Boritz Berger's daughter had no idea what symbolism lay behind borrowing Sande's retro blouse.

MY MARILYN MONROE BLOUSE
by Sande Boritz Berger

Every night, before bedtime, Jennifer, my younger daughter, plans her next day's wardrobe. This might entail the need to crawl past me, like a tiny soldier avoiding gunfire as she enters my closet, while I lie in bed, reading my book, dozing off.

There's just one blouse that I've warned her never to touch, try on, or borrow. Both my girls, Jennifer and Bari, refer to it as my Marilyn Monroe shirt. (They give a lot of my clothing names.) This particular shirt is pale pink, with rolled-up sleeves, in the style of the sixties. One of my favorite garments, not because it was expensive. It wasn't. It just fills me with nostalgia every time I wear it, reminds me of the time when I played my 45s and sipped egg creams without worrying about my waistline. I guess it makes me feel young again—a lot like my daughters.

One day, I search everywhere for the blouse.

While driving Bari to her after-school bowling league and Jennifer to her dance class, I try to sound nonchalant. I ask, "Girls, did either of you see my pink Marilyn Monroe shirt?"

I peek at them through the rearview mirror. Bari looks directly at Jennifer, which gives me my first major clue. I wait. Jennifer, right then and there, puts on an Oscar-worthy performance. She makes me feel awful that I've even suggested such a thing. I make a mental note to check the dry cleaners, thinking, "Maybe I forgot to pick it up."

Weeks later, while searching the bottom of my closet for a pair of boots, I discover a pink wad of fabric: my Marilyn Monroe shirt rolled up in a ball, sporting unidentifiable and indelible stains. Lunchroom pizza, perhaps? Kraft macaroni and cheese? Not in my diet. I am furious. My fingers are trembling as I put on the blouse and button it up. Stains and all, I march into the den where Bari and Jennifer are sprawled out in a rare moment, sharing a beanbag chair, watching TV. Seeing me, Bari gasps. Covering her mouth, she flies up the stairs, leaving me face-to-face with Jennifer, who begins throwing out apologies as fast as curve balls. But it is too late. There were two crimes here: first, the lack of respect for my personal property, and second, the deceit.

My younger one takes her punishment well, although she campaigns for me to *pul-lease* reduce the amount of her telephone-less days. She doesn't mind having to clean up the kitchen after dinner. Somehow she manages to employ the aid of her older sister, who had witnessed her mischief and urged her to come clean, all the time promising that she'd never, ever tell. And then:

Some weeks pass. On a windy, rainy morning, the two sisters miss the school bus. "Okay, I'll drive you on my way to the train station. Sure, I'll pick up Wendy, too." (She's Jennifer's best friend who lives down the block.)

At a traffic light, I glance at Wendy, noticing how pretty she's become. Is that lipstick she's wearing? And boy, that aqua sweatshirt she has on sure looks familiar.

"Wendy," I ask in a calm voice, "is that *my* shirt you've got on?"

A shivering silence holds my answer. ☜☞

S ometimes the conflicts can escalate to the point that even backstage isn't a safe haven. We forget that looking to our own needs isn't merely an option; it's a necessity. Nancy Hamel's place in her own world was seriously threatened by her daughter's shaky adolescence. In the midst of the upheaval, Nancy left home.

e∾

RUNAWAY MOM
A Story from Nancy Hamel

"God only knows what we were arguing about. I only knew I couldn't stay another night under the same roof as Amy. The tension was too thick. I was too emotional. She was too out of control. It was just too bad. One of us had to leave. Amy was too young. It had to be me.

"My husband said, 'Okay. If you're sure, but don't take yourself to some cheap motel. No dives. Take yourself someplace nice. Really nice. Go to the Lord Jeff. You deserve to be pampered.'

"I drove around for hours, up and down all these streets. I was crying the whole time." Nancy could hardly see the road through the flood of her own tears. She felt lost, even though she had traveled every road and passed every house a hundred times before. Finally, she exhausted herself.

"I drove up to the Lord Jeffrey Inn and walked up to the front desk. I must have looked like a total wreck, my face flushed and my eyes swollen. Well, I know the clerk. I'll tell you, she was so kind. She gave me the best room in the house and said, 'Nancy, I don't know what's wrong, but I hope it will be okay soon.'

"I settled into this beautiful room, sat there crying. Then there was a knock at the door. It was room service, with tea and cookies on a silver tray, and a note: 'Compliments of the house.'

"When you don't know where you belong, little things mean a lot." ∾

Good-Mother Guilt

Often, as our daughters push us into a lonely corner, our mistakes come into focus. Guilt becomes our most intrusive companion.

For mothers, guilt is inescapable. Psychologically, we are steeped in a belief that nurture, not nature, creates the character, personality, and emotional well-being of the child. This deeply instilled assumption assigns both credit and blame to the primary caregiver—the mother. If our children are happy, we're happy: We must have done something right. If our children are unhappy, we feel an involuntary constriction: Surely we're responsible. With the advent of adolescent growing pains, our mistakes come back to haunt us. The women who contributed to *Ophelia's Mom* sounded this theme again and again; even the "good" mothers, those of us who have tried to do everything right, feel we must have done something terribly wrong.

Around the same time Nancy Hamel retreated to the Lord Jeffrey Inn, I bumped into her at the local drugstore.

Nancy and I had lived in our lively little town for ages. We moved to this community for the same reason: It's a great place for kids.

Let me tell you about Nancy. This woman radiates goodness. As a mom, she's extraordinary. I know. I watched her nearly every day. From the time our children entered first grade until her younger daughter graduated from sixth grade, we both worked at their school. I was a psychologist. She taught library skills, but behind that professional role stood a personal agenda. Nancy intended to be fully available to her son and daughter.

She exercised her maternal priorities so discreetly: staying in the background, never intruding, not the slightest bit overbearing, quietly supplying forgotten lunch money, a joke, a hug. But give Nancy a crisis, and she burst out of incognito, saving the day. The sixth-grade graduation trip was about to be canceled due to lack of funds. Nancy single-handedly organized a massive pizza party, raising enough money to rescue the endangered adventure. A treasured teacher fell ill. Nancy orchestrated a letter-writing campaign, shaming the administration into acting humanely. Raindrops poured through the school's ceiling. Nancy mustered public enthusiasm for roof repairs. All the while, this good mom bathed her son and daughter in a constant flow of positivity. Every exuberant cell of Nancy's being lived to ensure the well-being of her children.

So when I saw Nancy, I felt the glow of my long-held admiration. Our conversation followed a predictable path. We talked about our kids.

I began, "How's Aaron?"

Nancy sparkled. "Wonderful. He'll be off to college in the fall."

Then, without warning, Nancy plunged in. "Nina, I saw Sara's book. I have to tell you: Amy, my little beauty, has sunk into the darkest place. She's my Ophelia." As Nancy spoke, optimism drained from her face.

Looking into her eyes, I traveled from shock to sadness and found few words. "I'm so sorry. Amy was the spunkiest, happiest little girl. Sara's always said, 'Amy's the coolest little kid in the entire school.'"

Nancy nodded, smiling weakly, as though conjuring up an image from the past. Then the memory appeared to flee. Her head moved from side to side as if she were trying to shake off her current reality. "Not anymore. She's so troubled. I'm awake nights trying to figure out how to help her. I hardly sleep, but I don't find any answers."

Without thinking, I blurted out my never-before-spoken admiration. "Nancy, you're such a good mom."

A short silence fell between us, just enough time to share pain. Then Nancy confessed, "I used to think I was a great mom. I really did. I tried, Nina. I tried my best. Now I wonder what I did wrong."

Sometimes the best moms feel the most guilt.

Riki Schneyer, who lives on the edge of an East Coast city, confessed that her feelings of guilt began the moment her daughter was born. "I'm endlessly forgiving myself for all the errors I made." Her daughter's attitude helps. Riki remembers her little girl—just three years old at the time—sitting strapped in her car seat. Looking pensive, the child studied her mother. Then the little one gave her mom a piece of her mind: "Stop trying to be the perfect mom."

Nestled in the mountains of northern New England, Wendy Elliot spoke in the same vein. "My daughter's just entering adolescence and she has this wisdom. She told me, 'Mom. You have to learn to love your imperfections.'"

On the West Coast, another mom had reached the far side of her daughters' adolescence. She had not come to the end of her guilt. "My older daughter told me a lot. She talked about her self-harming, her substance abuse, her sexual issues. I was devastated by her pain. But I was surprised and gratified that she talked to me. I thought, 'She must trust me and love me.' Still I felt powerless to help her.

"Now she's gotten better, and I feel all this angst. I wish I had done more. I wish I had been more confrontational. I wish I had made more rules and cut off her allowance. I wish I had set more stringent limits. I'm in this torn place. The fact that every mother feels guilt doesn't mean I should let myself off the hook. I can't just let loose on a culture that blames mothers for every bad thing that happens and doesn't give us credit for anything good. I have to figure out how to take responsibility for how I failed my daughter. When I say 'I'm sorry,' it's putting a huge burden on her. I don't want to burden her."

Still another mother talked about that burden. "I've come to this age when I look back and I can see all my mistakes. I want to tell my daughters, 'I'm so sorry.' But I can't. I'm afraid if I talk about *my* mistakes, they'll feel I think *they're* flawed."

The older my daughters grew, the more I was visited by remorse. I'm not the only mother whose daughters' adolescence gave birth to inconsolable regret.

At times, we mothers of adolescent girls feel like we're drowning in shame. A swirling mass of confusion sucks us into a desolate undertow, where we gasp for clarity and grasp at resolution. Mother-guilt swallows the soul. Unanswerable questions press in. "What did I do wrong?" "Why did I react?" "Why am I so scared, so irrational?" "Why do I feel so empty?" "Why does she have to treat me so badly?" "Why do I hurt so much when she pulls away?" "Do I deserve her rejection?" "Will she ever forgive me?" "Will she be okay?" "Will she come through all this without scars? Whole? Alive?" "Will we love each other again?" Swimming in these questions, we feel ourselves sinking.

The prejudice of Western psychology does nothing to save us from self-recrimination. I know. I've been schooled in the tradition of blaming the mother. The Freudians, behaviorists, and humanists all subscribe to one preeminent conviction: "It's the mother's fault." That psychological certainty has seeped into the collective psyche. When a child has a problem, minds scurry to figure out what the mother did wrong. She must have been too indulgent. Too rigid. Too close. Too distant. She should have stayed married. Or gotten divorced. She should have been at home with the children. Or had more interests outside the home.

Trapped between guilt and blame, we lose track of ourselves. While hoping to guide our daughters through adolescent insecurities, we can lose our way. At least I did. I had become so dependent on supporting my daughters that I didn't notice they held me up. I didn't realize how much of me had turned into "Mother." How much I defined myself by my relationships with my girls. How much I needed to be needed. I felt lost. So did Jill Morris.

A divorced mother of daughters, Dr. Jill Morris had accumulated a warehouse of accomplishments. Yet not one of her many degrees staved off the personal crisis she encountered when her older daughter entered adolescence. Jill lives at the southern tip of the States. I live near the north. But the length of a coastline did nothing to separate our experiences.

℮∽

THE SHIFT
A Conversation with Jill C. Morris

"A short time ago, I brought myself into therapy.

"With my older one reaching adolescence, there was a shift. I began feeling alone.

"I broke up with my boyfriend. I stopped wanting a relationship. I don't feel right about bringing a man into an adolescent's life.

"Now I have to pay attention. It's going to be over soon. I need to concentrate on being a mother. I feel I have only a little time left to be with my daughters, and I don't want anything to dilute my focus on them.

"I'm searching for a new approach to living in the world and in my house.

"My older daughter has changed. She no longer wants me.

"I faced not being wanted but still being responsible: to give and get nothing back. It hit me like a brick. I told myself: 'I'm going to have to be a different person.' It felt almost as significant as getting divorced—almost.

"I feel different, like I lost my purpose. Everything I've done professionally has been structured around my daughters' needs. I put so much energy . . ."

Jill's voice quivered. She confessed: "I'm going to cry."

She paused, then continued with a litany of motherhood's responsibilities: "Sleep lost, diapers, leaving work: all the sacrifices. But when they're little, you get something back.

"Now I'm giving and giving but not getting replenished. She needs so much space. I understand she needs to reject me. But emotionally, it hurts."

Jill recollected a childhood experience akin to her current struggle.

"When I was twelve years old, I walked into a toy store. I looked around at all the shelves and I didn't want anything. I knew I had changed. I knew I was no longer a child. I felt despair.

"Now I'm thirty-five; I have one adolescent and one near-adolescent. I have all this accumulation: friends, colleagues, professional success, a house. Do I want it? I can't even ask that question. I'm in a holding pattern, a transitional period.

"It's not as though I neglected my life. I never did. I got a Ph.D. I make art. I have friends. I've had boyfriends. Still, my life has shifted."

As our conversation came to a close, Jill stepped back and looked at herself through her daughters' eyes.

"I know one thing. I don't admire my mother. My daughters admire me. I hold on to that tightly." ✧

Jill Morris and Monica Breen could not have lived their lives more differently. Monica married right out of high school, gave birth to three daughters, devoted herself to full-time motherhood, and stayed married to the same man. Yet when their daughters reached adolescence, both shared a similar despondency. Both felt deprived of purpose. Monica wrote from her suburban home:

MY LIFE
by Monica Breen

My three girls have been my life.

My life has revolved around the girls. For years, every decision I made centered on how it was best for the girls. With a love bond so strong, how do you hold on to a child yet learn to let her go? How do you remain a mother and yet become a daughter's friend?

The challenge: to hold yet release.

Being a young mother, twenty-two years old, and a mother of three baby girls, I had hardly learned to be my own person. Whatever I had learned about myself in that short time, I put behind me. I became a mother. It was the only responsibility I wanted. It became my life. The girls became me. Or was it that I became the girls?

While I focused my attention and energy on the girls, I forgot who I was or what I wanted to do with my own life.

Now the time has come for the girls to each go in her own separate direction. Even though it's not a total loss, it certainly has left me with a feeling of being all alone. I no longer have those little girls who once were so dependent on me, no longer can use them to hide behind. So often I wonder: What is life supposed to be about? What am I going to do? Who am I?

I don't blame anyone for this. It's just something that happened.

I made the choice many years ago and now I have to make more choices.

I don't regret being so involved with my girls. I think what I most regret is that I wasn't involved with me. I wasn't involved with who I am as a person.

I now have the time to discover what I want from life, yet . . . how does a mother find herself after not knowing herself for such a long time?

Over years of devotion to motherhood, an insidious notion of selfless love seeps into the psyche. We're in danger of becoming women without faces or voices whose sole identity springs from our budding daughters.

Karilee Halo Shames's daughter made it perfectly clear that Karilee had to find a new identity apart from her mother role.

e⌒

"IT'S NOT ABOUT YOU, MOM"
A Note from Karilee Halo Shames

Another milestone was Shauna's senior year in high school. It suddenly dawned on me that she was leaving. I was devastated when she applied to six schools—all in the East (we were living in California). Soon the acceptances poured in—Bryn Mawr, Wellesley, Mount Holyoke . . . They not only wanted her, they were competing for her.

And where was I, the mother who people assumed was thrilled to death? I was in my room, sobbing my eyes out. My baby was leaving, and not only going away but doing what I had done, going across the country to make her own life.

I just couldn't stop crying. Finally, one day, after ignoring it for months, Shauna looked at me and said, "Mom, I really love you. I don't want you to be hurt over this. This is not about you: It's about me."

Another lesson in letting go of Ophelia. It was not she who was drowning in her petticoats; it was me. I was buried under expectations about what a loving daughter should do. I needed to remember to listen to Shauna, my wise and wonderful mentor. *⊷*

part one

Into Adolescent Territory

DRIVING LESSON
by Jean L. McGroarty

I hand her the keys and sit on the passenger side of the car. I think of her in the stroller, on the tricycle, in the bumper cars at the fair, and I see her now, ready to drive my car. She turns the key and I think of her playing with my keys before she could walk, making them jingle and squealing with delight.

The car starts and she tentatively tries to shift into reverse. I think of her on her first pair of roller skates, inching along, trying not to fall. She backs the car out of the parking space, shifts into drive, and moves ahead. I try not to gasp, try not to make any noise, high or low, try to be cool, to let her drive the car without comment or complaint from the passenger seat.

I think of the look on her face on her first day of nursery school, and it reminds me of the look on her face now, cool blue eyes looking into the future with confidence and curiosity. Her lessons in life go on, and for a while I'm along for the ride.

blood and tears

DAUGHTER TO MOTHER
for Alicia Alexandra
by Marianne Peel Forman

she doesn't fear the blood
but she doesn't want the hair
will cut it off, she tells me,
when it comes to her.

we bathe together
on a foggy thursday night.
she tugs the hairs straight,
releasing and watching them
curl back onto themselves
like cellophane Chinese
    noodles,
like black worms in spring.

she looks at the hair around
    my face
the color of coffee with
    unmeasured cream
and asks why the hair
between my thighs
is so dark, so black,
so like night.

and she doesn't want the
    breasts,
asks about the brownness,
the hardness of the nipples.

my body is sliced like the
    horizon
by glycerin and rose water,
breasts and nipples hard
from the cold above the foam.

she reaches below the surface
gathering up the warmth
like white wildflowers
in her tiny hands
and scatters it onto my
    breasts
and stomach
and thighs
to warm me
water petals
through the fog.

I lie in bed with my baby daughter nestled under my arm, nursing. I am perfectly connected to my baby's body, soothed by my biological purpose, wrapped in tranquillity. My mind rests on one thought: "For this alone, I would be reborn." I melt into sleep.

I never felt completely physically comfortable with another human being until I gave birth to Manju, my first child. She slipped out of my body into the world, a little girl, just like me.

We bonded in the bathroom. At first, in the bathtub, giggling at the green wind-up frog. Later, in front of the mirror, fussing with our hair. Then, one day, she shut the door behind her. I was no longer allowed to enter. Her body had begun to be too much like mine. The time had come for privacy.

The embarrassment that comes with leg hair and budding breasts and menstruation: It's as confusing to a mom as it is to her daughter.

For Sandra Hunter, a family practitioner in a western city, menstruation is the basic currency of everyday life. Every moment of her workday, she deals with the ins and outs of female sexuality. At home, she talked openly about menstrual woes and never thought to hide her tampons. Yet confronted with the sight of her daughter's first bloody underwear, she spoke of her bewilderment:

TOO SELF-CONSCIOUS FOR WORDS
A Story from Sandra Hunter, M.D.

"About a month ago, I walked into my daughter's room. Tina was packing for a camping trip with her uncle and his son.

"Her panties and jeans were on the floor, soaked with blood. I was shocked. I had no idea she'd started menstruating. I blurted out, 'Why didn't you tell me you had gotten your period?'

"Tina clenched her teeth and told me, 'I didn't want you to know.' Then she screamed, 'Go away.'

"She absolutely refused to talk to me. She was going away and I couldn't figure out how to give her pads. What could I do?

"I wrapped some pads in pretty paper, put a bow on the present, and attached a card. All it said was *Congratulations!* I figured she could just take them along with her, without having to talk, without having to admit she was bleeding, without feeling embarrassed.

"When she left, I walked back into her room. Her stained jeans were still on the floor. The package was open. Only one pad was gone.

"A few days later, my brother-in-law called, perturbed. 'Why didn't you tell me she had her period? You didn't send any pads with her.' She'd bled through while hiking.

"When she came home, I insisted we talk. After all, she needed basic information.

"I told her to take pads or tampons to school. She wouldn't hear of it. She yelled, practically stomped her feet. 'No. No. No. I'll never do that.'

"I don't know what she'll do if she gets her period at school. Does she think she won't bleed again? I worry she'll get her period in class. I send her off holding my breath.

"I leave books about menstruation and sex around the house in conspicuous places. I can't give her a book directly. I can't call any attention to them. If she suspects that I'm behind the appearance of the information, she'll absolutely refuse to read it. If I say nothing, she'll pick them up by herself, in her own good time.

"She's in denial. She's just not emotionally ready to menstruate. Her body's out of step with her identity. I don't know. Maybe it's about not wanting to become a woman." ◦━◦

Puberty can take possession like an invasion of body snatchers. Many girls aren't ready to become women, but emotional misgivings don't stop them from developing early. Behind the closed doors, girls are budding breasts, sprouting pubic hair, and menstruating younger and younger. In 1997 Marcia Herman-Giddens published a study of seventeen thousand girls in the journal *Pediatrics*. According to her findings, Caucasian girls begin menstruating at 12.8 years. On average, African-American girls begin menstruating six months earlier. Other studies dispute the findings that girls are entering puberty at younger ages.

According to *Girls Speak Out*—a study authored by Whitney Roban and Michael Conn and commissioned by the Girl Scouts of America—psychological maturity doesn't go hand in hand with the acceleration of physical development. Too-young girls can't possibly feel comfortable stuck in suddenly alien bodies. Surging hormones throw every girl into an unfamiliar state; even with preparation, it's a shock to bleed. A ten-year-old girl who menstruates might naturally want to hide or deny.

Judy Pohl ushered four daughters through the onset of menstruation. Her mid-Atlantic home brimmed with young women borrowing sanitary pads and teasing one another about PMS. Still, Daughter Number Three couldn't find the courage to ask her menstruation question out loud.

Judy speaks with the breezy confidence of a seasoned mother.

CONFIDED TO THE STEERING WHEEL
A Story from Judy Pohl

"My girls started menstruating early: one at ten. Some were more snarly than others. It seemed like they'd get real grumpy for about two years before they got their periods. I swear one little one had PMS at eight years old.

"Even the older ones noticed. They'd ask, 'Does that girl have her period yet?'

"In our family, we talk about everything in a crowd.

"One time Number One had a boyfriend over to dinner. It was like a first date. We were sitting around the table and somebody, one of my girls, asked about menopause.

"They ask; I answer. That's my philosophy.

"I explained, 'When you get older, your period stops. You no longer ovulate and can no longer get pregnant.'

"I was as matter-of-fact as possible, given that there was this would-be boyfriend sitting next to me. I tried not to look at him."

Judy paused. The pace of her words slowed, as if she were trying to fit an awkward piece into the family puzzle.

"Daughter Number Three: She's real private.

"I got into my car one day. There was this note taped to the steering wheel. It said, *I got my period. I've been bleeding since Wednesday. Is that okay?*

"That's how I found out Number Three started menstruating.

"I don't get it. With a mother like me, how does a girl get so shy about speaking up?"

Back in her own adolescence, Cynthia Peel Knight had been as self-conscious as Judy Pohl's daughter. Now a California mother with adolescent twins, a son and a daughter, Cynthia has a different story to tell—a tale of mother/daughter bonding, tinged with humor and embarrassment.

e◦

WINGS
by Cynthia Peel Knight

Driving toward Half Moon Bay with Camille and Jake in my company seemed surreal. The thick envelope of fog descended upon us, insulating the silence inside the darkened car. Nothing to see, yet so much beyond the wall. This darkness accentuated what I didn't know about my daughter. We never really talk.

I drove this entire trip, four hundred and fifty miles, with her in the backseat, her headphones clamped to her ears, not saying a word. She never asked to eat or to go to the rest room. I wanted to interact with her. All I ever got was a blank look. She couldn't hear me over the violent sounds of *The Cure*. When she did take the suction cups off her ears and actually listen to my questions, I got shrugged shoulders or "I really don't care" or " I didn't ask to be here on this lame nature trip of yours."

Then, just as we passed the Half Moon Bay sign, Camille spoke, penetrating the silence.

"Aunt Joni says to get *Wings*."

I guess I lost sight of the possibility of her getting her period.

Last year I had taught the sex-education class at her school. I knew most of her friends were already menstruating. All summer, any time she was tired or irritable, I assumed she was about to get her period. We interviewed many friends about tried-and-true types of feminine protection. We narrowed the wide selection down to two brands. We had gone pad shopping. The pads still waited in her bathroom back home. A lot of good they'd do us now.

Before I could speak, Jake, Camille's fifteen-year-old brother, faked confusion and teased, "What? Buffalo wings? What are these wings, big sister?"

Using my most threatening tone, I pounced. "Jake! Not another word."

Then I pulled in to the Lucky Supermarket and turned to Camille. *"Always Wings?"* I asked, citing the brand she'd chosen before.

She shrugged.

I responded, "Well, you'll have to come in and pick the ones you need."

"Mom! Wrong! No way am I going into there to buy pads. Just get *Always Wings*."

"Camille, there could be a dozen varieties. Those things mate and proliferate monthly. I don't want to waste time buying and returning the wrong pads."

"Okay, Mom. Just don't get those big honkin' pads made for fat ladies who nearly bleed to death every month."

"Camille, don't worry. I won't. 'Cause you're coming in," I said as I parked the car.

Jake barked, "Hurry up and get your new little wings so I can go to bed."

Walking through the gliding door, Camille recommitted to her non-participation, saying, "I'm not going to carry them."

"You will if I don't," I quipped.

"Then forget it, Mom. I don't need them."

I teased, "Oh, come on. Grow up. You can't go your entire woman-hood with toilet paper stuck in your underwear."

We found the feminine hygiene section brilliantly juxtaposed to the diapers. The subliminal message: "By the time you stop using these, you'll be putting on diapers." (I think they should bridge the two aisles with a condom display.)

Camille stood as far from the feminine hygiene side as possible, her back against the Pampers. She whispered, "There they are, to your left: *New Always Wings* in the teal-green package with pink writing. Get slender, regular absorbency."

I found the right package and walked back toward her. She stiffened her arms as if I were about to hand her a bag of snakes.

"I'm *not* holding them. Please, Mom. Please!" she begged me.

"Oh, Camille, calm down. I won't always be available to buy your stuff."

She pleaded, "I know, Mom. But it's my first time."

I took pity. "Okay. Come on then. There's just one other thing we must get to help us bear this monthly burden. It's my duty, as your mother, to initiate you properly."

Camille rolled her eyes. "Please, Mom, let's go. The toilet paper is crumbling in my underwear. My whole world is falling apart, and you have a little educational field trip planned."

"Okay, Camille, but you're the one that will suffer, forever."

She relented. "Okay. Let's go if it'll get us out of here sooner."

I led the way. "Over here. Aisle three. I must advise you that every time you buy a bag of pads, you need a bag of these. Chocolates. Choose your poison."

She was not amused. "Oh, great. Zits and more calories so I bloat up like a heifer."

I insisted. "It's the rule. One of these and one of those. It's the yin and yang of menstruation. I don't question the wisdom behind these things. I just heed the advice."

Camille picked up a bag of low-fat York Peppermint Patties. Obviously, I had my work cut out for me. But it was a beginning. I picked up a bag of peanut M&M's.

She objected, "What are you doing? It's not *your* period."

"It's called sympathy pangs," I explained.

"What?"

"It's my way of letting you know I feel for you."

"Yeah, right." She didn't buy it.

We headed toward the cashier. Camille halted dead in her tracks and pulled on the sleeve of my jacket. "Not that one! There's a cute guy ringing up the stuff."

"What do you think? He has a period scanner? How will he know they're for you if I'm carrying and paying for them?"

I moved forward. She lagged behind. Three other people waited in line ahead of us. I thought about how different this event was from when I got my period. I was so embarrassed I didn't even tell my mom. I used toilet paper for a couple of months, then moved on to my sister's pads for another seven months. My mom found a pair of my soiled pants in the laundry and outright asked me if I was having a period. As a lesson, she sent me to buy my own pads at Fred's Superette. My teacher's wife worked there. Everyone in our small community shopped at Fred's. I was so mortified that I paid my little brother a dollar to buy me my pads. I was so embarrassed that I couldn't even talk to my family or any other girls about menstruating.

Still in line, I picked up a home-improvement magazine and began reading. As our turn approached, I went to return the magazine to its rack. I turned around to find the young hunk holding the package of pads out toward Camille and asking: "Do you want to use this now?"

I felt like I was moving in slow motion.

Flustered, Camille forced a smile and pretended to get the joke. Then, unable to hold back tears, she bolted out of the store.

The young man turned to me. "I'm sorry. I mean the coupon here on the back. Did you want to use it now?"

"No, thank you. Maybe next time," I said casually.

I met Camille out by the car. She was red-faced. Pacing.

I tried to console her. "Come on, honey, he didn't mean anything. He probably still doesn't know they're for you. And what if he does? It's not like you'll ever see him again. We're four hundred miles from home."

I reached out to embrace her. For the first time in a long time, she let me hold her. She sobbed until she was empty. Then she began laughing uncontrollably. I laughed, too.

"Come on, let's get back in the car."

Jake was in the front seat.

"Jake, get in the back," Camille demanded.

He objected. "Why do you get the front seat?"

"Because I'm a woman now," she said as she pulled back her shoulders and lifted her head high.

We took off, my new copilot, this new young woman, and me. ◁○

Utter mortification comes in degrees. But Jan Schmitz Mathew is willing to bet that her tale, set in a bustling schoolhouse in a small city of a midwestern state, deserves its title.

℮↷

THE MOST EMBARRASSING DAY
by Jan Schmitz Mathew

When I answer the phone, her shaky voice answers, "Mom, please come get me. This is the most embarrassing day of my life."

I find her in the waiting area outside the school nurse's office. She sits on a giant-sized maxipad laid out to protect the vinyl-covered chair. *Damn*, I think. Poor thing must feel like she's sitting on a big diaper. Or a changing table. Waiting, literally, to be changed.

I hold my breath as she stands. I prepare to say the right words, to fashion the right look. Then I see. A deep red stain covers her left buttock. Her menstrual flow seeped through her underwear, soaked through her khakis.

I launch into a comforting cadence—the universal language of mothers. "It's okay, honey. We'll take care of everything. Don't worry, honey. We'll go right home and everything will be all right." I repeat the litany in a soft rhythm. My daughter breaks down, abandoning all semblance of bravery. Tears spill over and one sentence summarizes her humiliation: "Mom, everybody *saw*."

I lead a stiff and purposeful parade out the front door. The school halls are blessedly vacant, but we take no chances. I walk first. Mandy is in the middle, and the school nurse walks closely behind.

I say nothing on the drive home, but my mind is full. I sift through my thoughts, separating, prioritizing, returning to and rehearsing those I will share with my daughter. We'll track your cycles, I'll say. We'll make sure that, on your second day, you wear dark pants and that you tie a sweatshirt around your waist. You can try using a tampon. I'll remind you, and I'll help you any way I can. We'll make sure this never happens again. You'll be prepared.

I decide to reject sharing the two words that keep rising, like a rude interruption, to the surface of my thoughts: "Women bleed." We menstruate. We give birth. But we also bleed from the soul all our lives—for stray dogs; for white-haired, overweight joggers; for babies in Dumpsters; for the whole world and for our next-door neighbors. Monthly blood, like a stain on khaki pants, is simply one of the more obvious.

I silence these thoughts for now. Soon enough she will discover their truth on her own. I pull the car into the garage. I turn to Mandy. I begin to prepare her for next month. ⌁

W omen bleed. Mothers and daughters bleed. When there's no one else to comfort them, our daughters find themselves in our care.

When a milestone turned into a medical crisis, Jean L. French was called to the rescue. Who else but a mother prepared by years of changing diapers and cleaning up vomit could jump comfortably into emergency mode during a menstrual calamity? And have the presence of mind to make sure that her daughter gets the right take-home lesson?

⌁

TAMPON BLUES
by Jean L. French

Esmeralda didn't start her period until she was almost fourteen. When she was fifteen, she decided: "Tampons are much more comfortable than pads, especially for playing sports" (which was nearly all the time).

I warned her. "I had problems using tampons at your age." Actually, I wasn't able to insert a tampon properly until Playtex came out with those applicators with plastic all the way to the tip, like a slim penis. I was, by then, a nearly-eighteen-year-old virgin.

But Esmeralda was determined to try, so I bought her a box of tampons, the slimmest, lightest absorbency we could find. She opened the box, and we got out the instructions and went over them together. She wasn't on a period at the time, so I told her to put the tampons away until they were needed.

I didn't know she'd decided to sport her first tampon until I heard an anguished "Mom!" from the bathroom. When I knocked, Esmeralda opened the door and beckoned me in. There my daughter stood, straddle-legged, her underwear sagging. Crying. Of course, I was alarmed. Containing my panic, I asked, "What's wrong?"

"I tried to use a tampon and now it's stuck," she moaned. "I can't get it out. It's been killing me all morning. I couldn't find the right hole for the longest time. Then when I did, I couldn't tell how far to push it. You said when it was in right, I wouldn't feel anything, so it must not be in right, 'cause it hurts! I tried to pull it out, but it hurts too much!"

Not since her last diaper rash had I found myself examining Esmeralda's vagina. But in agony and with adolescent pride nowhere in sight, Esmeralda was again my little girl. At this point, modesty was the last thing on her mind. I had her lie down on the bathroom floor and raise her legs in the stirrup position—the one all women detest—the position associated more with the dreaded gynecological exam than with mother love. I could just see the very bottom of the tampon protruding from her vagina.

"You didn't get it in far enough," I told her. I tried pushing it in farther, but it wouldn't budge. She was bawling her eyes out. I pulled gently on the string, and she howled. I remembered the feeling of removing a dry-on-one-side tampon. Not pleasant. For a fifteen-year-old, it was a nightmare.

"I'm never going to have kids," she sobbed, her arm flung over her eyes. "How can women stand it? How can a baby fit through there when a tampon won't?"

That was a question I couldn't answer with any real authority, since both of my children were born by cesarean section. But my daughter needed me to act like I had a solution. This was one of those times when maternal confidence was mandatory. A bottle of aloe vera gel sat on the bathroom counter. I washed my hands, squirted aloe gel all over my fingers, and went to work.

"It's going to be okay, honey," I said. I told her what I was going to do and added, "Most babies make it through there, so I'm sure we can get this taken care of, too."

Little by little, the tampon began to ease free and finally slid out.

I told her to take a warm bath and relax. (Hey, it works in romance novels when the virgin has just been deflowered.)

The next day, Esmeralda thanked me several times for rescuing her.

"I'm never gonna have sex," she said seriously. "No *way* am I ever putting anything else up there again!"

"Uh-oh," I thought. "Time for damage control."

Esmeralda and I have always been able to talk about sex openly and honestly. My own mother was very shy about sexual matters. I couldn't talk to her at all about the things that concerned me in that area. I always wanted my daughter to be able to talk to me about anything she chose, and she has. So it wasn't difficult to explain: "Ultimately, sex is worth the initial first-time discomfort. Your body's made to accommodate both a penis and a baby's head. While you might choose for many reasons not to experience either event, you should not make those decisions out of fear, but out of a sincere conviction about what is right for you personally."

Because I shared my own experiences openly with her—my difficulty in using tampons, my first sexual experience, and my two cesareans (neither of which had anything to do with my being too small to deliver vaginally)—Esmeralda listened.

In true teenage fashion, she's decided to reserve judgment on the matter.

I figure that's about as much as the mom of an intelligent adolescent can hope for. ✑

mirror images: hormones, body shapes, and skin conditions

℮↷

ADOLESCENCE AND MENOPAUSE. WHO'S RESPONSIBLE FOR THIS cosmic scheduling blunder? Just too many hormones under one roof at one time. Acne and wrinkles. Diets and eating disorders. Liposuction and face-lifts. Cultural standards of beauty mangle the confidence of both daughters and mothers. The degrees of destructiveness vary wildly, from passing insecurities to life-threatening depression.

For many mothers, watching daughters debut on a womanly stage awakens flashbacks. We reflect our our own youthful body images and remember focusing on our blemishes. Seeing the folly of looking for flaws under the harsh glare of a magnifying glass, we hope our daughters will instead look in the mirror and recognize their fresh beauty.

Some of us admit that it's hard to comfort our daughters when we haven't learned to accept our own inevitable changes. It seems unfair that the permanent five, ten, twenty pounds or more that slide onto our hips and butts with our slowing metabolism arrive at the same moment that our daughters are revving up and becoming their most nubile.

In time, occasionally under pressure from a rude awakening or two, mothers put the importance of the body in perspective. In the end, most find maturity well worth the wrinkles.

Reflecting on Influence

Rachel sat with a small group of friends, leafing through the pages of a picture album. Her shining young face stared out from the photographs. Long black hair with flowers entwined. A vivid peasant blouse. She remarked, "When I look at these pictures, I think, 'I was so beautiful.' But at the time, I didn't feel beautiful. I felt so insecure about my looks. I was so self-conscious. Now I look at my daughter and I'm in awe of her beauty. I hope she appreciates how incredibly beautiful she is right now, at this age."

Some mothers are taken aback by how suddenly their little girls metamorphose into beautiful young women. A friend described walking down a city street with her daughter, who ran ahead to greet a neighborhood dog. As the mother walked by two young men, she saw them checking her daughter out. One of them said to the other, "Get a load of the ass on *that* one." She stopped in her tracks, detoured back to the young men, and said, "That girl is eleven. And I'm her *mother*." She told me, "I could have murdered them then and there. And no jury would have convicted me."

Mothers do their best to guide their daughters clear of the familiar pitfalls. Debbie Gaffney sees herself in her daughter's body. She hopes Amelia will never struggle with the same discomfort.

"I have always been awkward and uncomfortable with my body. My large breasts have been a source of much embarrassment to me. Finally, this past year, I had breast reduction surgery. What a difference!

"Like me, Amelia has large breasts. Even though I had surgery, I try to let her know that having large breasts isn't a bad thing. She developed in fifth grade. She's a very pretty girl. With her body, she has already received a lot of attention—jealousy from other girls, wanted and unwanted advances from males. Luckily, she has a very positive image of her body."

Not all daughters fit into the same developmental pattern as mothers. Some bloom on an entirely different schedule. When spring comes early, moms can miss the entire season.

MISSING THE FIRST BUDS
by Rita Harris

I wasn't prepared for hormonal changes in my daughter's body. Neither was she.

I expected her body to work just like mine. It didn't. I was almost fifteen before I got my period. Everyone, every single one of my friends, menstruated before me. By the time my period came, I was plagued with paranoid thoughts that something was terribly wrong with my body. My body never developed. Not really. For most of my life, I was five feet three and weighed ninety-six pounds. It was like I was always prepubescent. Except, of course, I had an eleven-year-old daughter and raging PMS.

I had this delusion that Vanessa's development would follow the same timetable as mine. I thought her body was a perfect reflection of me. I looked at her and saw this perfect petite doll of a child. I didn't notice that my delicate little girl had curves, lots of them. Somehow the budding nipples beneath the polo shirts never registered as breasts. Somehow I never realized there was a reason she wore baggy T-shirts over her bathing suit. I never gave her the message: Your blossoming body is a thing of great beauty. I just couldn't relate to a body that blossomed because mine never had.

I didn't give her any support for that time. I didn't help her find a perfect training bra. I didn't tell her how beautiful and lucky and womanly she was becoming. I was so blinded by the expectation that she would be me. I missed the process of her flowering.

Suddenly one day, I noticed. I thought, "Vanessa, you have breasts! Where did you get those? I don't have breasts."

Years later, when she had grown into the most amazingly shapely, delicate young woman, she told me, "It would have been nice if you had bought me a training bra. I needed one."

I felt the sadness that comes when a mom realizes she's missed a major milestone—like a first word, or a first step, or a first day of school. I couldn't resurrect a memory that never happened. I apologized. She looked at me with soft eyes. "It's okay, Mom. I could have told you."

I hate that I missed that very special shopping trip. Now I'm going to buy her any wedding dress she wants. No matter how much it costs.

＜◯

Other mothers do take note of the difference between their daughters' bodies and their own. At times the recognition of contrasts brings reason for concern. Riki Schneyer worries that the vestiges of her youthful anorexia might have created a reaction in her daughter. "My daughter and I both have eating disorders—subclinical, but still. . . . I undereat. She overeats. I'm so active. She resists activity. I worry about my influence. I'm endlessly forgiving myself for the errors I've made. When she was younger, I was more into my own stringent dieting. I thought she wouldn't notice my compulsions. Now she gets on my case when I fall into the same old behavior. I go to the grocery store and check out the labels. She calls me on it. 'Mom. I don't want to hear about fat.' I try to squiggle out of it and say, 'I was looking for ounces.' She gives me one of those exasperated sighs."

Five hundred miles down the coast, Jill Morris considered her history with food. "I was anorexic, then bulimic. I had the mind-set of eating disorders. My younger daughter talks about dieting. She scares me. I don't want her to think of herself as a body. That obsessive focus on food—you lose so much of the rest of your life."

Like these mothers, Ling Winston fears she might be communicating other subconscious messages to her daughter. She worries her daughter might sense her ambivalence.

ZIPPED LIPS
Thoughts from Ling Winston

"I look at my husband's family, and some of them are like Jabba the Hut. I'm worried my daughter will turn out that way. Without question, given the hereditary loaded gun and my own distorted view of body types, the fear is there.

"My dad said terrible, cutting things to me. He'd tell me routinely, 'You're fat.' 'Move your fat butt.' 'Get off that fat butt of yours.' My mom said only positive things to me about how I looked. I was never fat. But guess which parent I believed? Two or three years ago, I was wearing a sleeveless dress, and he said, 'Whoa, that makes your arms look beefy.'

"I've been so focused on staying thinner than I need to be. But I've always tried to curb what I say to my daughter about the body I began with and the body I have as it runs into the wall of forty. I'm sure she's heard me say things. Certainly the ubiquitous 'Does this make me look fat?'

"Lia has a very different body type from mine. I got over my disappointment over my small bust by thinking, 'Well, at least I don't have fat ankles.' But Lia has her dad's family's body type—sturdy legs, not-thin ankles. I've found myself caught in this place where I hope she gets the compensation—the big bust that goes with that family.

"Right now she's just a little bit on the chunky side. I know she's going to grow more, and she'll lose the weight. But still, I keep thinking about it.

"This is bat mitzvah year. Most of Lia's girlfriends are Jewish. So here we are shopping for much more dressy clothes than she's used to

having, which equals clingy clothes. I'm with her in this store. She's trying on this great cool nylon outfit. The clerk is telling her, 'Everyone
wants this one.' I look at Lia, and God strike me down, but I'm thinking,
'You need to cut back a bit, babe.' Am I evil? I did bite my tongue. I don't
think it even showed on my face. The clerk was great. She said, 'Here's
some things you can do with this shirt so it doesn't look . . . stuffy.'

"We have never said, 'You're fat.' We haven't restricted her in terms
of treats. But you can't be a parent and think something and not have
that something leak out to your kids, even if you've zipped your lips. This
bothers me." ❧

While Ling hopes that her silent judgments won't seep into her
daughter's subconscious, Trish wishes her daughters could read
her mind. In her thoughts, she bathes her girls with appreciation of their
extraordinary beauty and washes away every self-loathing impulse.

℮〜
MY GODDESSES
Thoughts from Trish

"To me, my daughters are like goddesses. I love seeing them all dressed
up. I admire their bodies. Both my girls are extraordinarily beautiful. But
it's nearly impossible for a girl to grow up loving her body in this culture.

"My older daughter is picture-book thin—gorgeous in that culturally admired way. But she has this incredibly distorted body image. She
cut herself. That's the embodiment of self-hatred. By cutting her body,
she felt like the pain of her imperfection came under her control. There's
an epidemic of girls cutting themselves. What does that mean for our culture? Beautiful girls feel like the only way they can accept their imperfections is by taking control, by inflicting imperfections on themselves?

"My younger daughter is a different kind of beautiful. She's sturdier.
She's an athlete. She deals with not having the culture's version of a perfect body. She uses substances to dull the suffering.

"So I don't feel only admiration when I look at them. I feel great
pain. It's the pain of knowing I can't insulate them from the culture's
messages of self-loathing.

"When I was a teenager, I asked my mother, 'Am I beautiful?' She
quoted Thornton Wilder. She said, 'You're beautiful enough for all practical purposes.' I wanted to give my daughters more than my mother gave

to me. I wanted my girls to feel like their beauty had no limitation. I didn't succeed." ❧

Ageless Imperfection

Some mothers come face-to-face with the limits of their own youthful beauty when they look at a daughter's emerging form. A friend tells me how jealous she is of her daughter. "Before I had Theresa, I had these perfect six-pack abs. During my pregnancy with her, the muscles separated, my belly button popped out, and it never popped back in. Now I'm all poochy and saggy, and she's got this little nipped-in waist and can run around in crop tops. It's not like I didn't know my bikini days were over. It's that I'm so depressed about my flabby belly, and at the same time, I'm trying to convince my daughter that looks don't matter, that she shouldn't obsess about her figure. It's like that Roz Chast cartoon where the character gets her first 'ma'am' from a sales clerk and she's freaked out. I have to accept that now I'm in permanent Ma'am Land."

Many mothers reach that awkward age—the time when you're no longer peach-perfect but not yet prune-dried—when it's hard to let go of being young but impossible to grasp being old. I remember a recurring scene. One of my daughters stood in front of one bathroom sink. I stood in front of the other. Both of us stared into the mirror. I bent close, examining the depth of my wrinkles. She leaned in even closer, preparing to pop an offensive pimple. I objected, "You'll make it scar. Just be patient. It'll go away by itself. You're young. You'll have perfect skin." I looked back at myself. My image betrayed a fact. I am no longer young. I'll never again have perfect skin. I can only hope my retinal cream and my electric face massager will slow the inevitable sag.

When I turned forty, I thought I had won the age wars. I figured, "Hey, I'm forty. Now I can rest in the serenity of low expectations." I figured, "As long as I avoid drying up like a prune or blowing up like a blimp, I'll feel beautiful *for my age.*"

Manju bolstered my confidence. Walking down the aisle of a local grocery store, we passed one of her classmates with her excessively overweight mother in tow. Manju tried not to stare. Once they had turned the corner, Manju looked at me and said, "I'm not ashamed to be seen with *you.*" I fully expected to be a role model for aging with grace.

I'm not. I don't like having a belly that pops buttons. I don't appreciate that my hair no longer fluffs. I don't treasure the crow's-feet around my mouth. Every once in a while, I have fantasies about "getting a little work done." I conjure up a memory. In a gallery, Sara and Manju by my side, I study a woman poised in front of a painting. Her skin is pulled taut, stretched into a grotesque mask. Her lips are swollen with collagen injections, plumped and painted red. I think, "Now, there's the menopausal version of self-mutilation. Cut my face? No!"

Amazing, really. The pressure to meet some culturally imposed standard of beauty. It never goes away. It's a pressure mothers and daughters share.

A mother speaking from California described an unexpected relief from the pressure of feeling not beautiful enough. "I went to this weeklong conference. There was this model-perfect woman there. She was drop-dead gorgeous. You just don't see people like this on the street. But you know, she was a really unhappy person. I thought, 'If she's unhappy, what's so great about being beautiful?' That thought freed me. With my daughters reaching the end of adolescence, I'm feeling my age. But I don't compare my menopausal experience, or my sagging skin, or my lost shape with my daughters' youth. I'm not jealous. Except about my knee. I wish I had a young knee."

Hormonal Passages

The hormonal scheduling gaffe wreaks havoc on many households. When I was a junior in high school, I came home every day, walked directly to my room, shut the door, collapsed on my bed, and sobbed. My mom knocked on my door, sat at the side of my bed and asked, "What's wrong?" My answer was always the same: "I don't know."

I also didn't know, didn't have a clue, what my mother was dealing with. Menopause: up all night, changing one drenched nightgown after another. I just thought she was grumpy and unstable. I had no idea we were both held hostage by raging hormones. Now I have belated sympathy for my mother.

But daughters? Few of us can expect our daughters to see our side of the hormonal battle. They just think we're neurotic and unpredictable. Sometimes they're right.

Tamara J. never anticipated that she and her daughter would end up taking the pill at the very same time for the very same reason. As she spoke, the medication's soothing effect was beginning to take hold.

THE COMPLEMENTARY PILL
Thoughts from Tamara J.

"This time is much more difficult than I thought. Not easy to live through. Not easy at all. With me falling apart and my daughter having a hard time, it's been harder than I predicted.

"My daughter's the girl I would have given anything to be. Jessie's really, really pretty. She's five feet five and weighs 105 pounds. She can eat anything and not gain weight. She has long legs and a long torso, perfect features, and flawless skin. Sometimes I think, 'Maybe I just see her as so pretty because she's my daughter.' Then my sister says, 'Don't you just love to look at her? I can't take my eyes off her. I could stare at her all day. She's so beautiful!' Jessie isn't just pretty. She's considerate and sweet, popular and bright, gregarious and self-confident.

"Then, for a few months, she got moody. That dip was painful for her. She fell into a depression. I thought, 'If Jessie can be depressed, the rest of us have no hope.' That thought scared me.

"Jessie was at the mercy of her hormones. Her periods got uncontrollably heavy. She bled profusely. It grossed her out. She actually got physically nauseated at the sight of the blood. She had terrible leg problems, cramps. She's a dancer, and she couldn't dance.

"I made an appointment for her with our pediatrician. This wonderful woman doctor prescribed the pill. Jess and I weighed the pros and cons. We decided to go with it. Now, she's on the pill—a low-dose estrogen pill.

"At the same time, I was going through my hormonal crisis. Every time my husband and I had sex, I got urinary infections. I thought, 'Okay, sex is over.' I felt very vulnerable, overwhelmed by my moods. Then I started getting really heavy periods and cramps—just like Jessie.

"So both Jessie and I are taking estrogen for the same reasons—to regulate our menstruation and even out our moods. I think it's beginning to smooth things out. I've stopped fantasizing about running away to the mountains."

Ruth's menopause did not coincide with her daughter's menstruation. She bought her last tampon long before Vivian needed her first sanitary napkin. Menopause had passed by the time her daughter reached adolescence. Excess hormones never flooded her home. Ruth

speaks with the slow cadence of a woman who is in no hurry to be somewhere else.

THE FRILLY AND THE COMFORTABLE
Thoughts from Ruth

"I was forty when I gave birth to Vivian. I was filled with new life and I
felt very young.

"I had my last period when I was fifty. Vivian had her first period
three years later. She was thirteen and I was fifty-three.

"We were swimming across this lovely woodland pond. When we got
to the middle, she whispered, 'Mom. I got my period.' I didn't make a big
deal out of it, but I did find the perfect gift—a lovely mirror framed in a
sculpture of two women swimming. I thought it was so beautiful. Vivian
unwrapped the box and said, 'What is *this thing?*' My husband assured
me, 'Don't worry. When she's twenty-one, she'll love it.' Then he gave her
a rose.

"I feel sad my daughter and I never menstruated at the same time. I
wish we had gone through our monthly cycle together. I would have liked
to have shared cramp bitch sessions, and tracked our cycles, and craved
chocolate together. All that girl stuff.

"But I do think, in some ways, having gone through menopause
gives me a calm in dealing with her moods. My daughter's hormonal
mood swings began at twelve. She's gay and giddy, dancing around the
house. Minutes later, she doesn't want to come out of her room. I watch
her go up and down, and I feel like a wise woman.

"These days I look at Vivian and see this fresh young woman. She's
full-busted and tall and thin. I'm losing my baby. It's wonderful and sad
and scary. I get concerned for her when I see how males of all ages look at
her. I'm afraid for her innocence. I want to wrap her in a blanket and
keep her in her room.

"I look at myself. I see my age. I pass a mirror and I'm surprised.
'Yikes. Who is that? My mother? My grandmother? Not me.' I don't feel
bad. I'm just surprised by how I look. My skin is losing its elasticity. My
breasts are sagging. I have salt-and-pepper hair. I don't have the body I
remember. It's almost like someone else's. I'm getting old.

"But I still love all the girliness. Buying bras with my daughter is
one of my favorite things. She's well endowed. We have fun with the joy

of blossoming. She picks out all these frilly, sexy, silky things, but she's actually modest. I don't go in the dressing room. I just tease her and bring her fancier and fancier, lacier and lacier, items. I shop for bras at the same time. I buy sensible cotton. She says, 'Mom, don't you want to be pretty?' I say, 'I just want comfortable. I'm not willing to do uncomfortable anymore.'"   ⬦

frozen affections

SEPARATION AND REJECTION. TEENAGE GIRLS DISTANCE THEM-
selves from mothers. Sometimes momentarily, sometimes sporadically, sometimes consistently, developmental separation
turns into disdain and disruption. It's normal.

Over and over, I've noted a pattern, an inverse relationship.
The closer, more bonded mothers and daughters have been
throughout the daughter's childhood, the more convulsive the
disconnection during adolescence. Daughters who have adored
their mothers feel a pressing need to tear away and weave the
fabric of their individual identity. One mother typified many:
"When my daughter was a little girl, she stuck to me like glue.
She clung to me. Really, sometimes I felt like 'This is a bit
much.' She was ten, eleven years old, always climbing into my
lap, snuggling like a too-big puppy dog. Then, at thirteen, she
turned on me, became vicious, snarled when I touched her."

I remember when both my daughters came down with the
defining symptom of adolescence: mortification at the possibility of being seen with me. More than once, I sat in a coffee shop
watching a girl, probably eight years old, talking to her mom.
Without deciphering a single word, I saw the intimacy between
them. Clearly, they were delighting in each other. Sara and
Manju had once scheduled "mother/daughter bonding time."
Then they became too embarrassed. No more teatime at the ice-
cream parlor. No more shopping at the local mall. No more
giggling at silly movies. Until, of course, they grew older. When
Sara was seventeen, she invited me to go to a movie. Incredu-
lously, I reminded her, "One of your friends might see us together." A bit disgusted, she informed me, "Mom, I could care
less. I'm not thirteen anymore."

There's hope. If we manage to accept our daughters' rejection as developmental, will we find it easier to respond without
rancor and escape without feeling wounded? We're given the
universal advice "Don't take it so personally." Still, in those
moments when we feel frozen out of our daughters' lives, it's
hard. How can we *not* take it personally? Humor helps.

Maria Nunez stood in her kitchen, spatula in hand, tending a mammoth black frying pan filled with scrambled eggs. When her three teenagers awoke, plus all the stray friends they had collected the night before, she'd have breakfast waiting. Now, while she and I were still alone, she pondered my question, then launched into her story:

"Me and Ruby? You want me to tell you about our relationship during that girl's adolescence. Well, let's just call this one: 'Ophelia Reeks.'

"As soon as puberty hit, Ruby developed this wooden-soldier response to my touch. Like it happened overnight: Suddenly one morning, she walks into this kitchen. I pull my head out of the refrigerator, put the milk on the counter, wrap my arms around her, and say, 'Good morning, sweetie.' Her body goes boardlike, completely stiff. Hands at her sides. Chin up. Feet planted. Like a soldier standing at attention. Like her mind orders: 'Remain rigid while the slobbery middle-aged woman tries to distract you.' So she stands there, frozen, waiting for me to stop hugging her.

"Sometime between sunset and sunrise, Ruby got paranoid. I had metamorphosed into The Enemy. She called my hugs *smell hugs*, like I was a bloodhound trained to sniff out the lingering smell of tobacco. Truth is: She did smell—a bit."

Maria paused and corrected her olfactory observation. "Actually, she reeked to high heaven. But me? Really. Smoke detection was just a by-product of being the same old mama, wanting to snuggle."

Maria put down her wire whisk, placed her hands on her hips, looked into my eyes, and said, sighing, "I realized later I was afraid of rejection. I caught myself rejecting Ruby before she could reject me. Night after night, I'd 'forget' to go up to her room to say good night. After I was sure she was asleep, I tiptoed into her room, studied my daughter's peach-perfect skin, whispered, 'Night-night. Sweet dreams.' I savored the day's only opportunity to kiss her on the cheek. I felt guilty about being too late for a proper good night, but I liked appearing in the absence of all possible rebuffs."

As Maria was ending her confession, a blurry-eyed adolescent, crowned by morning hair—drooping gelled spikes—wandered into the kitchen. Led by her nose, the girl found herself by Maria's side, sniffing the steam that rose from the frying pan. Maria reached out, pulled the young woman toward her and gave her a Mama Bear hug. The rumpled girl fell into Maria's arms, surrendering to her full-bodied warmth. Maria introduced Ruby's best friend, Ariel, and continued.

"Thank goodness for this one. Thank goodness for Ruby's friends. When Ariel and the others started coming around, I found surrogate dream-daughters—sweet honeys who lapped up my hugs."

For Ruby's many friends, walking into Maria's realm must have been like entering Marshmallow Heaven—soft, sweet, bouncy, airy. Ariel dashed in and out of Maria Land, romping up to Ruby's Marshmallow Mom for a free cuddle—affection with no restrictions, no judgments, no past to get stuck in, and no future commitments.

In their own homes, you can bet Ariel and Company wouldn't voluntarily give their own mothers as much as a peck on the cheek. Maria had only a vague suspicion that one of her surrogate huggers, her "cuddly, fuzzy bunny girl" turned into a "frozen, cold adolescent child" at the sight of her own mother. Lenore is another of Ruby's best friends.

Like most girls, Lenore had reached the age when adolescence obligated her to inflict hug deprivation on her mother. At exactly the same moment, she required a full-time, on-call chauffeur. Stephanie Palladino, her mother, was relegated to the driver function. Stephanie drove here, there, and everywhere, depositing her sullen daughter at the shrine of her best friends, where, miracle of miracles, Lenore transformed into a beautiful, bubbly socialite. Stephanie swallowed Lenore's preference for the company of her peers. But the vision of Lenore flinging open her car door, racing up the steps, and running into another mother's arms awakened pangs of loss.

That night, feeling starved for affection, Stephanie sat alone and scratched a message to her emotionally distant daughter:

LONGING TO BE THE OTHER MOM
by Stephanie B. Palladino

My mind turns to the long, tender hug your best friend's mother offered you this evening. Her arms softly wrapped around your delicate body and pulled you close. You stayed calmly in her embrace, placing your slender arms around her and meeting her gaze with a broad smile.

I remained below, in the driveway, uncertain whether to go away unnoticed or climb the bare steps and introduce myself—"Lenore's mother"—to this woman whose whisper-voice I have heard only by telephone.

When I left, you didn't even say good-bye. You stood outside the screen door by the deck, surrounded by your friends, turning your head from one to the next. They greeted you with words and kisses.

Lately we hug haltingly, if at all. You pull back almost before my arms close in on your shoulders, as if I were reaching out to hurt you. Sometimes you even wince at my clumsy efforts to draw you near. I weep inside and wonder: Will we ever hold each other close comfortably again, as glad for each other's embrace as when you were my baby in arms? ❧

Girls march off to adolescence and their mothers grieve. The same babies who looked up from our arms, their eyes bathing our faces in rapt adoration, now look past us. We capture their attention for fleeting moments. When they look in our direction, their hair tosses, their eyes roll, their mouths drop open, and they sigh "Mother" with that special lilt—the tone that lets us know how mortified they are by our very existence.

In all parts of the country, in all varieties of homes, little girls hear the call to an adolescent uprising. From an artsy corner of the metropolitan East to western farming communities, mothers experience the same grief. Riki Schneyer spoke about those commonly held feelings.

"I've loved every stage of my daughter's life. I was never the kind of mother who resisted her growing up. Until now.

"Suddenly, for the first time, I want my snuggly bunny back. Sometimes she'll cuddle for a minute. Then the next time I come near her, put my arm around her, she voices disgust: 'Mother! No.' 'Please. You'll mess up my hair.' 'Go away.' 'Oh my God.'

"I know. She's got to find me annoying, a pain in the ass. She has to distance from me, to get away from me, like when she was two. She wanted to sit on my lap without touching me. She'd climb onto me. Then she'd be irritated because my legs touched hers.

"I feel scrutinized all the time. She loves me to pieces, but she has to pick me apart, to find faults."

Stephanie Large, a thirty-year-old mother living in far-west farm territory, described herself: "Hey, I think I am pretty hip—I'm still young and fun—and all of my daughter's friends just love me." Still, like other mothers from coast to coast, Stephanie became an embarrassment to her own progeny. "Jamie was truly the best child. Never had a problem, never wanting to hurt anyone's feelings, always willing to lend a hand. People loved to see us coming. Then it happened: eighth-grade summer, right before her freshman year, total turnaround.

"No drinking, drug, or boy problems—just a *Mom Problem.*

"What happened? My kid doesn't like me anymore? I'm the most dorky, stupid mom anyone could have. What's up with that? I'm Public Enemy Number 1. She's out to humiliate me.

"You know, I don't think I even care if she really likes me or not, but she could at least *act* like it. Smile when she walks with me. Pretend. Have a great big smile painted on her face—kind of like Jack Nicholson as the Joker. Ha.

"I tell myself, 'This is how all teenagers act.' Well. As young as I am, you think I would remember myself? Nope. Can't remember."

Back in the East, in a small-town restaurant, Sandy, a midlife mom, spoke softly. Her communication with her daughter was no longer oiled with an easy affection. Conversations felt like laborious friction between two rusty gears. No matter how carefully Sandy polished her words, trying her best to fit them into her daughter's world, her questions always seemed to intrude.

"Sweetie, how was your day?"

"Mom, do you have to know what I'm doing every minute?"

"Sweetheart, how did you do on your history test?"

"Mother. Do you always have to pressure me?"

"Honey, what are you doing Friday night?"

"I do have plans, Mother. You think I'm such a loser."

No wonder Felicia Blasi, a rare and fine writer who lives smack-dab in the middle of America, had motherly misgivings. She shares her tongue-in-cheek thoughts with the kind of humor only a mother could offer.

ON SHOPPING
by Felicia Blasi

As far as I can tell, there are no logical reasons to have children. I have two of them, so I feel qualified to make such a statement. They're worse than men. They like you for a while, otherwise known as the "Happy Meal Years," when they can be bought for $1.99. Get 'em a package of those Ronald cookies and you're golden for at least an additional hour that day. They love you and then they leave you. And most often you're broke as hell by the time they go.

My daughter needed a dress for an acquaintance's high school graduation party. He was a senior this year; she was a freshman. "Who else from your class is invited?" I asked, worried she was on the high school fast track. "No one," she glibly replied. Hmm. I've always thought of this boy as a cad, and I've told her so myself, but she looked at me as if I were speaking Swahili when I said this. Her older sister said, "Jeez, Mom, did you have to use such an outdated word?" Well, yes I did, because the only other ones I could think of at the time were "little prick." At least the party would be adult-supervised, and more family than students had been invited. Besides, said Liz, "At Prairie High, you know everyone; it's not a big deal that I know Adam." Sure. "You know Adam because you're five feet eleven inches tall, five of those feet being legs, and you are beautiful," I think. If you were fat or had acne or some other defect, he wouldn't have given you a second look.

Nonetheless, we set out for the dress hunt. I've learned a few things in this area: Set a time limit before you leave the house. Say these words directly to the child: "If you can't make a decision in one hour, no dress." This strategy will benefit you greatly. Your arches won't fall as early in life and you won't want to curse the child in public. I mean, if you love malls, then you ought to have about eight daughters, because that's where you'll all live. A home would function as a mere pit stop in your lives, a flophouse at best.

We're in the mall. And it stinks, like all malls do. I've already used the limit: "One hour." Still, I'm wearing my best Birkenstocks. Here's why: Sometimes the one-hour strategy backfires. The child finds a dress that costs $800. (They can do that in a New York minute.) Then the mother breaks the rule and stays as long as it takes to find a budget-priced garment.

There's another rule about language here. When the kid pulls a dress off the rack that looks like it'd make Madonna blush, you do *not* say, as I have in the past, "What the hell is that piece of slut-wear?" I've found that the child's feelings are hurt when I say this, or that she gets real pissed. Not pissed enough to stop shopping, just enough to make the mission even more miserable. So instead you need to say, "I won't pay for that," which leaves an opening for, let's say, her dad to buy the dress, or for her to buy it, or for it to go back on the rack. These words leave less room for interpretation, especially on the big question of "taste." They make a simple, declarative statement.

Now, I have to admit that the kid and I have scored *twice* in the "Signature Dress" department at Marshall Field's. This happened because God is a single mother without much money who has a teenage daughter, and she knows when you're desperate. One time we bought a winter formal dress and a box of Frangoes and I'd written a check for $36.87. I was dancing my sad old feet out of that store. This grace had been with us earlier in the year at homecoming time. Forty-five dollars for a Jessica McClintock gown and a bit of a tiff over accessories, but in the end the total was about $65. A steal of a deal, even with the black feather boa she bought to wear around her neck. This good luck will not stay with you for long, though. It can't. Here's why: Our entire economic upswing is the result of teenage girls and their mothers buying dresses. If you think Alan Greenspan, interest rates, the Dow Jones, and the NASDAQ have anything to do with our nation's fiscal good health, well, you are wrong. Greenspan's job is gravy compared to shopping with a teenage girl.

Our most recent mall excursion, for that graduation dress I mentioned earlier, almost turned on me. Searching for a garden-party dress was easier than I'd thought, but the total package came to more money than I had. The child stepped into Ann Taylor at my suggestion, swished three dresses off the sale rack and into the dressing room before I'd had a chance to see that the clearance prices were, well, really high. One of the dresses was fine. She looked great: She looked like she had a mother with good taste, which is really the most important thing. However, the search for shoes had yet to be undertaken, and this was not going to be easy. She needed a pair of shoes with a heel of sorts, so that, she said to me, her calf muscles would appear more "defined."

While your kid is working on showing off her legs, you'll be bemoaning the force of gravity as you hope each morning that your breast doesn't get caught in your jeans zipper. This irony is not lost on me; the more beautiful your kid gets, the less young you look. And if age were really just a state of mind, you'd look even older. Trust me.

Bill Cosby once said, "People say they love children because their kids are so honest." Then he laughed one of those "hah!" laughs. I know he's right. Your kids will be so damned honest with you sometimes that you'd rather have a Chatty Kathy doll than a daughter. Five years ago, when my older daughter was applying to colleges, I was encouraging her to go to Madison. She obliged my idle chatter on this subject only so long. Then she finally said, right in my face, "I can't help it that you wanted to go to Madison but didn't. You cannot relive your life through me. I don't want to go there and I won't." I winced. She was right. But that's the thing: All of this conflict over dresses and colleges, calf muscles and cur-fews, makes you realize that you don't know where you end and the kid begins. They are, however, very clear on this.

They also know your wallet is a part of you. That's when they need to get close to you for a few hours, to get that dress, and shoes, and boa. Once the mission's accomplished, they're pretty good at drawing the boundaries again.

When I asked the kid about the graduation party, she said, "It was really well done."

I thought, "She's not going to give me one damn detail."

And I was right. ❧

A dolescent distance can stretch the limits of any mother's affection. Stephanie Palladino made note of the strain.

One brisk February morning, Stephanie wheeled into my driveway just as I was about to hop into my car. She parked, got out of her car, and handed me a manila eight-by-twelve mailer, the silver clasp shut tight. I took the envelope from Stephanie's hands. I didn't know she had entrusted me with messages written to her daughter, with silent thoughts a mother whispers on paper, the thoughts she can't quite speak out loud.

DO I LOVE YOU LESS?
by Stephanie B. Palladino

Do I love you any less tonight, so furious that I am driving wild with rage across town to fetch you once again, feeling so reckless behind the wheel that it exhilarates and astonishes me all at once?

No. A mother's love has roots so deep they cannot be clipped by such adolescent selfishness. Love abides, but alongside it trails the gaping hole of disappointment, growing larger with each half-truth crafted skillfully by such an articulate girl as you. You tell a story to serve one purpose and one strand of desires only—yours, now, all else be damned.

I feel tricked by you.

Suddenly sweet memories intrude—I was raking leaves. You were skipping through the piles in your red corduroy jacket, three big white buttons holding it closed against the November wind. We were both so much younger then. Thirteen years have passed, and it's come to this.

Tonight I attended a poetry reading—the featured poet began with poems dedicated to her two grown daughters, who now reside on the other side of this vast country. Since both were unable to attend in person, the poet explained, she would record her words on a cassette that she would send to them. This mother's pride and love were so evident. I ached. My mind wandered to your future and mine. I imagined you grown and living far from home. In so many ways, you have already begun to leave us. At home we talk of you now as if absent, even when you're in the house, behind a closed door. Lately, your sisters mention your name less and less. You are becoming a stranger.

I feel for you. I hope that one day soon your heart will open to those who love you more than you imagine. Even now, my love abides. ⌖

A biding love faces challenges during our daughters' adolescence. Carol Lawler felt on the edge of danger when her daughter confronted her.

TOUGH LOVE
Thoughts from Carol Lawler

"I can imagine telling a kid 'Not in my house.' I can understand telling a kid they have to leave home. A kid can reach such a destructive, violent place: drugs and weapons.

"I've never been there. It's never gone that far, but it's come close.

"Kyle and I were in the kitchen, preparing dinner. She asked to go to a coed sleepover. She was in seventh grade, just too young. I told her I wouldn't allow her to go.

"Kyle was slicing carrots. She looked up at me. Her face was stern, cold, confrontational; she said, 'How can you stop me.'

"I said, 'I can't stop you, but I'm not giving you permission.'

"She pointed the knife directly at me. She looked straight in my eyes and challenged me: 'What would you do if I threatened you with this knife?'

"I didn't flinch. I glared right back and said, 'I'd call the police.'

"She bolted out the door, ran down the street, and disappeared.

"I waited for two hours. I was shaking. Finally, I called the police. I told them, 'My daughter was upset. She's been missing for two hours. She's twelve years old.' That's all I told them, nothing more. They asked for a description and said they'd search for her.

"Her older brother came home. He took the car and drove from one friend's house to another. Finally, at the fifth house, she opened the door.

She didn't say a word. She got in the car and came home. She went directly to the family room, sat down, and switched on the TV. She stared at the screen all night, never said another word about the sleepover.

"A year earlier, when Kyle was eleven, she was this soft, cuddly, stick-to-Mom sort of girl. She always wanted to hold my hand, sit on my lap, tuck herself under my arm. She craved physical closeness. Sometimes, I felt, 'Just get off me. Give me a little space.' I never said anything, but I felt a little claustrophobic.

"Then, overnight, she changed. She pushed me away. She had to work really hard to get free of me. She treated me so badly.

"Kyle taught me unconditional love. She taught me to accept her no matter what she did, no matter what she said, no matter how much she rejected me.

"I'm a better person, stronger and more loving, for everything my daughter put me through." ⬤⬤

passing storms

THE COLD SHOULDER OF ADOLESCENCE ISN'T INVARIABLY INFLICTED with stony disdain. At times daughters repulse mothers with dictatorial flare and Technicolor tantrums. Inside our own homes, unavoidable irritations trigger raging blizzards.

Adolescence is by nature a time of heightened emotions. In a flash, exhilaration turns to fury. The impulses activating giddy joy and explosive anger reside within a hairsbreadth of each other. The slightest miscalculation and the wrong button is pushed, igniting a nuclear cataclysm. We mothers are thrown into a warped reality where whatever we do is wrong. Sometimes we head for cover, waiting for the all-clear. Sometimes we get caught up in the cross fire and shoot off a few defensive salvos of our own. But sooner or later, the rockets run out of fuel and the bombs stop falling. The challenge is to limit the casualties and reserve enough goodwill to heal the wounded.

The mothers I heard from often talked about tiptoeing around their own homes, doing their best to keep the peace. But walking around on pins and needles gets pretty uncomfortable. Most see that battles are unavoidable. The problem is, it's hard to see those clashes coming. More than one mom told me, "I don't know what will set her off. Sometimes I ask her to do something and she's totally civil. The next time, same request, she goes ballistic. Please. Tell me it's developmental. Tell me it's hormones. Tell me it's not me. Tell me it won't last forever." It won't last forever, but it can feel like it.

Barbara Murray wrote from her idyllic nest overlooking the Atlantic. Surrounded by nature's perfection, she felt like she was about to fall off a cliff, as if her daughter had shoved her out into the dark, swirling winds of a hurricane with nothing to hold on to.

The problem itself wasn't really the problem. Jessica, Barbara's fifteen-year-old daughter, had asked for a ride to town at noon. Barbara agreed. At noon, Jessica was far from ready.

Barbara gently hurried Jessica along, explaining her own time commitments. She offered to help Jessica move faster. Or, as Jessica might have said, "My mother nagged me."

An hour and a half after the scheduled departure, an argument broke out.

Later, with the storm barely subsiding, Barbara sat down and vented with an honesty nearly every mother can identify.

A MOMENTARY TEMPEST
by Barbara Murray

I hate it when:

~ I see the permanent frown lines on my face from being so sad and crying so much of the time

~ You get mad at me for not thanking you for cleaning your own dishes or doing your own laundry

~ You tell me you hate coming home and being at home

~ You blame me for your bad grades

~ You accuse me of yelling when I haven't raised my voice

~ I feel like a failure as a mom because of something you've said

~ I feel like I'm on an emotional roller coaster; one day (minute) up and loved, the next screamed at and hated

~ You take my time for granted and expect me to be at your beck and call

~ I put my own things aside to be there for you and you turn around to accuse me of not "having a life"

~ You don't keep a deal. Then you scream at me for reminding you of it and tell me that I don't "trust" you

~ You get upset about something and blame it on me

~ I feel like killing myself because I am in so much pain over something that has happened between us

~ You tell me that I've done things that will scar you *for life*

~ You tell me last summer was the happiest in your life because you were away from me

~ I feel like I can't do anything because I'm so depressed about our relationship

~ I don't think you notice or care that I've devoted a big part of my life to making your life work

~ You repeatedly tell me to "fuck off" and to leave you "the fuck alone"

~ You disregard the one request I've made of you and put me down as being "Catholic, Republican . . ." (neither of which I am) to justify your not doing what I ask

~ You are late getting up or leaving and blame it on me

~ I feel like becoming a parent was the worst choice I've ever made

~ Your struggles make me think that adoption isn't viable

~ I'm always arguing with your father about parenting issues ◄∞

After releasing her turbulent emotions, Barbara stuck her words into an envelope and sent them off to me with her assumed name attached. She had captured her swirling emotions, but she knew enough not to deliver the message of distress to her daughter. Such honesty might wound a child, even an adolescent girl. Instead, she hoped those same words, the honest spilling over of feeling, might soothe another mom trapped in lonely tumult.

For Barbara, the lamentations passed. Months later, I received a second installment. The other side of Jessica's adolescent coin was a girl who reawakened Barbara's mother-love. Again Barbara sat at her desk and wrote:

I love it when:

~ You tell me I am the best mom in the whole world

~ You take responsibility and say "It's my fault"

~ You share your excitement about your life with me

~ I think I must have done a good job of parenting because you are such a wonderful person

~ I look at you and see a teenager who is beautiful both inside and out

~ I see your kind heart in things that you do or say to me and to others

~ I feel close to you and you ask me for hugs or give me a hug

~ You tell me you are happy to have us as parents and to be in our family

~ I'm driving and you comment on the beautiful scenery around us

~ I see you using your energy to create awareness and positive change in the world

~ You stop midstream in an argument and tell me you love me and don't want to be fighting with me

~ You thank me for staying up late to help you to finish a paper/project

~ You catch yourself cursing in front of me and you both stop and apologize for doing it

~ You spend the weekend around the house, working, studying, and feeling happy and satisfied

~ You use your experiences to change your behavior positively

~ Your dad and I feel that we are the luckiest parents in the world

~ You tell me you love me ◀○

Over those six months, Barbara's daughter had softened the edges of youthful entitlement. That girl learned to say "Thank you" and "I love you." Barbara's brow lost its frown. She is again a happy mom, willing to do anything, absolutely anything, for her daughter.

Again and again, mothers fall into the "can't do anything right" trap. A writer with a humorist's flare and a gift for dialogue nearly got snared when she tried to rescue her daughter from a bad-hair day.

HAIR
by Cynthia Peel-Knight

The bloodcurdling scream: I am awakened. I bolt upright, the sheet scrunched in my hands, glued to my chest. I sit immobile without breathing. Every neuron in my body tilted on edge. I gasp quietly for breath. I shroud my mouth with my trembling hand, muffling the sound of my breathing. I wait. I hope I merely imagined the horrendous utterance, though somehow I know the scream actually happened.

The agonized shriek pierces the stillness again. Perfect guttural, primordial pitches. My heart pulsating like a windup toy wound too tightly, I spring into action. I move through the chilling house in uncontrollable motion, down the long, dark hall toward the door that leads downstairs to the kids' bedrooms. I reach the bottom of the stairs, breathless. I am a mother with that instinctual urge to protect my young in any way and at all costs. I am ready to negotiate, plead, maim, or kill.

Panicked, I call out, "Camille! Camille! Honey, are you all right?"

I grab the doorknob and open the bathroom door with so much power that I whirl myself back against the wall. I push forward and see her. I recognize the body, but the reflection of her face in the mirror is so badly contorted that I actually look away briefly in disgust.

Confused, I ask, "Camille, what's happening?"

"My hair! Aaauggggaahhh! I hate it and I don't know what I'm going to do with it 'cause it's so retarded!" In the throes of trauma, my daughter begins to cry. "I knew this was going to happen. It happens every time my hair gets this long. I can't control these curls or this stinking frizz!"

I'm still trying to recuperate from my fight-or-flight mode. Between hurried breaths, I manage to say, "Then use that antifrizz stuff you bought for a week's worth of wages."

"It doesn't work. Look!" She yanks the top of her blond hair in her hand. "Nothing works. Nothing is going to work. I asked you to take me to get a haircut. But no. You're just too busy. I can't stand it!"

She's growling, glaring at me with her flared nostrils and her lips pulled tightly to one side. I'm studying her face. I can't believe that this is the latest homecoming queen crowned for poise and beauty. I speak.

"Camille, calm down. It's only five-forty-five A.M. Everyone is still sleeping."

"Mom, I don't care what time it is. I can't help it! I don't know what I'm going to do." She turns abruptly and lunges toward me to castigate me. "And you're no help."

"Camille, it looks fine to me. What do you want me to do? Cut it? Your hair, I mean." (For one instant, I had fantasized *her throat*.)

She turns to me and bares her teeth. "Oh yeah, right, like you're some sort of expert with your big eighties hair."

Then she turns to face the mirror, still watching me.

I am feeling more composed. I speak in measured tones. "Why are you attacking me? I came prepared to save your life down here. And I am your mother. And I don't care if you woke up bald, you don't get to talk to me with so much disrespect."

"Okay, Mom. But I don't know what else to do!" She forces control, seething while sparks of spittle fly from her perfect mouth.

"Wear a hat," I suggest, but I think a brown paper bag would be just perfect.

This adolescent thing is so hard, more challenging than those long, sleepless nights of her infancy. I feel hog-tied. I have this conflict that registers every time she acts like this. I feel like I am so supportive of her. She doesn't seem to know I didn't get a moment of my parents' time for anything that even remotely resembled inner conflict.

If I even *looked* unhappy, my parents attacked me with "Oh. You look so pathetic. Like you have so many problems. You don't have any real worries. Try supporting this family. *Then* you'll know what real problems are."

There was no such thing as having a bad day in my youth.

I look at her. I try to avoid being condescending while reaching for a solution. I suggest, "Maybe you could just have a bad-hair day."

"Oh yeah, sure, right!" she retorts, nodding her head in sarcastic agreement. "Everyone will look at me like I'm a freak!"

I want to shout with all my pent-up frustration, "You *are* a freak!" But I just stand there with my poker face, choosing to say nothing. I recall my newfound resolve to change the way I usually react. I know this is about more than her hair. It's about more than I'll ever know. I feel trapped. I've done this wrong so many times before. I've returned her hateful insults with my own more clever ones. I've bullied her with my knowledge and experience, making her feel hopelessly powerless. I've lied to shut her up, to get her to move past her crisis. I want to do better. I want to make this about her, not me. It's not about me.

The big round globe lights over the vanity seem to penetrate my soul, revealing my past blunders. Is this redemption? Will I do or say the right things for the right reason? I've given this a lot of thought. My intention is to recognize that this is a real crisis for her. Her young life of fifteen years is still intensely centered on herself. She doesn't know that someday she'll be lucky to have time to take a shower, let alone style her hair. I can only throw her a life preserver. She needs to feel that I really mean to save her.

"Camille, I'm here if there is anything I can do for you right now. I'm willing to look at my schedule to see when we can get you in for a cut. I need to have you treat me with respect. I know you can do it because you do it often. I'm sorry you feel so frustrated about your hair. I can see how crazy it makes you. It must really make you feel helpless to try to get your hair to cooperate without success. I'm wondering if you think you could accept your hair like this for today."

I'm desperate to end this uncomfortable exchange. I want the conversation over, with or without solutions.

"Mom. Will it be fixed by tomorrow? I have to work today, and I can't get it cut." She's gesticulating wildly with the hairbrush as she speaks.

"Camille, it most likely won't get cut in the next two days." I close my eyes and sigh. "But please, know we are working on a solution. Your haircut will be a priority. Look, we can't change your hair today. Can I ask you to change the way you think about it? I'm afraid you'll let this taint your whole mood and make you miserable today."

"Oh yeah. Right. Did you learn that one from *Oprah*?"

With this remark, I feel the strain of the conflict. I'm tempted to react—to abruptly end this exchange or make her feel more uncomfortable than I do. I pause. I choose instead to encourage her.

"Camille, you can decide to accept that your hair isn't your ideal style but that you are still a dynamic, beautiful person."

"I just hate it." She says it without the vehemence, more matter-of-factly. The energy is draining out of her.

I respond, "I'm going upstairs. I think you just needed to get my attention. Next time, do you think we could work at talking it out rather than acting it out?"

I feel myself getting preachy. So does she. She pushes past me. "Could you please just leave? I have to get to school and I'm not even half ready yet."

Not ready . . . when will I ever feel ready for all that it takes to support this young woman? I feel unsettled. With the pressure still in my stomach, I lumber up the long flight of stairs. My legs seem weighted, as if a child is wrapped around my ankles for a free ride.

What I did wasn't perfect, but I know she will come home after school and neither she nor I will feel threatened and insecure. I want to keep her close, in dialogue with me. I don't want to push her away because of my own unrequited struggles. As I reach the last couple of stairs, I feel less pressure. It does feel better to have come from a more conscious place. ⋘

Jean McGroarty found that unconditional love needed a boost from some mother-imposed conditions.

Jean lives in a quiet town in a serene part of the country. The thousand residents of her village have lovingly watched over her twin girls since their birth. Jean overflows with pride when she describes them. Yet behind closed doors, teenage tantrums came in stereo. In her contribution, Jean writes for the first time about how the Surround Sound bombardment taught her to turn up her own volume, to insist on respect.

TWIN TEENS, DOUBLE TROUBLES
by Jean L. McGroarty

I am the mother of twin seventeen-year-old girls. Both are beautiful, blond, blue-eyed young women: talented actors, writers, and artists, conscientious and excellent students. Everyone outside our immediate family loves them.

Until recently, they drove me crazy.

From the time Emma (one minute older than her sister, Ginger) turned ten years old, she began to exhibit what I considered hormonal emotional outbursts. I could almost time them, even though she hadn't started to menstruate. One time I said to one of my friends, "I just wish she'd start her period!"

I remember her stomping so hard on the floor in her room that I thought she'd come through the living room ceiling. I remember her climbing a tree so she wouldn't have to go to some appointment, screaming "I hate you" all the while. I remember her shutting herself in the bathroom all evening so she wouldn't have to go to her room. After hours and hours, I relented. She wrote me a triumphant note saying: "I won. You lost."

Four hours in our little tiny bathroom? Okay, she wins.

Ginger was slower to anger. Her rages were less frequent but more intense. She launched into foul language. She struck out physically at her siblings or at me. She threatened to call Child Protective Services while she raged abusively at all of us.

At times they both exploded. I joked with friends, "I feel like a tethered goat with two velociraptors circling around me, each alternating the attack." The snaps usually started with "You never let me . . ." or "You always . . ." or "You like our brother better!"

As the girls grew older, the synchronized attacks became more frequent. I found dealing with them harder. The day after any upheaval, it was difficult for me to concentrate, to wake up, to function. I felt like every bit of air and energy had been sucked out of me.

Meanwhile, my daughters acted as if nothing had happened. They were winning the bizarre power struggle, and I was sinking a little deeper every day.

I found myself trying to appease them just to stop the arguments and the accusations. I looked for compromise at every turn. I gave in more and more often.

The summer of their sixteenth year was the worst. Ginger erupted during our family vacation and trashed the inside of our car. Throwing maps and receipts everywhere, sobbing and telling us how much she hated us. Emma complained about having to be in the car with "these people" (her family).

On our return, I realized that I had become depressed. I didn't laugh anymore. I had no original thoughts. I prayed each day that we wouldn't have a scene. I had no enthusiasm for anything. My work suffered. Our home was a mess. My girls had become tyrants in my life.

All the while my friends and acquaintances were telling me what nice girls they were. I jokingly asked, "My daughters? Do you mean *my* daughters?" But really, I was sick inside. Why did everyone else like them? Why did I feel so ambivalent toward them? What was wrong with me? What was wrong with them? I wept frequently and for no reason.

The October after that terrible vacation, I had my epiphany. We were taking a day trip to visit my uncle. I told the girls' brother he could come with us. They started screaming at me: "It's a girls-only trip." "Why do you always let him do what he wants?" "It's all your fault." "We're not going. We refuse." I tried again to appease, to compromise, to do anything to stop the yelling and the anger.

We finally took the trip, sans little brother, in sullen silence. We had no fun. The girls chatted with each other, but I couldn't bring myself to even look at them, let alone forget what they had done and said. The trip was short. By the time we returned, I had come to a decision. I was going to once again become the mom in the family. I would no longer let them tyrannize my home and my life.

I made my announcement the next day. "Anyone who curses at me will no longer have the privilege of riding in my car. Period. If another uproar like the last one happens, I will walk out the door with your brother and leave you behind. You will abide by written rules. Above all, you will remember that I am in charge, that I am the mother in our family, and that you will treat your parents with respect." Amazingly, they listened. Things started to improve.

Of course, that wasn't the end of the emotional scenes or the yelling at their brother. However, when they started to snipe at me, I simply told them to back off immediately, and then I walked away. They slowly came to realize I meant what I had said. They were refused rides to certain key events because they had used inappropriate language. Their brother got to do things that they couldn't because of their outbursts. I went to movies alone when they started histrionics.

The funny thing is, I think from that point on, they became happier. I know I became happier. I realized that boundaries and limits are necessary in mother-daughter or parent-child relationships. I had allowed my daughters to take over. They had no clear boundaries. I felt I couldn't control the situation, so I was unhappy. In a sense, they couldn't control the situation either. They weren't able to rein in their emotions.

My daughters are now entering their senior year in high school. Our relationship is not perfect and surely never will be. But there is more respect in our home. My girls waste less time and energy in petty anger. And I am stronger. I can take what they dish out philosophically and with grace.

I joke, "I'm the mother of three teenagers, and I'm not afraid of anything."

You know, I think that may be true. ⟨∽⟩

For Jeanie French, reason wasn't enough to quell one particularly stormy confrontation. Water and good humor were required to put mother and daughter back on an even keel.

⟨∿⟩
THE PERFECTLY HORRIBLE STORM
by Jean L. French

Cold water. It's good for separating fighting dogs and cooling sexually frustrated males. Who'd have guessed it would also be good for calming teenage female hysteria?

I have two children; my son, the firstborn, has always been "the difficult child." Not that my husband and I didn't love and enjoy Joel. But right from the beginning, he's always been work in a way that Amy, three years younger than her brother, wasn't. Amy could amuse herself for hours. Even as a toddler, she created games and songs and dramas and acted them out with dolls or puppets. She made the puppets herself out of paper bags. If you told her to do something, nine and a half times out of ten, she'd do it with little or no complaint. She was never one to throw what my mother called "walleyed fits." She was cuddly and sweet and, yes, compliant.

That's why this particular event, when Amy was thirteen, caught me completely off guard. I'm not sure now what we were arguing about.

Some months later, I asked Amy if she remembered what set her off. She thinks it was something to do with cleaning her room (which she hated). I still maintain it was the time I tried to show her how to do a math problem (she was sure that her teacher had shown her a different way).

Whatever it was, Amy went into a tizzy.

I remember we were sitting on her bed. She leaped to her feet and threw something, a book or papers, to the floor and started shouting at me.

I'm sorry to say I don't have a slow temper. When somebody yells at me, I yell right back. It wasn't long before both of us were standing there yelling at the top of our lungs. Neither of us could hear a word the other one was saying. It struck me as funny. Finally, I started to laugh. That just made her madder. So I was standing there laughing and trying to calm her down, and she's letting the rage run free. After a while, it started to scare me.

Amy was petunia-red in the face, her eyes were rolling, and spittle was flying out of her mouth. This was definitely a walleyed fit.

I didn't know what to do.

I thought about slapping her. I remembered how my mother had slapped me occasionally when I became disrespectful—"sassy," she called it. I could speak my mind to my mother, but I wasn't allowed to sass. I always hated it when my mother slapped me; it humiliated me, which is why it worked, I guess. And in the movies, when a woman gets hysterical, you slap her. I thought, "Okay, I'll slap her." But my heart wasn't in it. The gentle tap I gave her low on her cheek didn't have any effect.

Maybe the next idea also came from the movies or television or cartoons. I don't know. I do know I had this image of a woman turning a garden hose on two fighting dogs. And inspiration struck.

I grabbed Amy by the arm and started pulling her toward the bathroom. She was screaming, "What are you doing? What are you doing to me?" but not really resisting. She could have resisted, easily. Although I still outweighed her by twenty pounds, she was already several inches taller and quite a bit stronger, due to her athletic prowess at volleyball, basketball, and gymnastics. But I don't think resisting even entered her mind. Her mind had shut off. She wasn't capable of rational thought.

I got her, still screaming incoherently, into the bathroom; pushed until she stepped, fully clothed except for shoes, into the tub; and then I turned the shower on full blast—cold. Her screams stopped immediately under the shock. She stood there for a few seconds, absolutely silent.

I said, "Are you calming down?"

She nodded and shivered. "Can I get out now?"

I told her to wait a minute. I adjusted the water to warm. When she stopped shivering, I helped her out of the tub and out of her soaked clothes. Then I wrapped a big towel around her skinny body and just held her. She was weak, exhausted from that crashing storm of emotion she'd just weathered.

I got her back to her bedroom. We sat on the bed, her dripping-wet head on my shoulder, both of us holding on as tight as we could. And we talked.

We talked about growing up and hormones and how they can make you just feel wild sometimes. We talked about learning self-discipline and how that doesn't mean you can't express how you feel about something. And I told her that as much as I respected her as a person and appreciated her budding womanhood, I was still her mother. I'd have the final say about things for some time to come.

And it was okay for both of us.

After a while, she lifted her head. "Why'd you put me in a cold shower?"

"Well, slapping you didn't work," I said. "I couldn't think of anything else to do. You were so out of it, I was afraid to just leave you alone."

Then I told her that we'd laugh about this someday.

And we have. ∞

limits of power

LETTING GO
by Veronica Golos

My daughter is fourteen.
She has thirteen earrings
in one ear
another in her nose—
a dragon in red, green and
     blue, tattooed
on her—thigh.
She is as colorful as the
     spin-wheels,
the ones we put on our bikes
     when we were young.

Now she is wearing bracelets
     on her ankles
chains on her waist
a necktie in delicate lace.
I can't understand
her words
she seems to have learned
     another language
while I was sleeping
so that bad is good
and fat is fine
and wack is—wack
and I don't know where to
     find
her.

She stands for no crap and for
     that I'm glad
she brings home women-
     who-are-men-who-are-
     women, people

who are peopling in the
     world as more than
     women and men and
I should be glad because
but I am scared because
I want something I can
     recognize
I want that daughter I can
     see when she
washes—the green eyeliner,
     maroon eyebrow pencil,
purple hair tint, and wicked
     black lipstick off—
and is soft, for a moment.

I try to hold on but it seems
     I'm slipping
she is the rainbow fish the
     flying fish
the one who slid from my
     womb like she wanted
     to run—
and ever since.

As she goes to the door,
     I suddenly see:
her bones are too delicate
     for wear.
I don't know how they
     hold the muscle, the
     tendon,
how she continues to stand.

I weep when I imagine
(and I do, nightly)
of her becoming *gone*
of her being *not here*
not to mention all the rest.

Even though when she looks at me
with those eyebrows of hers
in the *manner* of hers
in that
*Mother, some things I just can't
     explain* way of hers
I could brain her! But I always
     give in.

And she walks out and into
and, sister, I know what is out
     there

waiting for her
because she is too
bright too brilliant too
full of color
I want to hide her from it—
but I think she already knows it.
So I must let her go
this tinted girl
this lilac fuchsia fashioning
     herself
this curled passion wrapped
     in black
this moment that comes and
     goes all at once
this seed
this me
this
daughter.

ᴄ☙

Until children reach adolescence, setting limits is among the primary tasks of parenting. With adolescence, that task changes. The challenge becomes letting go of our daughters—gradually, with a safety net below them.

From the moment our children are born, we enclose them in limits designed to keep them safe. We set the rules—when to sleep, what to eat, where to go, what do to—parameters firmly placed for their own protection. Making boundaries, keeping children secure, practically defines the role of parent. With our children securely limited, mothers feel at ease. Our protective instincts idle comfortably on standby.

Then adolescence enters. Our daughters' bodies develop and the world beckons. Suddenly, we face a new and frightening responsibility— to release our daughters. All the years of nurturing lead to this point; we raise children to launch them. Yet when we actually are required to loosen the strings that bind them to us, confusion and fear set in. Confused, we don't know exactly how to let go, how to accept our daughters' sailing off without abandoning them prematurely in treacherous waters. We vibrate with anxiety.

No wonder one mom reported, "I look at my daughter—this beautiful, vivacious creature. I just want to lock her in a cage and feed her chocolate mousse. I know I can't. I know she has to explore the world. But I fear for her. I really do."

Another mother said, "I understand now why my mother always waited up for me. She couldn't sleep. I can't sleep until my daughter's home. That's why I set a curfew. I know she can get in trouble before midnight, but I need her to come home. So far, she does."

What's a mother to do? At the very time our daughters are most at risk, they are more attracted to experimentation, adventure, and danger. At the very time they are most in need of reasonable limits, they are most unreasonable. The answer is never clear. The parental progression from guardian to mentor takes different turns in every mother/daughter relationship. But nearly always, there's a tug-of-war along the way. My daughters and I had our moments.

I had painted the living room pink. A thirteen-by-twenty-four-foot room, all in two shades of pink. It wasn't cotton-candy pink. I could not, would never, associate myself with too much sweetness. No. Not too pink. I had stirred just enough black into the gallons of paint to make the walls mature, sophisticated, creative, daring, and warm.

Manju, my older daughter, fit in this expansive space. When Manju's school day was done, she nestled in the far corner of this room. She spread out. She read. She studied.

Then one day in eighth grade, she did something she'd never done. She brought a boy home. And that day I did something I had never done. I made a rule.

I walked into the living room, her dad by my side, and made an announcement: "When you're in here with a boy, the door stays open."

I suspect, though I can't quite remember, we used the opportunity to assert more authority. My husband, Michael, and I stood shoulder to shoulder, listing our demands. "No telephone conversations until homework is complete. Straight home after school. No phone conversations longer than thirty minutes."

The pastel glow drained from Manju's face, leaving the dark pallor of mistrust. She screamed. For the first time in her life, she screamed at us. "You used to be my friends." She paused before delivering the next salvo. "You've turned into *PARENTS*."

She hurled the final word—*parents*—with vehemence usually reserved for obscenities.

I had betrayed her without warning. Until that moment, every parenting mistake I had ever made fit into a different pattern. Over and over, without variation, I gave her too much responsibility too early.

Manju had emerged from my body, laid on my belly, looked around, and drunk in her environment. I nursed my firstborn, her eyes wide open, studying my face. I held this vision: my daughter, a wise old soul. Since the day she was born, I had burdened her with trust. I treated her like she was older than her years. I put her in day care too early. I gave her a clothing allowance too young. I sent her on buses too soon. Each time I imposed a premature responsibility, Manju carried her load with laudable competence.

For twelve years, I had reasoned with Manju. Discussed options. Asked for options. Given advice. I had listened. I hadn't dictated rules. I wasn't about enforcing regulations. I had never acted like a *parent*.

Suddenly I had changed.

That day she had walked through the door with a boy, a symbol of her new maturity. For the first time in her life, I didn't trust her judgment. Afraid her emerging sexuality would overpower her reason, scared her impulse toward freedom would crush her stability, I tried to bind her with rules.

For the next four years, I behaved like a faltering disciplinarian. I succeeded just well enough to evoke Manju's occasional wrath, send her into fleeting periods of alienation, and teach her selective secrecy. That's the best I could muster.

Still, the distance between *parent* and daughter saddened me.

Rebecca Newman had once prided herself on instilling a respect for education: "I was the perfect elementary school mom. I set up a place and a time for homework. I brought Allison hot chocolate. I corrected her spelling and helped when the math eluded her.

"When she was in ninth grade, I followed the same routine. Allison christened me with a new identity—*Domineering, Vindictive, Nonaccepting, Intolerant, Emotionally Abusive Control Freak*. But the vilification didn't scratch my Good Mother veneer. Then she said, 'You don't want me to succeed for myself. You want me to get good grades for you. You need me to be on the honor roll and to go to an Ivy League school. It's your last chance to prove that you're not dumb. Well, Mom, that's your problem, not mine. Besides, you can't do algebra to save your ass.' She was right."

Jill Morris, a therapist, lives a thousand miles away from me and Rebecca Newman, but she spoke of a similar melancholy. "I know I have to set guidelines and make rules." In the shadow over her words was the message "It's a tough job, but somebody has to do it." A parent has to parent. Jill's voice softened. "My daughter doesn't confide in me. She's not a friend. That's a disappointment.

"Strange thing is, I like teenagers. I really do. But with my own daughter, our history makes her unable to use me. She could. She could trust me. It's my profession. I know how to keep confidences. But she needs to do her own thing. It's really hard for me.

"My influence becomes so much less direct. I just cross my fingers and hope."

Maybe there's no escaping the conflict that brandishing protective discipline brings to the relationship between mother and adolescent daughter. Even a young California mother like Stephanie Large lost her playmate when she began wielding parental authority.

 ॐ

FROM PLAYMATE TO PROBATION OFFICER
Thoughts from Stephanie Large

"With me being so young and all, Jamie and I were more like sisters. I mean, I was pregnant with Jamie when I was fifteen. I deal with life every day with humor. Jamie and I skipped down streets, went to the county fair, had a ball.

"Now Jamie's fourteen, nearly fifteen. She calls me her *probation officer*." Without a breath of hesitation, Stephanie described how she tracked her daughter. "Jamie goes to a party or dance. She has to call me every two hours until ten o'clock. After ten, she's got to call every forty-five minutes. She misses a call and I just might show up. I told her, 'If you even just think about drinking, doing pot, or going too far, I'll storm in there and drag you home by your hair.' She knows it's true."

From the resolve in Stephanie's voice, I heard her message: When it comes to protecting my baby, I don't care a hoot if I embarrass her and humiliate myself. I noted her pride and chuckled, impressed by her ability to intimidate, when she announced, "All the little boys, they're scared to death of me."

She continued speaking, finding security in her daughter's honesty. "Even though I'm her probation officer, she still tells me stuff. Like the other day, she came home and told me some of her friends went behind the pizza place to smoke pot. I just listened. Now I restrict how much time she's allowed to spend with those kids."

Stephanie knew she couldn't stop temptation from crossing her daughter's path. A touch of fear invaded her tone as she confided, "Jamie's a sweet girl. I don't worry about her causing trouble. I am afraid she'll follow. Other little girls have fewer rules. I try to plant small moral messages in her head. I hope she'll hear a little voice when she needs it."

I envisioned Stephanie as a pint-size angel sitting on her daughter's shoulder, poised to whisper messages of conscience, just like in the cartoons. ❧

Sometimes we might as well save our breath. No words, no amount of lecturing, cajoling, or reasoning will rescue our daughters from adolescent insecurities, those devils poised on the other shoulder, whispering words of mischief or misery.

Writing from the Midwest, Denise Crumrine expressed melancholy resignation as she watched her daughter enter adolescence.

WATCHING THE STRUGGLE
by Denise Crumrine

Being a mother is weighing heavy on my heart these days.

My daughter is twelve. I see her struggling for independence and remember my own struggle. I want to allow her the freedom to find her own way, but I'm terrified of the pitfalls in her path.

I thought we females had come along in the last generation. Now I see that some things never change. I want my daughter to be strong and confident and empowered. Instead, I see the same weaknesses that my friends and I experienced—the insecurities of adolescence, wanting to fit in with the popular group, and the desire to be liked by the right boys.

I want to gather her and her friends and beg them to find themselves, to explore the wonderful people they are and feel the power they have. But they wouldn't listen any more than we did to our mothers.

That is what breaks my heart—I have to sit back and watch them struggle to find the truth that I already know. ❧

At times even the best daughters don't respond to the most wisely chosen guidelines. Or maybe girls who live within arm's reach of big-city sophistication grow into trouble earlier.

Meryl Brownstein lost all feeling of parental power. She felt defeated. She pondered her daughter's transformation from "the bubbliest child on earth" into a burdened soul. Meryl wondered when, and where, and why she lost control.

SOCIETY'S SEDUCTION
Thoughts from Meryl Brownstein

"What do I think happened? I know it's too simplistic to attribute my daughter's difficulties to any one thing, but I'm going to speak in the general sense. Basically, I think the problem was that my daughter was too good, too kind, too compassionate, and probably too naive.

"I carefully screened the movies she watched. I limited TV. We went to shows, watched old musicals, and read the classics out loud. I tried to protect her from all I saw in the culture and thought was toxic and destructive.

"In the end, I couldn't compete. Outside influences poisoned my child.

"I couldn't compete with the media, with parents who didn't have a problem renting R-rated videos for ten-year-olds, and teachers who showed MTV during school lunch periods.

"I couldn't compete with irresponsible mothers and fathers who made my husband and me look like we were crazy—overprotective for insisting on curfews.

"I couldn't compete with her friends who used justified anger at their own parents to convince my kid that I was awful.

"Throughout this siege, my husband and I held on to each other. But we began to question every decision we had to make. We felt confused by every unreasonable request. We had to struggle through, ask ourselves, 'When do we give in? When do we hold firm? When to say yes? When to say no?' At times we gave in, even when we thought it was bad. We feared another alternative would be even worse. We said yes when all we wanted to say was no.

"We're not controlling parents. It's just that we're trying to hold on to a value system that seems to be melting away all around us.

"I don't want to come off as lecturing. My daughter hates a lecture. But someone has to be the voice of reason." ∾

Adolescence comes. Mothers deliver reasonable messages. Daughters slam the door in our faces, put their foot down, and swear, "Mom, I'm doing what I want and you can't stop me." No mother is immune.

Karilee Halo Shames is the author of *The Nightingale Conspiracy*, on nursing in the twenty-first century, along with a list of other titles. Karilee is also a professor, a medical practitioner, a psychotherapist, and a feminist. Still, her daughter simply refused to follow family guidelines. Shauna (now a women's studies major at Harvard) challenged Karilee to the depths of her motherly attachment. Sitting with a pile of exams on one side and revisions for her thyroid book on the other, Karilee wrote about their hard-fought time.

BEYOND CONTROL
by Karilee Halo Shames

For months, Shauna had been telling me that she needed me to trust her more, that my attempts to establish curfews were upsetting to her. I felt I was doing the "proper thing" as her mother. Honestly, inside I was terrified at having a fifteen-year-old daughter, given the tremendous risk of violence for girls of that age. Also, knowing what I know about the cycles and patterns of families, I sensed that this age could be as turmoil-filled as my teen life had been (when my mother broke her arm on me at age fifteen—but that's another story).

On this particular Thursday, Shauna had a cold, and it was a half-day at school. I told her to please come home at lunchtime, when school was out, and rest. Rich and I are both health professionals, so this is a very important focus in our lives. We had raised the children to pay attention to their body messages, something Shauna simply "didn't have time for."

That day at noon, however, something unusual happened. I was state coordinator for a national nurses' association, and the president had come to my town for a visit. I had offered to meet with her for lunch and was joyfully driving her to a restaurant. As we drove past the high school Shauna attended, I happened to catch, out of the corner of my eye, a glimpse of my intelligent, passionate daughter climbing into a car filled with teens. Shauna had specifically asked me if she could do something with Amanda, her best friend. I had said no, that she needed to come home and rest.

I couldn't do anything about Shauna's defiance at that moment, with the visiting president in my car. However, that evening I told Shauna that we needed to talk. She refused to stop at that time. (Shauna was always doing twelve things at once.) So I told her that we would need to discuss what happened before she made any plans for the weekend.

The next day was Friday. Our family made a habit of turning off the phones Friday evening, renting some fun videos, and having a Sabbath together, where we shared our stories of the week and laughed and rested. We always looked forward to this as a time to relax and focus on enjoying being together. I knew it wasn't the time for Shauna and me to process her obvious disobedience, so I again told her that we could postpone our discussion until sometime over the weekend before she did anything with friends.

On Saturday morning, however, I heard a "clunk, clunk," sound from the hallway. Much to my surprise, when I went down the stairs, I saw Shauna on roller skates, with a backpack on. "Where are you going?" I asked her.

"To the library. I'm meeting Sara."

I said, "Shauna, we have to talk about what happened on Thursday. You deliberately disobeyed me. You have never done that before. You cannot go to see Sara until we discuss this."

Shauna, looking obviously disgusted, kept clunking down the hallway. She marched down the front steps and over the rock driveway to the front gate. I followed her, amazed at this uncharacteristic behavior of the daughter I had nursed for two years, who had always been independent but reasonable.

She turned and glared at me as she opened the gate, and said, *"What are you going to do—lock me up?"* And with a slam of the gate, she was gone. Never before had she been unwilling to discuss anything.

I figured she'd go the library, get her work done, come home mid-afternoon with a sheepish grin. But as afternoon melted into evening, Shauna did not appear.

To further complicate matters, the tension in the household precipitated an argument between me and my husband, Rich. We were supposed to go to his friend's party, and he ended up going alone. As I sat home with the two other children, I became more and more agitated.

Finally, it was nine P.M. and I was beside myself. I called Sara's house, got the message machine, and left a message there. Sara later called, saying she hadn't seen Shauna for hours.

In desperation, I decided to check my office voice mail. There was a message—one that chilled me to the bone. "Hi, Mom, this is Shauna. I've decided to take a few days away with some friends of mine. You don't know them, so don't try to find me."

Now I was panicked. We simply had never had to deal with anything like this from our straight-A student. All the teachers raved about her, she was best friends with the counselors and principal at her school, and was the only youth ever selected to have a full-cover photo on our local community tabloid, the *Pacific Sun*. I honestly didn't know what to do. I thought about myself at age fifteen and remembered the verbal abuse I experienced at the hands of an overwrought, undersupported, and immature mother. I had worked so diligently to have a respectful relationship with my daughter and simply hadn't seen this coming.

Just then the phone rang. My heart leaped, and I jumped to answer it. No, it wasn't Shauna. It was my friend Dorothea, a very strong woman who had single-handedly raised her own four children. I told her what was happening, and she said in her strong, clear way, "You have to call the police. That's the only option."

I struggled to make sense of this. My fear was overpowering, and I just wanted my daughter home safely. I imagined monsters in the night, depraved humans, preying on the child I had guarded and protected all these years. I was unable to come up with any better solution.

I called Rich and told him he had to come home and help me. Then I called the police and discussed options. Fortunately, the policeman who came to our home was very experienced in this type of situation and extremely competent. He told us what we needed to do. I had Gigi, our younger daughter, look for numbers of Shauna's friends. Gigi found an electronic gadget on which Shauna had listed her friends alphabetically. We called everyone on the list, late at night, telling them if they heard from Shauna to please tell her she had to call home right away, that the police were looking for her.

Then we sat and waited. Within an hour and a half, the phone rang. Shauna was furious. "What's going on?" she asked.

I said, "Shauna, I don't know what's happening with you, but we have a policeman here. He wants to talk to you. He says if he doesn't see you in person, he is obligated to put your name on every computer in the country, listed as a missing child. He says this will give you a record. You have to come home."

Shauna kept saying, "I don't want to."

And I kept saying, "I hear that. And I respect that. But you have to. Think of the future you have planned and college scholarships you want. Is this worth it?"

She talked to the officer, who told her to come home so he could see she was okay.

Then I got back on the phone. I told her she could talk to the officer then go to bed. I said, "Your room can be your safe place. I won't come in there. But you will have to talk with me at some point. Not tonight."

Another hour or so passed. We heard the key in the lock. She came in, threw down her things, looked at the officer, and screamed, "Mom, this is the lamest thing you have ever done." She talked to the policeman and went to bed.

We slipped food into her room via her siblings for the next day or two. On Monday I stayed home in my pajamas. Eventually, she came out. We had an uncomfortable dance around each other for a while, and finally, when she plopped on the living room couch, I joined her.

Shauna and I talked, quietly. I followed her lead. I had always known that Shauna was one of my best teachers. She didn't let me down. She pulled herself together and picked up where she had left off as if it had never happened. She didn't want to talk much, except to reiterate that she felt we had her on too tight a leash and didn't trust her.

After a couple of months, I asked her to come with me to a therapist I knew who specialized in girls' groups and parent-child communication. I thought it was very courageous of Shauna to readily agree, since this was someone I had used for my own counseling in times past, and I had a professional relationship with her. Shauna was very willing. I was grateful.

By then I felt very distanced and estranged from Shauna. For me, a delicate bond of trust had been severed, and I didn't know how to repair it.

When we arrived at Ilene's office, Shauna and I sat across from each other. Ilene asked me to start. I took a few minutes to describe what was going on. I told her how fearful I was. I trusted Shauna, but not others who could do her harm. I rambled on about my multitudinous fears and my sense of inadequacy in attempting to mother a fifteen-year-old, since I had experienced such volatile mothering myself. Finally, I paused for a breath. Ilene and Shauna were staring at me.

Ilene turned to Shauna, whom she had never met before, smiled, and said, "Shauna, do you ever feel like your mom is straight out of the fifties?"

I looked at Ilene with a puzzled glance, interrupted by the gleeful laughter of my daughter. "I can't believe you said that!" Shauna screeched in mirth. "That was exactly what I was thinking. How did you know?"

Ilene and Shauna had bonded. I realized the wisdom of Ilene's maneuver. As a therapist myself, I felt slightly uneasy, but I trusted Ilene. She knew what she was doing. From there on, things went well.

Shauna was pouring out her side of the story. At one point, passion overwhelmed my better judgment, and I interrupted her. She turned and glared at me and in a very sharp tone said, "Don't interrupt me. I'm not done!"

Ilene turned to me and laughed. She said, "You know, Karilee, somehow I really don't think you have to worry about Shauna. She seems quite capable of taking care of herself." We all laughed.

At the end of the session, Ilene pulled me aside and said something I will never forget. "Here's how I see it. You have two options. Either you let her go or she'll go."

Those words rang through my brain for days. I had raised Shauna to be strong and to feel powerful. She had learned to use her strength in service for the betterment of the world and was now using it to salvage her own life, something I was unable to do at her age. My mother, in her rage, would have—and almost succeeded in—killing me at fifteen. I knew I had to do it another way, but I didn't know how to let go.

The next few years were spent under Shauna's wise guidance, learning this lesson. There were many times I felt scared and wanted to hold on to her, to direct her life, to advise her. But she had stopped asking me and was learning her own way.

I began to realize that to mother a strong daughter means following your own intuition when she is young and allowing her voice and intuition to begin guiding her as she matures. I realized we have few manuals for raising strong daughters. I saw that it's up to us, as mothers, to learn to release and let go with grace, to trust the world to support our daughters' strength. ◀◦

In Shauna, that strength has risen up and triumphed.

Like Karilee, all mothers face an obligation to loosen the strings of attachment, stand back, and let girls learn their own lessons. Daughters walk onto the adolescent stage. Mothers are left behind the scenes. No matter how much we crane our necks and strain our eyes trying to get a clear view of our daughters' lives, we can't.

By accident, I've had a glimpse or two of how blind I really am. Those flashes of insight have done nothing to dispel my fear of being left in the dark.

Fear of the Dark

Manju sat in the driver's seat, her learner's permit safely tucked into her wallet. I sat beside her. We reached the end of the driveway. Manju braked and asked, "Right or left?"

I considered the options. Turn right toward the narrow, slippery bridge and the hairpin curve? Turn left to the blind entry on busy Route 63, followed by the five-way intersection with the obstructed view? There and then I had a pang of near-paralysis. "There's no safe way to leave our house. Which way do you go? I have no idea."

Two years later, Manju had survived turning left and turning right. This day, she sat in the passenger seat as I crept into the five-way intersection with the obstructed view. Guiding me through, looking right while I looked left, Manju commented quite offhandedly, "This intersection is so dangerous. I'm lucky that accident wasn't worse."

I stopped dead in my tracks. "Accident? You were in an accident? What accident?"

Manju put her index finger sideways between her front teeth, nodded, and mumbled, "Oh . . . yeah . . . I forgot. I never told you." Then she tilted her head reassuringly and, without the tiniest wee bit of remorse, said, "There were a lot of little things I never told you. You would have worried."

I sat, stunned. What little things? What near-fatalities had I missed?

Mothers never see the whole adolescent movie. Obviously I didn't. Throughout Manju's teenage years, I delivered a stock line: "Manju's wonderful. So mature and emotionally available."

With Sara, my younger one, I felt I knew more than I wanted to. I thought, "Maybe it's weird that Sara tells me so much." Then, after *Ophelia Speaks* was published, Sara was interviewed in *The Boston Globe*.

The reporter's question: "How much do you think even the most perceptive parents know about their adolescent daughters?"

Sara's answer: "Nothing. I quite honestly didn't talk to my parents about anything."

So there you have it. My daughter announcing to the world: "My mother's deluded."

It's hard not to feel spun by our apron strings. How much privacy do we give our daughters? How much do we investigate? When does a secret become a lie? Where should the boundary between a mother and a daughter be drawn? How close is too intimate? How far is too distant? What's normal? What's healthy?

Robin thought she knew every nuance of Jessica's life. She bragged to her friends whose daughters hid under a stony silence: "I value Jessica's honesty above all else. Yes, she tells me to go to hell. Sure, she berates me. But she tells me everything. No secrets. No lies."

Then one day Robin had to admit how little she really knew. "My husband found a letter. He read it. I never would have read it. I respected Jessica's privacy. Besides, I thought she was completely open with me.

"Then he told me, 'She steals. She steals clothes and makeup.'

"I felt like a fool."

INESCAPABLE TRUTH
by Jan Marin Tramontano

Which are the most desperate lies?
The ones she tells me
Or those I tell myself.

I, the mother, she, my child,
A teenager, barely a woman
Who is me, was me.
Exposed, unarmed.
Searching for herself in shadows.

I, the weak protector; she slips
Beyond my grasp.
Those tiny fingers no longer
    entwine mine
Now she wrenches her rigid
    fingers free.

I stretch to hold on, frantic to save
    her from
The slippery slope, calling hollow
    warnings
Into the air.
She hears nothing and flies
    recklessly away.

I, the hapless detective, like a
    suspicious wife
Looking for traces of betrayal.
A magnetic force field pulls me into

The piece of her world within
  ours.

Clinging to the hope my real
  daughter lives.
Fearing I'll find evidence
I can't pretend is something else.
I sift through her bedroom floor
  piled high,
Scattered pieces of her life.

Ashamed, driven, I search for
  solace among
Her smoky black shirts sporting
  symbols of death,
The flimsy lingerie trimmed
  with leather.
I press them to my face,
Searching for my baby's scent
That child of mine
Whose light brightened my world
Whose loss I mourn.

I, the inquisitor, she,
The unwilling confessor.
Where were you? Who were
  you with?
I demand.

My heart racing, her eyes darting
No time to plan a good story.

Can't be so, must be so, need it
  to be
So it is. . . .

Let it be. No. Let her know
  you know
Hold back words, swallow the
  tone.
Afraid she'll run again to them
  from me.
I trade truth for a temporary
  truce.

I, the reluctant collaborator, she
Eager for anyone and
Anything else.

A pause, a brief searching of
  each other's eyes
As if to say, I know you know
It has to be this way.
For now.

I, the mother desperately drawn
  in, she
My woman-child wanting to give
  me peace
On her terms, and I accept.

Operating half blind sends mothers careening from one worry to the next.

Then one day, most of us step on the brakes, stop our overinvolved minds, and take a good look at our daughters. We give up the illusion of control. We see. A woman now lives in the girl's skin. Gail Seligson wrote about the day that she had a new vision of her daughter Joelle. That day she realized Joelle was in control.

SUDDENLY READY
A Contribution from Gail and Joelle Seligson

Joelle just graduated from high school this past June. I am having the usual mother challenge of letting go, [having trouble] believing that she is actually ready to live on her own at the University of Florida, which is a thousand miles from our home. Not once since her last day of high school did I see Joelle awake before two-thirty P.M.

Then, one Friday morning, Joelle appeared on our screened porch wearing a professional outfit of white pants and blue top, résumé in hand. It was eight A.M. She informed me that she was off to an interview at a temp agency. I was surprised but simply smiled and wished her good luck.

Joelle arrived home several hours later. She asked which I wanted to hear first—the good news or the bad. When I opted for the bad news first, she told me that due to construction, she was uncertain where to park for her interview. She left her car in an outside lot for a few minutes as she ran inside to find out where to park. The temp agency told her she was parked illegally. As she ran downstairs to move her car, she saw a tow truck pulling it onto the street. She waved at the tow-truck driver. He waved back at her and continued down the street.

After Joelle got over the initial shock and finished her interview, she thought, "Well, it's a nice day for a walk." She inquired about the towing fee. Then she walked the three miles to the bank, withdrew the necessary $85 from her account, and walked home.

Listening to how she handled herself—the finesse she used when talking to the tow-truck man, trying to convince him to just give her back her car (which didn't work), the fact that she had money in her account to pay for the tow on her own, and her willingness to take matters into her own hands with poise, grace, and optimism—was truly a turning point in my seeing Joelle. She has grown into a young woman ready to face the world and deal with the many complexities and challenges of adulthood.

And the good news: She got the job and begins temping next week.

part two

Disarmed Bodyguards

Sometimes I feel like my daughter's standing in the middle of the road. A huge truck is speeding toward her. I scream, but she doesn't hear me. My feet and hands are tied. I can't move. I can only watch.

—JUDY POHL, MOTHER OF FOUR DAUGHTERS

Feeling paralyzed while our daughters suffer: That's the hardest, absolutely the hardest.

Yet that's the plight of every adolescent's mom. As our daughters make their way in the world, we lose the ability to protect them. More and more, their lives proceed independent of our control. We're no longer welcomed into their classrooms. We often lose track of their friends and seldom know their friends' parents. They rarely consult with us about their flirtations, romances, or sexual entanglements. They deal with the lure of intoxication in secret. Faced with their depression or illness, we can't fix them. While we mothers still feel every protective impulse we have ever known, we're increasingly disarmed. We stand vigilant, always on watch for our daughters' well-being, but we have little power to fend off the hurts that the world may inflict upon them. Instead, we hope that forces outside our door will be kind to our daughters. If not, we stand ready to rescue them.

the culture of school

"IN ELEMENTARY SCHOOL, I WAS TOTALLY WELCOME IN MY daughter's classroom. Any time there was the slightest problem, I called the teacher. We talked. Or she'd call me. Now my daughter has seven teachers. I see them once a year for seven minutes on Parents' Night. The classroom is packed. And get this! There's a rule: Don't ask anything about your kid. I have no idea what's going on in that building. And you know what? The teachers don't want me to know. And my daughter's certainly not going to tell me."

I heard this sentiment nearly universally. In almost every community, large or small, the difference between elementary and secondary school comes as a shock. In elementary school, where daughters generally spend their days with one teacher, mothers feel able to influence a child's environment. Parents and teachers can work together to improve faltering self-esteem, wavering social acceptance, sinking grades. In secondary school, the model changes. When the school bus arrives in the early morning, mothers often feel like they're sending their daughters into alien territory—an impersonal zone beyond their grasp and outside of their control.

One mother described the common sense of alienation. "You know me. When my daughter was in elementary school, I did it all. The field trips. The PTO. The fund-raisers. The volunteer work. I loved it. I practically lived at that school. I adored every teacher. I could walk into any classroom, any time. I trusted those folks with my daughter. Then junior high. Now that was a rude awakening. I was persona non grata. A busybody and a bother. When my daughter started to have a hard time, that was the worst. The *worst*. I had no place to turn. No power." No wonder few mothers spoke or wrote positively to me about their daughters' school experience.

Only one mother, Theresa Henderson Gilstad—who had suffered from a devastating stroke—found support in the comments of teachers. She wrote, "I realized I'm doing a fairly decent job, despite being handicapped. At the end of last year, a prize-winning teacher pulled Erin and Jessica aside and told them that they were two of the most well-raised students in the school." Others found their daughters' schools alienating and judgmental. "I came away feeling, 'School's tough on a girl. And on a girl's mother.'"

Suzanne Jackson sat in my kitchen, all smiles, beaming with pride and joy as she spoke about her daughter, Kyle.

"At Kyle's sixth-grade graduation outing, all these kids, boys and girls, lined up for a race. The whistle blew, the runners took off. Kyle pulled out in front. She won. She was the fastest runner in the school, even faster than all the boys.

"The next fall, in junior high, she joined the track team. I thought this was great, a way for her talent to be nurtured.

"One day, not long into the season, she came home and announced, 'I'm quitting the team.'

"I asked why. She said, 'I don't like beating other people.'

"Kyle's too kind for competition."

With that vignette, Suzanne's attention turned to Kyle's junior high and high school days. She paused and bowed her head, as though searching for words beneath the waxed sheen of my oak table. She gathered her thoughts and looked up. Her expression changed to sadness as she recollected the stories.

TOO CARING TO BE CARED FOR
Stories from Suzanne Jackson

"In elementary school, Kyle's teachers were enthralled by her. They nurtured her. They saw her goodness and encouraged her talents. They had only one complaint: 'Kyle does somersaults across the classroom.' She was so happy in that school, she couldn't contain her joy.

"In less than a week at the junior high, I knew her new school would not value and nourish her.

"Kyle walked through the door, upset. She told me that she and her friend Tina had been walking in the hallway between classes. Tina bumped her head on the edge of a locker door. The metal corner scraped her forehead. Tina was bleeding, and Kyle was comforting her when the bell rang. A teacher saw the girls. This woman barked at them, ordering them to get out of the hall and on to class. Kyle objected. She explained that her friend was hurt and called the teacher's attention to the blood. The teacher showed no sympathy. Instead, she repeated the rule: 'No students in the hallways after the bell rings.'

"That day, Kyle had been made to feel like a rule breaker, like a bad kid."

Suzanne's story faded into self-examination. "Did I call the teacher? I can't remember if I called the teacher."

Suzanne's fingers covered her lips as she felt the special horror reserved for mothers seized by sudden guilt. "I had to have called. I must have supported her."

Suzanne's eyes darted back and forth, looking for a memory. The recollection came. Her tightened shoulders relaxed, and she returned to her story. "I did. I called the teacher. She isn't a bad person. The system, that system, dehumanizes people.

"By ninth grade, Kyle went into a darker place. Cynicism entered. School felt like alien territory to her.

"One afternoon when she was in the cafeteria, some friends came running, yelling to Kyle, 'Tina's fallen down a flight of stairs.' Kyle sprinted to the stairwell, found her friend, knelt down, and took Tina in her arms.

"A teacher arrived and ordered all the students to disperse. Kyle continued to comfort Tina. The teacher demanded that Kyle leave. Kyle refused. The teacher repeated his orders. Upset by his insensitivity and militaristic manner, Kyle screamed, 'Fuck you.'

"Of course, Kyle was sent to the dean of students for discipline. She described the circumstances, explained why she had stayed with her injured friend. The dean understood. He told her he'd need to give her a minor punishment, a detention.

"At that moment, the teacher burst into the dean's office. Right there and then, he insisted that Kyle be suspended. He argued that she had interfered with a medical emergency by not obeying his orders. The dean relented and suspended Kyle.

"Kyle wanted to appeal the suspension. I felt totally supportive. I wanted to affirm her commitment to her friend. I was proud that she had the courage to confront authority. We had to meet with a panel, including the principal. This man was an authoritarian, huge and gruff, with a reputation for intimidation.

"I sat next to Kyle as she explained. She had responded to her friend's need. For Kyle, comforting her friend was more important than following orders. The principal actually listened. He appreciated Kyle's dilemma. He told her, 'You did the morally right thing.' Still, he's an authoritarian. He was incapable of giving in. His rigidity took over. He issued his final judgment: 'You broke a rule and the punishment stands.'

"Kyle decided to appeal to the next level. I admired her, told her I'd go with her and stand by her. We made an appointment with some higher-level administrator.

"At the appointed time, a secretary ushered us into this small formal back room. Nearly the entire space was filled with a long wooden table. We were instructed to sit at one end. This administrator sat at the head of the table. He stared down at Kyle, and I'll never forget his words. He said, 'Kyle, I see your grades have dropped lately.'

"She slumped, and I deflated. At that moment, he punctured our will. It felt so calculated. Like my brother, the police officer. In training, he learned transactional analysis. They taught him to make other people feel like children, to manipulate himself into the authoritative parental position.

"When we left that room, Kyle said, 'I give up. I'll never win.'"

Repeating her daughter's words pierced the thin barrier between composure and tears. Wiping the moisture from her cheeks, Suzanne confessed, "I regret I didn't encourage her to fight on. I felt beaten down. I wish I had been stronger.

"After that, school became more and more defeating. I felt pained sending her off to spend her days in such a soul-ravaging place." ⬤

School can be so oppressive that mothers worry daughters will turn violent.

Marla Jacobs spoke from a determination to warn other mothers about the danger.

THE PRESSURE BUILDS
A Conversation with Marla Jacobs

"One day Kelly told me, 'Mom, I can't go back to that school. If I do, I'm going to hurt myself or somebody else.'

"I said, 'Then you're not going back.'

"I understand Columbine. The pressure builds and builds inside kids. No adults notice. They explode and . . .'"

Marla's voice trailed off without describing the scene evoked by the word "Columbine," without mentioning the guns and the killing. She did not speak the unthinkable, that her own daughter could have turned to violence on others and on herself. Instead, Marla chronicled her struggle to find a safe place for Kelly.

"In elementary school, Kelly's teachers and I shared the same goals. In junior high, I think they thought I wanted them to give her an easy pass. They didn't see that I also wanted to teach her to be responsible. But I knew they couldn't teach her anything unless they paid close attention, unless they took the time to listen to her.

"You see, Kelly has this way of talking. You think she's saying one thing when she means something else. She can look like she's being stubborn when she's really just being slow, trying to understand and get it right. She asks questions. People hear attitude. Really, she means to ask a sincere question. If adults get into a 'because I said so,' authoritative-type thing, well, that just doesn't go with Kelly.

"The whole atmosphere of her junior high had that kind of reform school atmosphere. I'd go into the office. Even the secretaries treated the kids like criminals."

Marla straightened her body, feigned a tight-mouthed scowl, and mimicked a woman behind the counter at her daughter's junior high school.

"'And you. What do *you* want? So? Aren't you supposed to be someplace else?'

"Those secretaries grumbled at everybody, not just to the kids. That's the way they talked to me.

"Why do people who hate kids teach? Kelly had this one teacher. He told her, 'Next time you come to class, bring your brain. If you have one.' Can you imagine a teacher saying that to a student? Kelly came home, her spirit broken, and told me. That guy hurt her. Not just once, but over and over. He kept saying cruel things.

"I felt helpless. Kelly didn't want me to interfere. All I could do was listen and say, 'That's awful.' At least she talked to me. I didn't make her wrong.

"Sometimes I couldn't stop myself. I did interfere. There was this other teacher, Mrs. Herman. She was a decent human being, really, but she just wasn't able to break out of the system to see Kelly's needs.

"Kelly fell behind in Mrs. Herman's class and needed after-school help to catch up. The makeup sessions were scheduled for the same days as basketball practice.

"Kelly was on this tri-community girls' basketball team. She loved it. She was good. Playing hoops was the only thing in her life that really worked for her. She wasn't sleeping. She wasn't eating. Her whole life was miserable except for basketball. She had practice two days a week. It was mandatory.

"I called Mrs. Herman. I explained, 'Kelly needs to play.' I tried to get across how vital this one positive activity was for my daughter. Practice involved a whole team of kids from different towns. Scheduling changes was impossible. So I asked Mrs. Herman if Kelly could come in on other days. She sounded sympathetic. She said, 'I understand. I'll talk with the administration and see if I can schedule Kelly for other days.' When she called me back, her attitude had changed. She'd gone all cold and formal.

"I could just imagine the discussion that went on behind my back. 'That mother is so indulgent. The kid is so spoiled. Somebody's got to teach her responsibility.' And 'Goddammit! If her mother's not going to do it, we are.' So Kelly had to give up basketball.

"There was nothing good left in her life. She got more and more sleep-deprived. She sat at the table, night after night, not eating a thing. She messed up more and more. She turned into this sullen kid. Kelly can be so mean. I know she was mean to me. Really mean. Maybe she started smoking dope and drinking. I don't really know. But she was just a little kid, just twelve years old."

Marla paused. Her face trembled. Tears fell from her cheeks as she struggled to find her next words.

"I had to love her. When she was messing up everywhere, when she couldn't do anything right, I had to love her. I had to give up everything I wanted from her, all my expectations, and ask myself, 'What's right for her? What does she need?'

"Kelly taught me to be clear, to cut away all my own crap, to just see her. I had to set goals and limits and love her. That's what I wanted from the school. I didn't want them to cut her slack or make special deals. I wanted them to discipline her but at the same time see the good in her. I wanted them to look behind her attitude and attend to her needs. They couldn't do it.

"At her school, they couldn't give her anything she needed. They didn't have time for her. I took her out of that place." ⬯

It's the nature of motherhood to feel remorse for our daughters' pain. When they're hurt, we're compelled to wonder where we went wrong.

When school became a burden for Becky's daughter, she looked for cause and effect. What had she done? Had her role-modeling been responsible for her daughter's attitude toward school? As Becky sorted through the reasons for Chrissy's anxiety, she told a story saturated with humor and warmth.

⟿ CONSCIENTIOUS TO A FAULT
A Story from Becky

"I had Chrissy when I was still in college. Can you believe it?

"Nobody who got pregnant in college graduated. Everybody, absolutely everybody, dropped out. But me? What do you think I did? I just dug in my heels. I finished. Then what did I do? I went straight to graduate school. Got my master's. Chrissy was brought up with me studying, studying all the time. Her first memories are of me with my head stuck in a book. I think it affected her.

"Chrissy's hyper about school. She's got all this intrinsic motivation. Really, she's too hard on herself. She gets stressed out.

"Like the other day: I pick her up after school. I'm late. I'd run into some colleagues, had to pick the baby up at preschool. Anyway. No excuses. I'm late. Just a little late. I pull up. She hops in the car and she's crying. Poor kid. New high school and adolescent hormones—she's overwhelmed.

"The system doesn't help. In this city, kids have to test in to the best high schools. Chrissy's young. She skipped a year in elementary school. So last year, at twelve years old, my child had to face this exam to determine the next four years of her life. She didn't get into the school she wanted. All her friends did.

"What could I do? I told her it was a chance for her to charge forward with a whole new life.

"That's what I said to her, but that's not what I said to the principal of the school she didn't get into.

"I confronted him: 'How can this be? All her friends, kids with the same grades, got in and she didn't. Why?'

"He said, 'Different day. Different test.'

"I told him, 'Hey, this is a kid's life we're talking about.'

"I had no recourse.

"So with Chrissy, I stressed that she'd been given this opportunity to reinvent herself.

"Chrissy had gotten self-conscious about the way she looked. She wanted to stand out, to be more noticed. She wanted to dye her hair.

"I figured, 'Why not?' I took her over to this friend of mine. We dyed it red. Now Chrissy's got this one little radical thing: She's a redhead.

"Red hair actually works. The funk was history. Her self-confidence came back. Whenever my husband and I get in a funk, he says, 'Let's dye our hair red.'

"And at her new school, Chrissy got the ultimate consolation prize: These girls asked her, 'Are you a *real* redhead?' She loved that they didn't know. She could be a *real* redhead.

"It's just the beginning of high school. She tested out of freshman algebra, biology, and English. My daughter should be in eighth grade. Most of her classes are with sophomores. The pressure gets to her.

"I took her to a psychologist. You have to understand. Out here in the Midwest parents don't send their kids to a shrink. Only people who are totally whacked out, running around naked, get sent to psychologists. Going to a shrink because you're way too conscientious about school? No. Never. Just not done.

"My daughter was falling apart under the strain. So I sprang for a psychologist. Hey, maybe it helped. I don't know. This Ph.D. gave her profound advice like 'Break your assignments up into small chunks.' That cost me a hundred dollars an hour.

"Now anything she asks for seems like a bargain. 'You want drum lessons? Twenty-five bucks a shot? It makes you happy? Sure. Great. It's a deal.'" ❧

E ven the finest schools money can buy don't always account to parents for their actions.

I had been talking for an hour, maybe more, with a mom. Before hanging up the phone, this mom gave me one instruction. "Nina, please disguise the details. Don't use real names. Except I wish you could use the real name of 'That Fine School.' I'd love for you to tell the truth about That Academy. I hate the place." She had her reasons. Here's how she told her story.

PRESTIGE WITHOUT A PLACE
A Story from Rural America

"My daughter got kicked out of That Academy two months before graduation.

"That school was everything to Larissa. She loved the preppy scene. She had created that life for herself, all by herself.

"In the spring of eighth grade, she decided she absolutely had to go to that prep school. I tried to discourage it. I wanted her home. But she begged. I relented just enough to call the admissions officer. He said, 'It's past the deadline.' I thought, 'Good.' I asked, 'Will you look at an application?' He said, 'It's very unlikely. We already have a waiting list, but your daughter can send her application along.'

"I figured I was safe. I'd let her apply. She wouldn't get in.

"That night Larissa went straight to work. The application asked her to include her two best essays from the last semester. She came downstairs to show me one essay. It was entitled, 'Why Our School Should Have a McDonald's.' I suggested she look for another essay. She was gone for two minutes and returned with 'The Lame Social Life of Rural Teenagers.' I advised her to write a new essay. She went back to her room and came back in five minutes flat with a letter:

> DEAR ADMISSIONS COMMITTEE,
>
> I am submitting my two best essays from this past semester. I wrote them both in ten minutes and received As for both.
>
> As you can see, I will not realize my potential without attending your fine school.
>
> SINCERELY, LARISSA

"I was home free. They'd never take her. But they did. They actually accepted my daughter at the academy based on *that*.

"I called and protested. 'You said you had a waiting list. You said she'd never get in.'

The admissions officer said, 'Never in the history of This Fine School had anyone submitted such horrendous essays. But what your daughter did with them was so clever, we couldn't refuse.'

"Larissa loved the place: the sports, the students, the whole posh environment. It was *her*. From freshman through senior year, she was away from the unsophisticated hicks of hill country. Larissa was in her element.

"Then, two months before graduation, I get this call. 'We're expelling your daughter.'

"I was floored. I thought, 'Larissa's done something outrageous. Really outrageous. Unforgivable. Drugs. Alcohol. Violence. I asked, 'Why?'

"This dean says, 'She put a quote in a paper without a footnote.'

"I couldn't contain myself. I said, 'You've got to be kidding. Give me something meaty here.'

"He wasn't kidding. He said, 'At Our Fine School, we don't forget footnotes by senior year.'

"I still don't believe that was the reason. I mean, *really!* They must have had something else, some suspicions they couldn't prove. They were just looking for an excuse to get rid of my daughter.

"Suddenly Larissa was home, back in public school with only eight weeks until graduation. She was so torn up. She had no friends. I felt really badly for her." ☙

At times, mothers and schools do reach an understanding without rancor. Anna Samson's tie to her daughter Stacy was reinforced with hope, remorse, and anxiety. Eighth grade marked the beginning of Anna's worries. For the next five years, she struggled to keep Stacy physically safe and emotionally afloat. Rather than buoy Anna's efforts, school—the students, the system, and the teachers—pushed her daughter deeper and deeper into trouble. Anna spoke about that grief-filled time.

LOVE THE ONE YOU GOT
Anna Samson's Story

"I'll never forget the day Stacy ran away from school. Literally ran scared. She burst through the door in the middle of a pouring-wet, windy, miserable day. She was soaked through. Her hair was dripping. She stood in front of me shivering and said, 'I can't go back. They'll hurt me. They'll beat me up.'

"I didn't know what she was talking about. We live in this really civilized suburb. It's not exactly gang territory. But it turned out that there are really tough girls in this town. They had threatened to beat Stacy bloody.

"Not that Stacy was an angel. Not that she was incapable of being provocative. But violent? No. Stacy wasn't violent. At least not back then. Not in eighth grade.

"I wanted to call the principal. That possibility scared her more. She said that if she 'ratted' on these girls, she'd be 'dead meat.' She assured me that she could take care of it—that she'd be able to protect herself better if I stayed clear.

"After that incident, Stacy got tough. She surrounded herself with the protection of streetwise, scary-looking kids."

Anna paused, trying to figure out the sources of Stacy's transformation from elementary school star athlete and honor roll student into a high school borderline delinquent with failing grades. She offered every mother a bit of advice.

"Don't let anybody ever tell you there's no difference between the advanced track and the standard track.

"At the very beginning of eighth grade, Stacy came down with a serious case of mono. She was out of school for three months. When she started back, she had fallen behind terribly. The teachers insisted she make up all the work, three months of advanced papers, tests, and projects. Stacy couldn't do it. No way. She was still recovering, still pitifully weak. She had no choice. She had to drop down a level to standard classes.

"In the standard track, that's when she got scared and got tough.

"I'd go to Parents' Night at school. The halls were packed with parents. But when my husband and I walked into Stacy's classes, the rooms were nearly empty. So few other parents. Just me, my husband, another mom or dad or two, and Stacy's teacher. I looked around at all the empty desks and said, 'This explains it. This is why these kids are so lost.'

"But you know, it wasn't just that her friends' parents were neglectful. And it wasn't just that the kids were out of control. Most of the teachers didn't help.

"Like this one teacher, who had loved Stacy's brother, Randy. Randy's two years older. Now, he's no rocket scientist, but Randy's hardworking and polite. Every teacher he ever had thought he was an angel.

"At Open House, this teacher says, 'I just can't believe Stacy is Randy's sister. Randy was so well behaved, so conscientious, so likable, and Stacy . . . well . . . Stacy's . . . so the opposite.'

"There were other parents in the room. I couldn't believe a teacher talked that way about my daughter, especially in front of other parents. If he was so negative in public, he must not have given Stacy any respect in class.

"All through high school, Stacy came home with these horrible grades and these friends who were real 'winners.' I'd drive through town and see her hanging out on street corners with these frightening-looking guys. Stacy was so out of the mainstream. To me, her life looked like a nightmare.

"I felt so sad. High school had been wonderful for me, filled with sports and dances and honors and good, good friends. I look back at those years and I'm flooded with warm memories. I expected it to be the same for Stacy. I thought she'd be a star—an athlete, a cheerleader, in the honor society, the prom queen.

"Instead, by the time Stacy turned sixteen, she wanted out of high school as soon as possible. She applied to this special program—half days at the high school and half days at a local community college. Her guidance counselor wrote her a reference.

"This man saw through Stacy's front, straight through to her goodness. He understood her. He wrote about her maturity, about her need for experience in the real world, about her insight. When I read the letter, tears rolled down my face. It meant so much to me that at least one adult at the school appreciated my daughter.

"During those years, I'd burst into tears all the time. I'd be working. I'd be fine. Then someone, anyone, would say, 'How are you?' And I'd start crying.

"My friends didn't understand. They thought their kids were so much better than Stacy. They'd say, 'Don't allow her to behave that way. Kick her out if she doesn't get her act together.' How can you kick your sixteen-year-old daughter out? Really. You can't.

"Then my husband and I found a Tough Love group. Those parents were the best support for me. I met all these good people from every socioeconomic level and cultural group you can imagine. We were all going through such horror. I listened to their stories and realized I wasn't alone.

"Tough love taught me to give up the kid I wanted and accept the one I have.

"And now Stacy's just out of high school, but she landed this hostess job at this outrageously elegant resort hotel in Hilton Head. She's eighteen and looks like a million bucks. That girl can work a room like you wouldn't believe. I stand back in awe, watching. The charm bubbles out of my girl." ☜☞

the influence
of friends

From I WISH FOR YOU, MY DAUGHTER
by Marianne Peel Forman

I wish you friends with
   no-care hair,
unplucked eyebrows,
and eyes that make you
   laugh and laugh.
Someone with whom you
   can sip iced tea
on a hot summer porch
comforted in each other's
   silence
like old salt and pepper
   shakers
on an antique oak table.

I wish you a place where
   everyone knows you
where their voices chorus
   together
and become the music in
   the room . . .
nothing shrieking out of
   the radio
from a faraway singer,
but friends, like old aunts
whose words harmony into
   song
as they swap the stories
in their party without music,
finishing each other's
   sentences

as they slap their knees
and laugh into the night.

I wish you faces in your life
that you want to photograph
   or film
because you want to
   memorize
the smile or the eyes
or the way the folds come
together when people laugh
   or cry.

I wish you an afternoon
of hat-trying and scarf-
   flipping
in a secondhand store.
Perhaps in front of antique
   mirrors
with an old friend who tells
   you
you look good, so very fine,
   in old hats.

I wish you good-byes that are
   difficult
because we all need people
we don't want to leave
but to whom we yearn to
   come back.

Good-byes that choke your throat
until your hands begin to shake
and you just can't hold back the
    tears
anymore.

I wish you a gracious friend
who will want to paint your
    portrait someday

in oils or watercolors,
capturing the gist of you
more real than a photograph
more lasting than a snapshot
revealing an honest vision of who
    you are
and what lies behind your eyes.

When daughters plunge into the adolescent social scene, mothers often feel crowded out. Friends take on greater importance and exert more influence. We hope our girls will surround themselves with "good" kids who shy away from dangers. We fear they'll land among troubled adolescents with an attraction to risky behavior. We know they won't escape the coercion of cliques.

When Sara was in sixth grade, she still explained her world to me.

"Mom, I'm not one of the popular girls."

"Sweetie, I think kids like you."

"I know, Mom. I have lots of friends. But I'm not even sure I want to be a popular girl."

"Sara, I don't understand. What's a popular girl?"

She straightened her body. Her eyes grew bright with the pride of a daughter who is about to teach her mother a lesson.

"Mom. A popular girl is a girl who thinks she's better than everyone else. And everyone else believes it."

I was blown away. I had never understood the tyranny of the in crowd. Sara had just explained the source of its oppression. Still a little slow to grasp the full social ramifications, I asked, "Do kids like popular girls?"

At this question, Sara flashed one of those incredulous looks that mean "I'm almost a teenager and you're almost more stupid than I ever imagined."

"Mom! Nobody *likes* them. Everybody just wants to *be* one of them."

That's the coercion of cliques. To feel acceptable to themselves, girls believe they need to be accepted into an exclusive sorority whose creed is disdain for other girls. Our daughters are either inside or outside. Either way, many of us find it hard to watch.

When daughters wiggle their way into a position of elevated adolescent status, we see them vying to maintain their place and sneering at those below them. A woman with a "my house is your house, the door's always open, everyone's welcome" attitude talked to me with dismay. "My daughter has become the most popular girl in her school, and I don't like it. She's become this cruel person. I hear her with her friends. They sit around *my* house, making snide comments about other girls. How did she get so catty? How much courage does it take to be kind?"

When the centripetal force of the clique flings daughters to the outside, we see their self-acceptance under siege. Paula Dawkins watched while a gang of girls pushed her daughter into a downward spiral.

OPEN SEASON ON APRIL
A Story from Paula Dawkins

"April's always been a larger-than-life personality. No one could squeeze her spirit into a conventional mold.

"In seventh grade, she had this confidence that made other mothers blush. One time we were on a family vacation. Another couple, a little older than us, really dear friends, tagged along. This other mom—her daughters are all grown up—was just digging April, couldn't take her eyes off my daughter. April was at the top of her form—dancing from one room to another, doing pirouettes down the path to the beach, performing one-woman Broadway musicals for herself, all by herself on the deck of the cabin.

"On a quiet afternoon, I noticed my friend had been sitting alone staring toward the bathroom for the longest time. I thought, 'That's cool; she's lost in her own thoughts.' She noticed me noticing her. She put her index finger to her lips, gently telling me to be quiet. Then she motioned for me to sit next to her. I snuggled close and she pointed to the bathroom. April was standing in front of the mirror, talking to herself. Actually, my daughter was performing for herself, primping with the most outrageous aplomb. She mouthed words, cocked her head from side to side, ruffled her hair seductively, feigned alluring laughter, even, so help me God, winked at herself. My friend whispered, 'Your daughter is so fabulous.' With that, April registered that she was being watched. We'd been caught. My friend blushed. But my daughter just waved and skipped over to the couch. My friend told her, 'Girl, no one's going to dampen *your* spirit.'

"Wish that were true. Other girls have incredible power.

"That fall, we moved from a kind of yuppie suburb to a picturesque country town. With the extra cash from unloading our house, my husband and I figured we could send April to one of the small private schools in our new community. We thought, 'It'll be perfect—a nurturing environment to prepare her for the inevitable ego-bashing of high school.'

"As it happened, April already had friends at one of the schools. When she was younger, she had gone to performing arts camp with a handful of them. They had had a wonderful time together, writing and performing their own plays, dancing and painting. During those summers, April and these girls had been inseparable. The choice of a school for April was clear. I really thought everything had fallen into place perfectly for our move.

"Within a month, I realized the school wasn't a good fit. I don't know how the mismatch escaped me. April is flamboyantly sophisticated for her age. She's like Madonna in a thirteen-year-old body. These girls are the most overprotected children you can imagine. I actually didn't know kids like this, families like this, schools like this had survived the fifties. The girls dressed in these sweet lacy dresses. They carried their books in pink backpacks and wrote poems in baby-blue diaries. They imagined themselves as ballerinas and memorized show tunes. I swear they had never even heard of Eminem. With a profile like this, I assumed they would be sweet. They were sweet, but they had no taste for anything sour, or bitter, or pungent. They spat my daughter out in disgust.

"Of course, April did have her insensitivity. She didn't exactly enter that scene like a wallflower. After the first day of school, she stormed into the house. 'Mom. I can't believe it. These kids know *nothing*. I'm going to have to teach them *everything*.'

"So she took it upon herself to instruct them in the finer points of cool. Only problem was, they had a different notion of cool. I don't know the details, but I can imagine. Her curriculum probably included little graphic lectures on safe-sex practices, drug choices and paraphernalia, transgender identity, hip-hop versus gangsta rap. Those kinds of things. Things she learned from her older brother and sister. Anyway, she expected her generosity would elevate her to a place of unassailable popularity. She imagined unending gratitude for her efforts to guide these girls out of the land of the geeks and into the new millennium. Apparently, the scene didn't run according to script. I can just see it. These little girls with their eyes popping out of their heads, saying 'That's disgusting.'

"By two months into school, she was a pariah. They closed ranks. They wanted nothing to do with her. They were brutal. I'd hear her calling them. One after the other, five girls in a row slammed the phone down on her. Sometimes the girls actually called her. That was the worst. She'd answer the phone, I'd see her face drop. She'd fight back tears. I'd say 'What's the matter, April?' She never told me what they said. My daughter was so wounded.

"I decided I had to meet with her teacher. He had all the appearance and manner of a gentle man—just the kind of person you'd expect in a small country day school with spiritual foundations. I liked him. He wasn't without compassion. He described how the girls excluded April, how she had no one to eat with, no one to do cooperative projects with, and no one to play with. I saw my daughter spun off into a lonely corner. He said, 'It's actually good for her.' He seemed to think she needed lessons in humility.

"I'm her mother. I didn't see the awakening of humility. I saw the dawn of self-loathing.

"I tried prying open the door to that girl clique by talking to their parents. No such luck. I got the message 'We're down-to-earth folks and your daughter is a bad influence.' They worried that April was exerting 'negative peer pressure' on their precious little girls. I ask you, who was feeling negative peer pressure? Not that tight little covey. All the negativity was raining down on April.

"I worried terribly. April was completely isolated. For such a gregarious girl, the loneliness was devastating. I saw the self-esteem drain from her body. She slumped around the house. And she wasn't easy to be locked inside with. She's always had a Dr. Jekyll/Mr. Hyde sort of disposition. Now Mr. Hyde pummeled Dr. Jekyll into oblivion. I got stuck with Mr. Hyde—April was nasty on top of depressed.

"I had to find her a therapist, a good therapist, and quick. I tried to drive up to the subject slowly: 'April, sweetie, I think you should see somebody. I think you need somebody to talk to.' She jumped right on the wagon. Not a moment's resistance. She was really lonely.

"It's really weird having a teenage daughter in therapy. I felt so strange knowing another woman knew more about April than me. I felt so in the dark.

"Then we had this unexpected breakthrough. I had promised April's older sister and her friends I'd take them camping in the Florida Everglades during February vacation. No way was I going to leave April home. She was just too vulnerable. I figured she and I could share a tent. The older girls would still have their privacy. I thought, 'Oh well. She'll be an outsider again, but at least I'll be there to protect her.'

"As it turned out, the older girls didn't distance themselves from April. They thought she was a cool little kid. When they squealed at the sight of an approaching alligator, she counseled them on running sideways. When they were frightened in the night, she soothed them with lullabies. When they fought, she talked reconciliation. She was amazing. Dr. Jekyll to the max: optimistic, wise, patient, friendly, uninhibited, polite, fun, flexible, energetic, happy.

"After the trip, I had a harder time getting worked up about April's problems. I still have to send her off every day to the Den of the Little Witches. But she seems to have discovered her own version of psychological Teflon—some magic that keeps the insults from sticking.

"As for me, I realize: 'It's the environment, stupid.' I know that deep down she's really okay. Those girls can't squash her insides. But the best is, I think she's learned real compassion. April's not about to declare open season on another girl." ⟿

We hover on the perimeter of our daughters' social lives. We've made every mistake they're about to make. If we step in to advise, will we push them further into the arms of the undesirables? If we don't step in, will they be lost?

When I asked mothers for stories of their daughters' friendships, I expected to hear about the redeeming power of best friends, the comfort of running with the pack. Instead, I heard far more about mothers' fears of their daughters falling in with the wrong crowd. Angela Lunt was the first of several mothers to talk about the dark side of adolescent friendship.

THE SLEAZE QUEEN AND THE FUNGUS
A Conversation with Angela Lunt

"In fifth grade, I got a preview."

Angela's story began, like so many mothers' stories, by searching the past. Her eyes rolled up ever so slightly, looking for the precise moment when her daughter had veered from the balmy course Angela had so carefully plotted.

"One day, my younger daughter, Julia, skipped in the door and asked to go to Natasha's sleepover party.

"Back then, Julia was the happiest, most innocent kid you could ever imagine. She didn't speak. She bubbled. With total naïveté, she enthusiastically announced that boys were invited to the party."

Angela, her husband, and their two daughters had settled into a nice neighborhood, one with southerly sensibilities and a staunch devotion to American values. Anchored in this protected enclave, Angela steered her family toward goodness. She hadn't anticipated the allure of steamier possibilities entering her daughter's world, at least not in fifth grade. With Julia's prepubescent interest in a coed pajama party, Angela sensed the breath of temptation. She decided to access the situation.

"I didn't know this girl Natasha or her parents, so I called Natasha's mom. This mother sounded nice, nice but young and flaky.

"I asked her about the party.

"She said, 'Oh yes. I know about the party.'

"I asked if she knew about the boys.

"She said, 'Oh yes, I know about the boys.'

"I asked if the boys would be sleeping over.

"She said, 'Oh yes, the boys will be sleeping over.'

"I asked if they'd be sleeping together.

"She said, 'Oh yes. They'll sleep together in a tent in the backyard. I think it will be so cute for the boys to stay.'

"We declined the invitation."

For another year, all remained calm. Angela basked in bonding with Julia, her bubbly princess. Pausing for just a moment, Angela luxuriated in nostalgia, then continued.

"When Julia was twelve, I finally met Natasha. This child had frosted hair. Her belly button was pierced. She wore a tight crop top.

"Despite first impressions, I decided to reserve judgment. I treated Natasha like I did all of Julia's friends. I chauffeured. I drove them here, there, and everywhere.

"I'd be driving. Natasha refused to speak to me. She wouldn't say hello. She wouldn't say good-bye. She'd sit there, sullen, the entire time. Then she'd get out of the car and slam the door. I'd yell after her, 'Thank you.'"

After a fair number of such rides, Angela's repressed opinion of her daughter's new friend leaped into consciousness. She had to admit, "I hated her from the beginning."

Not so for her daughter. Julia felt intensely attracted to Natasha. Soon the two girls were entangled. Natasha tutored Julia in the art of wearing excessive makeup and extreme outfits. Angela lamented.

"All the happiness fled from my daughter when Natasha, the Sleaze Queen, became her best friend."

Angela's home, once filled with show tunes and symphonies, turned toward the clangorous sounds of frenetic darkness.

"Natasha introduced Julia to loud, horrible music. I'd hear this misogynistic noise blaring from Julia's bedroom. I'd think, 'How can they link themselves to this women-hating vibration?' I felt everything my generation fought for in the women's movement had been lost.

"My husband had always deferred parenting decisions to me. He believed in me—thought I was the perfect mother. Now he turned on me. He'd shake his head and say, 'I trusted your instincts and look what's happened.'

"I thought Julia's dark rebellion was my fault. I felt paralyzed.

"It was a nightmare. Natasha split Julia away from us. My daughter challenged every value we upheld. She 'hated' us. She rejected everything we stood for.

"Natasha convinced Julia to give up every fun activity she was involved in.

"Natasha got Julia off the dance floor. That was the worst.

"My daughter had been an amazing ballerina. She had this intense love of ballet and this adoring relationship with her dance teacher. She spent hours and hours practicing under her watchful care.

"Natasha was jealous of Julia's ballet. The girls went to different schools. After school and on weekends, Natasha wanted my daughter to be with her every minute. The Sleaze Queen wanted more influence over Julia.

"When Julia started wearing all the heavy makeup, her attitude changed. Finally, the tension escalated to a showdown with her dance teacher. The teacher told her, 'If you come to practice tomorrow looking like that, I'm not allowing you in the studio again.'

"Julia was angry and hurt. She felt betrayed and stopped dancing.

"Natasha had won."

Angela sighed as she reflected on the loss inflicted on her daughter by divided loyalties.

"Even now, years later, Julia keeps all her ballet pictures on her walls, her dance slippers on her shelves, and local reviews of her performances in her scrapbook. Julia still thinks of herself as a ballerina."

Freed from the constraints of practice, Julia spent more time under Natasha's sway.

"Natasha introduced Julia to a whole new crowd. Natasha didn't go to Julia's school, but these kids did. This group came over to our house on Friday afternoons and stayed until Sunday. I'd try to get ahold of their parents, but I couldn't find them. No one would answer the phone. So I kept the kids. I couldn't send them home to empty houses.

"Through Natasha's crowd, Julia met a boy—the worst kid in the school. His entire family was in trouble with the law. He'd been arrested. His brothers had been in jail. But it wasn't his background that really bothered me.

"Mostly, I loathed the way he treated my daughter. He'd call and just grunt 'Julia.' No hello, just a grunt. I nicknamed him the Fungus. I'd yell to Julia, 'It's for you. It's the Fungus.' They'd talk. Then argue. He'd break up with her. I'd hear her in her room crying. They'd get back together. Argue again. Break up again. She'd cry again. The heartbreaking cycle repeated itself over and over. The Fungus was so bad for her.

"I'd devoted myself to keeping my daughter safe, but I couldn't protect her from her boyfriend, the Fungus, and her best friend, the Sleaze Queen."

During this ordeal, Angela needed a break. To get away from the pressures of her own home, to relax and take stock, she and her husband flew off to the sunshine. They had barely settled into their hotel room when the phone rang.

"It was Julia's guidance counselor, saying, 'I don't want to alarm you, but there's been an incident.' How can that not be alarming?

"We rushed home.

"Julia's new group had entered into a suicide pact. Julia had cut herself, but only superficially. Fortunately, she told her guidance counselor, and the guidance counselor called us in."

Sitting in her daughter's school, Angela heard the details of her daughter's aborted suicide pledge. The last threads of her confidence in her mothering were torn away. Angela did what was needed to protect her daughter, but she questioned herself at every turn. Angela looked to her husband for support. Together they found no easy answers.

"Throughout this siege, my husband and I held on to one another. Still, we began to question every decision we'd make. We felt confused by Julia's every unreasonable request. We struggled to respond to each one. Sometimes we said no and felt guilty. Sometimes we gave in and felt compromised. We'd say yes when all we wanted to say was no.

"We practiced hypervigilance. We watched Julia's every move. We limited her privileges.

"It's not that we're controlling parents. It's just that we were trying to hold on to a value system that seemed to be melting all around us."

Angela stopped, caught her breath, and went on to describe a turning point beyond her control.

"During the summer, Julia went to camp. She bonded with a guidance counselor from another school. One day they were out in a canoe. Julia burst into tears. She confessed her unhappiness. She told him everything that had gone on. He said, 'Julia, you cannot go back to that school.' He was absolutely unequivocal.

"Julia returned home from camp convinced. She insisted on transferring to the school where this man was a counselor. I resisted.

"Natasha, the Sleaze Queen, went to this school. I worried that Julia would be with her twenty-four hours a day, not just after school and on weekends. And the school was located in what seemed like a bad neighborhood.

"My husband and I met with this guidance counselor and with the principal. They assured us, 'We'll watch your daughter like a hawk.'

"We decided to give it try.

"Within a month, she was happy again.

"Julia made friends with another crowd of girls, nice kids from working families with good values. These girls, the ones who actually went to school with the Sleaze Queen, couldn't stand her. They didn't want anything to do with her. These great kids did something I couldn't do. They kept Julia away from Natasha.

"Amazing. By then I had actually tried to be more open to Natasha, to include and accept her. As soon as I stopped trying to push her out of Julia's life, Julia pushed her away all by herself. Now Julia agrees with my very first impression. My daughter thinks the Sleaze Queen is horrible.

"By the end of the year, Julia was voted the happiest student in the school.

"And get this. The Sleaze Queen started dating the Fungus." ⬡

In Angela's darkest days, she felt her daughter had been wrenched from her, stolen and brainwashed by a band of delinquents. Faith MacFarlane never worried about bad influences. She absolutely supported her daughter's choice of friends. A woman with an enormous heart and a welcoming home, Faith held no prejudices against the weird or wild. She looked below the surface and saw all kids as good kids. That is, until experience taught her to put conditions on commitment. Faith spoke about the reevaluation of unqualified acceptance.

"What did I care? So Anita had purple hair and talked with a pierced tongue. None of that mattered. She was my daughter's sweet lost friend. She needed a home. I invited her to move in. Three months, two days, and four hours later, I ordered her to leave. In those intervening months, days, and hours, I leaned on my friends. We talked and talked and talked. I called them at all hours of the day and night. They soothed my nerves and bolstered my decision to eject her from my home. I learned: Not all my daughter's friends deserve loyalty, and all my friends merit eternal gratitude."

Cheryl Thompson didn't question the strength of the influence of her daughter's friends. Instead, she worried that she herself had become a bad role model.

AT THE HEART OF TROUBLE
Thoughts from Cheryl Thompson

"I'm a psychologist. I've devoted my life to helping disenfranchised and disturbed people. Maybe my daughter's too much like me. Maybe I've led my daughter astray.

"Beth has this huge heart. She's attracted to troubled kids. She thinks she can help them. Her savior complex gets her in trouble.

"Last spring she came home from school.

"I asked, 'How was your day?'

"She answered, 'Fine.'

"That very same night, another mother called me. This mom tells me my daughter has information about a boy who's been stalking her daughter.

"I confront Beth.

"She says, 'Oh, that.' As though nothing happened.

"Then, in the most blasé manner you can possibly imagine, she tells me she spent six hours in the guidance office with three adults.

"School administrators found a note from Beth in this stalker boy's locker. My daughter had taken this wounded specimen of an adolescent male under her wing. The school authorities suspected she could shed some light on his obsession with this other girl. They called Beth into the principal's office to glean information. A guidance counselor, an administrator, and a teacher talked with her. At first, all three reasoned with her. No luck. She refused to abandon her friend. It was like she had taken an oath of confidentiality. Then they took turns. Hour after hour of tag-team interrogation with a soft touch. She was convinced she was the only person who could help him. Finally, they persuaded her that this boy needed professional help.

"I couldn't believe she said nothing to me, not a word."

The next time, Beth's overzealous commitment to protecting the oppressed landed her in bigger trouble. Angela described another spring-time scene.

"I'm sitting in a meeting with a colleague, the president of a state psychological association. I get this call from the state police. This husky voice says, 'Dr. Thompson? We have your daughter at the station. We have to ask you to come downtown.'

"This officer is talking. I'm nodding, making indecipherable re-sponses like 'Yes.' 'I see.' 'Certainly.' 'Of course.' 'I'll be right there.'

"Then I get off the phone, give a limp little smile, make some lame excuse, and get out quick. Can you imagine? I live in this little conserv-ative midwestern town. I counsel families. Sometimes I see adolescents. If word got out—'Dr. Thompson? Oh. Did you know? Her daughter's a juvenile delinquent.'—I can wave my practice good-bye.

"All the way to the police station, I'm driving in a blur.

"I get there to find my daughter and a friend. This friend of hers is pitifully poor. I mean really poverty-stricken. This child has no money, as in *none*. I feed her, for God's sake.

"So she and Beth were in the mall. The cash-strapped friend stuck a pair of jeans in Beth's backpack. Alarms went off. They got caught and dragged to the police station."

Cheryl paused and sighed. Then she put the whole debacle in per-spective.

"You know, it turned out to be the best thing. I grounded Beth. She didn't resist. I cut off all contact with this girl. She didn't object. I got to keep my daughter home. We spent time together. We took this great vacation. She got up early and rode her bike. We walked and swam. We talked about boundaries, about whom you can help and whom you can't. She actually listened and learned from me.

"Now my daughter seems less intrigued by troubled kids. She's seen enough trouble and is really trying to make better choices. Our relation-ship is much improved. Thank goodness. I pray she'll be okay." ⊂○

While Cheryl continues to worry that her daughter's compassion opens the door to trouble, other mothers ache over the wounds inflicted upon their daughters by popular girls. In the Gap-Nike-Tommy Hilfiger-uniformed culture, peer acceptance requires antennae finely tuned to the subtleties of "cool." The conformist mentality has been resurrected from the fifties—only today the badges of belonging have a higher price tag, and the bodies beneath the clothes must be skinny and buff. Retro comes with an escalation of tyranny. To be other than Buffy or Britney or Barbie rouses a doglike instinct for dominance in other adolescents. Girls who don't fit in become targets.

Ellen Harris felt torn apart by the catty brutality of her daughter's classmates. Ellen objectively assessed the sources of her daughter's isolation, honored her daughter's uncompromising attitude, and felt compassion for her humiliation. Mostly, though, she—like other mothers—blamed herself. "Andrea's picked on. When I got divorced eight years ago, she began comforting herself with food. She put on weight. Now she has to endure all these fat-fearing comments. It's so hard.

"I see how she gets in her own way and how she invites the abuse. She makes no effort to conform. She'd rather go her own way. She figures it's their problem.

"But when they do get in her face, she cries. They get satisfaction from her defensiveness and tears."

Hundreds of miles away, Penny Kaplan has concerns that mirror Ellen's. Penny's daughter Tamara had suffered from the conformist wrath of peers through her entire childhood. Tamara's search for acceptance among peers was a prolonged and bruising pilgrimage. By the time she reached midadolescence, Tamara was bound to trek farther from home. Her daughter's comings and goings left Penny lonely and scared.

IN A TENDER PLACE
A Conversation with Penny Kaplan

"I feel isolated, like I failed."

Penny's voice quivered as the confession came out haltingly. She had entrusted me with the most personal of confidences, a guilt felt at some vulnerable moment by every good mother. She inhaled, exhaled, and told her story in words chosen with care.

"What a week. It's been a hard road.

"When I look back, I see my daughter's always lived on the edges, on the borderline. Even in day care. I'd come to pick her up. I'd stand back for a few minutes without letting her see me. She'd almost always be involved in some kind of parallel play, or she'd be hovering on the outside, watching, looking in. I think some part of Tamara always felt rejected. She didn't quite know how to fit in. To this day, I don't think she knows what it truly means to have a good friend. Her pain, and the pain of her feeling like an outsider, has been transferred to me.

"I've never understood why her peers reject her, why her self-esteem is so low. Tamara's so smart, so interesting, so expressive.

"I love the way she says what she's feeling. I've never had to guess what's going on with her. We've been so close."

But Penny took no comfort in her intimate bond with her daughter. Instead, she questioned the value of her love.

"Maybe that's the problem.

"My husband says, 'Tamara doesn't know how to separate, so she's pulling away violently, in extremes.' There might be truth to that: Her whole life, we've been so attached to one another.

"Maybe she's too much like me. Maybe I haven't shown her how to make friends. I'm really not that social. I have only a couple of really close friends. I was never the popular type. But I never had her pain. I had a few good friends. That's really all I needed to feel supported. My daughter hasn't ever had a friend she could depend on. I'm the only one who hasn't betrayed her trust, the only one who accepted her, and the only one who rejoiced in who she is. She's talked only to me. She says, 'If you're not my friend, Mom, then who is?' That breaks my heart.

"When she says, 'We're just alike,' I think, 'Yeah. Bad genes.'"

Penny sifted through details of her daughter's history:

"She's never been happy in school. Still, she's gotten good grades. She's shown her talents. Teachers have loved her and consistently remarked that they're looking forward to seeing what kind of adult she becomes. The adults adored her, but not the other kids.

"Then in sophomore year, Tamara found a boyfriend, a kind of arty senior. He and his friends accepted her. She was really happy for a while. In the end, this older boy turned on her. I don't really know the details, but I think he emotionally and verbally abused her.

"Before her junior year, with the first boyfriend and most of her friends going on to college, she became hysterical about returning to school. I was in anguish. At the last minute, we arranged for her to go to a Catholic girls' school. The only private school we could manage on such short notice. She joked about being a Jewish girl going to Catholic school. But this school turned out to be a warm, easy environment. The teachers supported her intelligence and talent. Still, she had no peer group, formed no real connections with other girls. The parochial school wasn't all we had hoped for, but it seemed to be working. At least it seemed to be better than the alternative.

"Outside of school she started seeing another boy. A boy she met through her first boyfriend. This new boy has been out of high school for a couple of years. He's a lost soul who never made it through college, who lives on his own in a rented house, supporting himself through part-time jobs. He's bright, self-educated, and does wonderful things. He's a social activist who works hard for the causes be believes in. From the moment Tamara met this second boy, she admired him. When he became interested in her romantically, she fell in love.

"On a day that began as any other, she went off to school. Things seemed smooth for the first time in ages. I went to work. I'll never forget that day. How routine it felt. Just as I got off the phone after reordering her contact lenses, I got a call from school. Tamara had forged a note and left. I was frantic. Where had she gone and why? I called everyone I could think of, leaving messages everywhere for her to call me.

"Finally, at eight o'clock that evening, she phoned. She just wanted me to know that she was all right. She hadn't been in a car crash, but she wasn't coming home. She refused to tell us where she was. She slammed down the phone when I tried to find out what had happened.

"My husband went to her boyfriend's house. She was there, of course. But when he tried to convince her to come home, she was defiant: 'I'm seventeen. I'm staying here and there's nothing you can do about it.'

"On my husband's way back to our house, he stopped at the police station. Tamara was right. The police could do nothing. We could do nothing except wonder why she had left and how to convince her to come back to us.

"She called me after a few days to come get her, but things had forever changed. For the remainder of the school year and the summer, she pretty much stayed away, just touching base, not respecting curfews, sleeping at home but not coming in until three or four o'clock in the morning.

"Tamara's adopted her boyfriend's life. With him, she's found a group that accepts her. She's enthralled with the people in her new life, six or eight young adults all living together at this house. They tell stories about childhood abuse, about breaking out and finding their own way. She romanticizes them.

"But who *are* they? Metal heads dressed in black leather who listen to violent music? The boyfriend is the only one I know. What goes on in the house? Drugs? I don't know. I don't think she takes drugs. She's always been afraid of losing control. Or so she says.

"Now she's a senior. She's back in the original public school and still feels unconnected. She's home, but I'm afraid it won't last. I can feel her just waiting to leave.

"I'm afraid she'll go back to her 'friends' at the house, the ones who accept her for who she is. School is just too isolating to tolerate. She walks into the senior lounge. Girls inspect her and turn their backs on her. I'm afraid she's being stripped of her essential self.

"I hear about and read about kids who make it through a troubled adolescence, who flourish later. Still, I find it hard to see the good. I feel covered by a thick layer of clouds. I strain to see tiny, distant bright lights."

Once again, Penny paused. Then, as though focused on one of those tiny lights, she continued.

"It's strange. I do see her happy, really happy in one place: at her work. When she's at the doughnut shop, she's outgoing and friendly. She smiles. She laughs with the customers. Everyone likes her. Is that weird?"

Hearing about Tamara's work life, I sighed in relief and answered, "No, it's not weird. It's wonderful. She's found a safe haven, a protected island, where she's comfortable and confident. In that place, she has a purpose and she's valued."

After speaking, I hoped I hadn't sounded simplistic or preachy or too much like a psychologist. As I hung up the phone, I just hoped Penny felt less alone.

In the days that followed, I reflected on Penny and on her daughter. In her voice, I heard love—its strains tinged with a quality of guilt and fear only mothers know. Through her words, I had come to envision her child, now a young woman whose every pore has been saturated with her mother's tenderness. ◁∞

the quest for love

From I WISH FOR YOU MY DAUGHTER
by Marianne Peel Forman

I wish you someone in your
    life
who will send you odd gifts,
peculiar gifts of the heart,
like a rock that gleams in the
    sunlight
of your bedroom window,
shining for all its African
    worth
bringing you good luck,
or like olives from Greece,
or street crepes from Paris
smothered with bananas,
    Nutella, and almonds.

I wish you someone
who understands the inside
    you.
Someone whose patience
    draws out
what needs to be said,

like a person with two
    different-colored eyes
both light and dark in one
    face
both evident and hidden,
much like the essence of you.
I wish you the knowledge
    that suffering
is just one part of life,
like joy,
unexpected,
unasked for,
not cursed on you for
    something you did
or didn't do,
but just there
to be handled and understood
like the desert air
or the noon-stinging sun.

Mothers wish their daughters love. Yet that wish has fear embedded in it. Every woman understands the dangers of an open heart.

A mother's hopes for her daughter are usually very simple. We hope our daughters will be blessed with sensible attractions, that they'll want to be with good boys who treat them right. We hope they'll revel in romance, delaying the complications and dangers of sex. We hope they'll never settle for less than they deserve. We hope they'll never be brokenhearted.

Even though we know the road to mature relationships comes with practice and cost, we hurt every time our daughters learn another hard love lesson. It's painful to watch them dive headfirst into the shallow water of immature relationships. We know they'll be bruised.

Sara fell in love the first time when she was nine years old. The cutest little boy gave her a teeny-tiny white teddy bear with the words "I Love You" embroidered on its little red bib. There was a sweetness in this first infatuation. And in the next and the next. By the time Sara was in eighth grade, she'd been in love one, two, three times. Each for a year or so. Each with an innocent abandon that came and left without leaving scars or even second thoughts.

But in the second year of junior high, the tinge of sexuality attached itself to her. Adolescence transformed her from "just so cute" to "drop-dead gorgeous." And the next boyfriend had a different smell.

I didn't really like David, didn't fully trust him. But what could I do? He wasn't a bad kid. Actually, he was a nice kid. It's just that . . . well . . . his voice had dropped.

He courted Sara in all the right and respectable ways. Took her to dances. Talked to her every night on the telephone. Was properly attentive. Reeled her in and trapped her. Sara fell in love. Sara and David were the most admired couple in their circle, the equivalent of the prom queen and the student-body president, the cheerleader and the football player.

I was sitting in our living room, reading, when I heard Sara's piercing scream. She ran down the stairs and threw herself into my arms. I escorted her to the love seat. She draped her legs over my lap and tucked her head into my chest, trying like an adolescent Saint Bernard to fit where she had once belonged. She wept and wailed and sniffled. She didn't say a single word. She didn't have to explain. I knew: David had dumped her.

Eventually, gasping for breath, between sobs, she spoke. "My heart, Mom . . . it hurts . . . it hurts so much . . . my chest . . . it feels torn apart . . . I'm brokenhearted . . . I never knew what it meant to have a broken heart . . . it's so awful . . . worse than I ever imagined . . . I never . . . never . . . want to feel this way again."

My shirt soaked in the sweet bond of her salty tears, I thanked the god of coincidence that I was home to hold her.

The world has changed. The distance between puppy love and sex has shrunk.

The sexual genie was let out of the bottle sometime in 1967. And since that fateful time of flower children and free love, parents haven't successfully stuffed him back in. In this generation, nice girls don't automatically become sluts when sex enters their lives. Innocence overlaps with experience when girls are young. Too young. Mothers worry about their daughters' increased vulnerability.

One mother snatched a clandestine peek into her daughter's heart. Her voice went soft, as though the phone connection had receded thousands of miles into the distance. "This is a secret. You can use it. But for *this*, I'm Anonymous."

In sheepish tones, Anonymous Mom confessed, "Sometimes, not often, just once in a while, mostly if I'm worried about her mood, if I feel I really have to know what's going on, if I'm scared I need to protect her, I peek in her diary."

With the essence of her secret revealed, this anonymous mom continued, still apologetic.

"A few days ago, she left her diary wide open. It was just lying on the bed waiting to be read. Anyway, maybe I shouldn't have, but I did. I didn't even turn the page. I just saw the words: 'I've never loved anyone before Jason.'

"I worry. She's so young, immature, vulnerable. This relationship is so emotional for her. She's thrown her whole self into it. She's such an innocent. I'd hate to see sex thrown in the mix. I was fourteen when I first had sex—much too young. I hope she waits."

Sometimes the issue isn't that our daughters will be hurt. Sometimes the issue is that our girls choose to shower affection on boys who are beneath them.

Sharon Madison spoke for herself, but I heard her sentiments from other mothers. Dismayed by her daughter's attraction to boys who simply aren't "good enough," Sharon fears self-deprecation will draw her daughter into a lifelong commitment to mediocrity, or worse.

SETTLING
Sharon Madison's Concern

"My daughter has this twenty-seven-year-old boyfriend. I don't like him. Still, he's better than any of the others.

"My daughter is beautiful—gorgeous. She's brilliant. She's talented—writes prize-winning poetry. But she's had this series of really horrible boyfriends. These were guys who stole money out of telephone booths to buy drugs and alcohol—juvenile delinquents who treated her badly.

"One told her she was fat. This guy had the body of a speed freak. He looked like a concentration-camp victim. He thought she should look like him.

"I worried that she didn't feel worthy of being treated well. She'd tell me she was ugly and stupid. She settled for these guys, and they reinforced her every insecurity.

"So now she's with this really smart man who's sweet as can be. And he treats her really well.

"But I find it hard to feel really good about him. He went to this Ivy League school, got great grades but never graduated. The school wants him to graduate. They've tried to make it easy. They want him to do an independent study in P.E. But he doesn't seem to care. He just works at some nowhere job. If this relationship lasts, she'll probably support him for their entire life." ❦

When our daughters' search for true love turns physical, the motherly bond loses its grip. For some of us, it's as though a primal force lures our daughters in, lays claim to their bodies and washes their brains. Swirling around in never-before-felt arousal and gushing emotion, they let themselves go.

And we, their mothers, worry ourselves sick. We know they've abandoned more than us. They've abandoned themselves. From the moment they were born, we poured love into them. Now they anoint some sleaze with their affections. We know they'll be smashed against reality. We know they'll be forced to patch together the shattered selves they've given up with such wantonness.

No longer able to protect, cajole, or influence, every mother harbors the same worry: Will my daughter be drawn in to a self-destructive pact with love? Few women escape the devotion trap entirely. At one time or another, we have surrendered our affections and been mistreated by our generosity. Anita Singleton wrote about the stark images that spiked her anxiety.

℮

TABOO
by Anita Singleton

I heard whispers from her bedroom: his husky voice, hushed by his sleazeball intentions; her sweet muffled giggles, accentuating his sordid motivations.

I sat on the couch, my every breath drawn slowly, consciously quieting myself. For what? Why should I calm myself? To hear the sound of my daughter's lost innocence? To center my being? To find an answer? What am I supposed to do?

Then I heard, or at least thought I heard, my angelic child whimper, "No. Not here."

My breathing stopped and all thought obliterated, I flew up the stairs. I tore open her bedroom door.

There my baby knelt in front of this monster, her hands tied together.

I screamed with the bloodcurdling anger that only a mother confronting a child predator can muster. "Get out of my house. Never come back."

My rage transformed the man. Suddenly he was what he truly was—a doglike sixteen-year-old boy. Tail between his legs, he scurried down the stairs.

My daughter beseeched him, "Don't go. Come back. Don't leave me." Tears streamed down her face. Abby was left with only me, her mother, to free her from her bondage, from this sniveling immature idiot who didn't deserve her and treated her badly.

At least that's how I saw it: the bound hands a symbol of his malicious dominance and her lovesick subservience—a precursor of his sado-masochistic fantasies.

Of course, that's not how she saw it.

Abby sat down with me. I loosened the knots that bound her wrists together. She pleaded between sobs, "Mom. It's nothing. We're not into any weirdness. We were just sitting here playing with my scarf. I put it on him. He put it on me. I swear it was a silly little game."

I freed her hands. I believed in her innocence. Her childlike explanation gave testimony to the power that he held over her. She was sixteen years old, and she loved the creep.

That night, a dark foreboding fell over me. I left my husband's side and sat in the living room. Tearfully paralyzed, my mind could not even find a prayer.

My daughter sensed my wakefulness.

Gently, Abby came to me, stroked my head, and said, "Mom, I can see you're in pain. I'm sorry. You don't understand. You can't understand how I feel about him."

She kissed my hair and went to bed.

I sat alone. I did understand. I had once been swept away to emotional devastation by my own brand of bad boy—a rock-and-roll musician whose raw emotion magnetized me. I would have followed him anywhere. But I was lucky. He was too unstable to be loyal. He deserted me four times, enticed by the fresh smell of other young women. After his final desertion, he went on a bad trip. One tab of acid too much, or maybe it was angel dust—he never returned. He took up permanent residence in the haunted world of paranoid schizophrenia. He prowled around campus, no longer recognizing me. Mercifully, I was no longer the lovely blonde who faithfully soothed his tormented mind. By then he had captivated another. I watched them sitting in a field, his head cradled in her lap, her fingers caressing his head. My mind bursting with relief: Thank God he left me.

By the end of that affair, I had learned not to trust my instincts. I knew I wasn't immune to the destructive allure of a forbidden boy. Now, with my daughter under a similar spell, I was frightened for her. Would Abby ever be free?

As the sun rose on my sleepless night, my husband joined me on the couch. He came with wisdom and a cup of tea in hand. "Look. I hate the kid. I just think about him and my blood boils. But Abby's crazy about him. Maybe yesterday was just one Jerry Springer moment. Maybe we have to look beyond it. We can't force her not to love him. If we don't allow him here, she'll sneak off and meet him other places. We've got to take her out of this loyalty bind. Let's try to start over. We'll invite him over for dinner, go to a movie. Better they meet here, better we have some influence over him."

So that's what we did. We invited the slime to dinner and a movie. And we did it nicely. He got the invitation via Abby. He replied via Abby: "He's not sure he should come. He's afraid you'll lay a trip on him." I assured her we'd be totally charming. And so the messages went back and forth for several weekends, until suddenly the slime did something unforgivable.

I still have no idea what awful thing happened, but Abby wanted nothing more to do with the creep.

Within a week, a new name had entered her vocabulary: Luke. "Mom, he's this really cute guy. I think he likes me. He's from this big family and he works after school. Mom, I think you'll like him."

The next Friday night, I heard the sound of Abby coming in, just before her midnight curfew. I stumbled down the stairs to give her a good-night hug. In my pajamas and bleary-eyed, I peered through sleep to catch a glimpse of the cutest teenage couple I have ever seen: Abby and Luke. Even through my embarrassment, I caught the vibe. Luke radiated sweetness. I wrapped my arms around Abby. She introduced me: "Luke, this is my mom." I extended my hand to Luke. And Luke, in the most well-mannered, large-immigrant-family manner, held my hand, kissed my cheek, and said, "Hi, Abby's mom."

I was nearly giggly with approval. I can't really remember, but I think I gave a happy little hop as I left the room and involuntarily said, "You two are just so adorable." Maybe I didn't. Maybe I only thought it.

Luke became a member of our extended family—the son I wish I had given birth to.

A month later, Abby and I and my sister, Abby's favorite aunt, sat drinking latte and sharing chocolate mousse. My sister looked at me sideways and bragged, "Abby told me about Luke before she told you." Maintaining that mock air of "I'm Abby's favorite," she jumped right into a forbidden topic. "So. Abby, how do you feel about the old boyfriend now?"

A serious mood engulfed Abby. She delivered her message with the determination of fired steel: "I will never let another man mistreat me. Never."

My baby had matured into a strong and determined woman right in front of my eyes. All worry that my daughter would be enticed into an abusive web vanished. ❧

sex: the carnal consequences

POEM TO BECCA AT AGE TWELVE
by Rhonda Morton

You are twelve, a melding of
    opposites:
frightening, beguiling,
under a spell and bewitching,
serious, silly.
Belly round and soft—still
    my little girl's,
but every day your legs
    lengthen
like shadows stretching away
    from me,
your shoulders become a new
    horizon I can barely see
    past.
When you hug me,
press hard buds into the
    opened petals of my
    breasts,
your blood whispers to mine,
sets a stone into my well-
    worn flow.

I'm late. I'm early.
Rough water, this narrow gap
    between us.
You flirt with sexiness,
try on a look that will
    someday make men go
    weak in the knees.
For now, it is only me who
    sees it.
At times you storm, raging
    thunderous waves,
splitting the sky with
    lightning,
then sit becalmed, miserable
    in your doldrums.
I am tied to the mast, a stoic
    smile painted on my
    mouth.

Girls look like women while they're still children. One in seven Caucasian girls develop breasts and pubic hair by age eight. One in seven African-American girls show breasts and pubic hair by age seven; by age eight, one in two do.

Just looking at their blossoming bodies is enough to send mothers from coast to coast into a mass panic. It's human nature: Mothers protect their children. When girls enter adolescence, their maturing bodies still need that protection. But guarding them from harm is complicated by their innocence and their delusions of maturity. Lecherous vultures swoop down on our innocently pubescent daughters. Little girls love attention. They don't understand that beneath the attention lurks danger.

Debbie Gaffney had looked forward to celebrating her brother's wedding. She never expected to spend the evening guarding her daughter from dirty old men. Two men—one in his fifties and the other in his sixties—circled round Amelia. They cooed lasciviously, "Amelia, you are drop-dead gorgeous." "I want to dance with you." "You beautiful creature." Debbie was stunned: "Amelia is fourteen! She's not emotionally ready to understand and handle the male attention she receives."

UNWANTED ADVANCES
Thoughts from Catherine Hellmann

Catherine welcomed me into her life with an irrepressible enthusiasm akin to game-show host Bob Barker's daily invitation to "Come on down!"

I asked about her fears.

"Fears? I've got lots.

"Like the other day, just the other day. It's pouring rain. Emily's waiting for me to pick her up after school.

"I'm late, just a little late.

"She hops in the car and tells me this story: 'Mom, a man drove up to me and tried to get me to go in his car.'

"Emily, my thirteen-year-old child, is standing in the rain, this guy pulls up, rolls down his window, gives her a nod, and issues this invitation: 'Hop in. I'll give you a ride.'

"We're talking in front of a high school. Right in front of a high school.

"Well, she had the good sense to ignore him. She did the right thing.

"But I wasn't about to ignore it. I called the school, told the secretary. She got the police right on the case.

"Next day, a policeman comes to school and calls Emily out of class. That was a shocker. The cop was good. He asked Emily what happened. Took a description of the car and sleazeball. What more could he do? Now the school will be on the lookout for the jerk."

Pushing the car creep to the back of her mind, Catherine Hellmann spun off in the boyfriend direction.

"The police can't do anything about the everyday horny-adolescent-boy stuff.

"My daughter inherited my figure: short and large-breasted. The fashions today do too much to accentuate the positive.

"She walks out of her room in a tight tank top with her midriff showing. I do a double take and rein her in. 'Where do you think you're going in the hoochy wear?'

"She says, 'Mom. There's nothing else in the stores.'

"So. I take her shopping. She's right. She's absolutely right. There's nothing else. Why are we dressing our girls like whores?

"What do I do? I don't want to take her to Lane Bryant and cover her up like an overweight matron. We compromise. I've developed this language to censor what she wears, like 'That's too boob-bastic.' Or 'Just too bustulous.' Then I make her change.

"My neighbor, she's so awesome. She warns me, 'Don't make her feel ashamed.'

"I agree. I want her to love her body.

"*But.* I don't want older boys checking her out, going, 'Wow! Look at those hooters.'

"Don't get me started on Hooters. What is wrong with this country? A chain of restaurants, an entire chain, where the most appetizing attraction is big-breasted women. Please!" ⋘

How do we protect our daughters from the real harms of sexuality while instilling in them a healthy regard for its pleasures? We worry most about their initiation, fearing it will be the bellwether for every future relationship.

THE REAL CONVERSATION
A Story from an Anonymous Mom

"We haven't had any sex talks yet, except about structure and function. We haven't started to talk about relationships and how interest in someone is going to change her attitude toward sex. She's still pretty much at the 'Ew, gross!' stage.

"I haven't yet really made myself think about whether I'll tell her about my herpes.

"I still don't know where I got it. It was from one of two guys who were sort of deliberate flings in my senior year of college. We didn't grow up conscious of STDs. It was 'Ha-ha—syphilis' and 'Ha-ha—gonorrhea.' Risk felt pretty remote. I knew about herpes; it was even a joke on campus when there was an outbreak on the football team. The message 'Nice guys can have STDs' never sank in. I felt I was being responsible by protecting myself against pregnancy.

"So I felt extraordinarily angry and burdened when I got herpes— certain it would dog me my entire life. That hasn't been the case. It wasn't a problem during pregnancy. I haven't had an outbreak in years. It's been such a nonissue for so long. Recently, I found myself filling out a medical form and almost forgot to put it down.

"About speaking with my daughter: I've felt a certain perverse sense of relief that STDs are such a big issue now. AIDS and chlamydia are such huge threats to kids. I won't have to necessarily personalize the discussion.

"I've thought about whether my experience with herpes is going to affect the messages I send my daughter. Is it going to make me more protective? Am I going to try harder to hold her back?

"Surprisingly, I worry more that her heart will get broken. She's too smart a person not to take physical precautions. But so many of us aren't smart emotionally, especially with those first outings.

"I think I did okay about when I chose to have sex. No one broke my heart over sex. But I don't know how that will come into play with her. Maybe my experience will help me be more sincere and clear. I'll talk to her about waiting until you're completely on your own emotional footing, sure that it's what you want, and not doing it just to keep someone. My hope is that my solidity on that ground will inform the emphasis on trust, her need to know herself and trust someone else before she has sex.

"I have a lot of faith in her. If she gets into relationships, I know she's going to feel tremendous pressure. She's very hard on herself. This is a place where the demands she makes on herself can do some good.

"We're at a tipping point. She's having her first crush. So far it's just e-mails and look-at-me boy behavior. But it's like quicksand. Everything is going to shift, and someone needs to tell her—goody-goody, it gets to be me—that sex feels good.

"That's how people get sucked into sex before they're ready. At school, they never talk about how things feel. They didn't with us, and they don't with them. They don't discuss the extraordinary physical pleasures of sex. I'm sure if the sex educators did, the school would torch them in a second.

"My mother never came close to that conversation. She took instant refuge in the anatomy-professor role. Everything was explained to me extremely clearly in terms of physiology. There was never a hint beyond procreation why people do these things.

"That's the real conversation I need to have with her. Responsibility to herself is going to be my number-one emphasis." ∝

More often than mothers know, daughters are stripped of their right to make their own choices about when to become sexual. Men inflict their lechery on our daughters with alarming regularity.

For six years, Katrina Blumberg had no idea that an elderly man, perhaps even a relative, had sexually violated her daughter. She wrote about the day she found out.

A MESSAGE FOR EVERY DAUGHTER
by Katrina Blumberg

Megan and I were having tea in the breakfast nook. By then she was sixteen, over the worst of her adolescent distrust of me. We had returned to mother/daughter bonding moments, times like this, when we just sat together talking. That morning she told me a secret.

"Mom, something happened when I was about ten, still just a little girl. I was on vacation at Grandma and Grandpa's house. I was in the kitchen making pancakes. I was standing on a stool so I'd be tall enough to flip the pancakes.

"This old couple came to visit. I think it was one of your uncles and his wife. They all went into the living room to talk. Then the uncle or whoever he was came into the kitchen. He was all red-faced and he smelled of alcohol. He kissed me, Mom. He grabbed my face in his hands, forced my head to stay still, and he stuck his tongue in my mouth. I struggled. I tried to turn my head, but I couldn't. Then he went back into the living room. He just sat down and visited with Grandma and Grandpa again. After a few minutes, he came back and did it again. Kissed me. Pushed his tongue into my mouth. Grandma, Grandpa, and his wife were all in the next room."

As I listened to my beautiful teenage daughter, grief engulfed me. The image of my delicate child coerced into an adult act sank my heart. I said the only thing I could say: "Megan, I am so sorry."

"I'm okay, Mom. Worse things happen."

I could not imagine worse at the moment. I could only see the too-soon, forced introduction of sexuality inflicted on my perfectly innocent little girl. I told her, "Megan, it's sad. It's very sad. That was your first kiss. He took your first kiss away from you and made it into something ugly and scary."

Megan nodded. "That's true. He did."

We paused, silent in that sorrow. Then Megan continued.

"After the second time, I went to the bathroom and locked myself in. I stared at myself in the mirror, sat on the floor alone, just staring at myself."

The story told, Megan tried to figure out who had thrust his perversity upon her.

It had been a long time ago, and Megan simply wasn't sure. But as we considered the possibilities, I thought of one relative who would have been capable of such a hideous act. With that recognition came a shock. "Megan, that man had two daughters." Megan acknowledged that possibility: "I know, Mom. I thought of that." We both stood there silently, thinking the unthinkable.

I wanted to do the right thing, to put Megan in charge, to restore the tiniest bit of the power she lost that long-ago afternoon. I asked, "Megan, what do you want to do? Do you want me to confront him?"

"No, Mom. I'm not even sure it was him. I can't be certain."

"Megan, do you want me to tell Grandma and Grandpa, to get them to help you remember?"

"No. It's been too long."

That ended our conversation, but the facts still haunted me. My daughter had been violated right in my parents' home, with my mother and father in the next room. How could a girl be safe anyplace in this world? I was determined to protect Megan's younger sister, Terri. I sat her down in the breakfast nook and asked her the questions I should have asked Megan.

"Terri, has anyone ever touched you sexually or kissed you when you didn't want them to?"

Terri saw my seriousness. She answered thoughtfully, "No, Mom. Never."

Relieved, I gave her my next message, the one I was too late to deliver to Megan. "Terri, if anyone ever sexually abuses you, please tell me right away."

"I will, Mom."

Later, I told Megan about my conversation with her younger sister. She stamped me with approval. "Good, Mom. Every mother should warn every little girl and ask every teenager." ⟳

S ome mothers are forced to turn their daughters' devastating tragedy into goodness and healing.

Erika Coughlin explained why she contributed to *Ophelia's Mom:* "Maybe another mother and daughter will feel less alone, less desperate, more hopeful. Maybe some good can come out of all this horror. Maybe something I say will help another woman. I'm willing to talk with you and I'd be willing to talk with them."

⟳

PLUNGED INTO THE UNSPEAKABLE
Erika Coughlin's Story

"Right under my eyes, a man raped my daughter. It wasn't until she was in residential treatment, many months later after a pregnancy, abortion, and attempted suicide, that the truth came into the open. Finally, when she was far from home, where he couldn't hurt her, she felt safe enough to tell me, to trust me. Away in her container, she was protected. I couldn't save her in mine.

"My daughter is outgoing, vivid, dramatic, yet she was born anxious and vulnerable. I couldn't protect her. When she was fourteen, a friend of a friend needed a baby-sitter. I interviewed the family before allowing her to sit for them. She and I and my son went to the house. We met with the father and his little girl. The wife wasn't home. Everything seemed fine.

"The next time she went to baby-sit, the father touched her inappropriately. As soon as he left, she phoned and told me immediately. She trusted me. She was so responsible and considerate. She didn't want to leave the baby alone. She didn't want his wife to know. She didn't want to cause a divorce. She didn't want the baby girl to lose her father.

"I got her home and we called the police.

"After this baby-sitting incident, she became nervous. She didn't want to walk by the man's house or be alone. I wanted to protect her, to keep her away from this man. I brought her to work with me.

"I have a very nurturing work situation. We often bring our children. My daughter's bright and focused. I kept her nearby and gave her assignments. She'd go from office to office collecting mail and running errands for our staff.

"A man who seemed kind and sensitive, who was married with two children, worked for my company. I thought he was a fathering kind of person, but he raped my daughter more than once. He threatened to hurt her. She was afraid to tell. He forced her to a drug house, made her go inside. Awful things happened to her. I had brought my daughter into a situation that caused her pain.

"My daughter was in therapy when she was raped. She never told the therapist. She kept all that explosive fear inside. She was a ticking time bomb. I'd pick her up from her sessions. She'd be angry. I should have taken her out right away. I didn't know when to stop, when to find someone who could actually help her, someone she could confide in.

"Even when she tried to kill herself, she didn't tell. I didn't know. I took her to the emergency psychiatric ward at the hospital. She stayed for eight days. The staff helped me to realize I couldn't keep her safe at home. I had to place her in residential treatment. The best facility for adolescents was hundreds and hundreds of miles from our home. Leaving my child in that place was the most painful experience of my life.

"But it had to happen. She had to be far away, locked away from the dangers of the world. She was in that institution for three months before she told. The healing process began because she finally felt safe enough to speak. She stayed in residential treatment for six months.

"Now we're dealing with all the legal problems. She went to a detective, told all the details in a deposition. The district attorney took on the case. Fortunately there was still material evidence, lots of it, all over [the man's] office. They've done matching DNA tests. The man who raped her has been charged. When it comes to trial, I hope she can face him without fear. I'm in awe of the courage that will require.

"With all these mind-consuming distractions, her ability to focus and complete tasks astounds me. We just moved into a new house. She unpacked and organized the entire kitchen. With everything she's been through, she's a fabulous creative writer. She accesses herself, finds the perfect words to express who she is in poetry and stories.

"There's been a lot of guilt. I've questioned what kind of parent I am. Why didn't I see the signs? There were signs everywhere: scratches on her body (of course they all had explanations), dark moods, dramatic and dreary artwork with fire and anger and rage. The rebellious behavior I thought was normal was much more than that. Once I was in the tunnel, I could not see the light. She was frantic, frightened, and lost. And so was I. An earthquake had gone off inside my body. It must have been an eight-point-oh on the Richter scale. And I didn't even feel the tremors.

"I've learned to listen, to look for the truth, to know adolescents don't always exaggerate or manipulate. Now when she starts spinning, I pay attention. She's talking in circles, preparing to pierce the surface. I know it's about something underneath, especially her fear of men.

"The bond between us is almost frightening. She sees what I'm thinking. She tells me what I feel almost before I can recognize it. She's so intuitive. We've become so intimately connected.

"The struggle has been long. Now I can look back more clearly. It is only now, all these months later, that I can forgive myself. I know I could not control the situation. No matter how dedicated a parent I was, no matter how much I loved my daughter or how much I was really there for her, I could not prevent the world from hurting her." &cn;

With the horrific possibilities lurking in our minds, how do we allow our daughters to find the healthy side of their sexuality?

For every girl, sexuality is a new frontier. Mothers fear predators, both boys and men, bent on their own gratification. Girls dream of princes and rock stars, cute boys, exciting bad boys, and caring men waiting to be discovered. As the terrain of our daughters' bodies takes shape, we can do our best to fortify them with healthy attitudes. We can't hold them back.

When do our daughters cross into the danger zone? When does buying lacy underwear to flaunt at all-girl pajama parties turn the corner? When does flirtation turn into sex? When do boys turn into men? When does affection turn into broken hearts, pregnancy, rape, sexual diseases, and AIDS? Maybe never—maybe today. How's a mother to know?

I learned Sara's time had come when she presented me with a choice.

Sara's Ultimatum

Within an hour of giving *Ophelia's Mom* her blessing, Sara was hatching ideas. "Mom, you could write about the time you took your sixteen-year-old daughter to the family-planning clinic."

My eyebrows raised. I looked over my half-glasses and amended her memory. "Sixteen, Sara? How about fifteen?"

Her body gave a little jerk, like a doe-eyed puppy with a singular hiccup. "Fifteen?" She paused. "Was I really just fifteen?" Then, chin bowed, with just a touch of belated self-consciousness, she conceded, "Oh yeah. Fifteen."

As I remember the moment—though Sara might recall it differently—I was standing behind the kitchen counter about to switch on the food processor. At the time I was obsessed with ridding myself of hot flashes by transforming tofu into chocolate cheesecake. I had thrown all the estrogenic ingredients into the magic medicinal mixer when Sara bounced into the kitchen and announced, "I've made an appointment with Family Planning: Friday at four. I'd like you to go with me. But if you won't, Josh will take me."

Leaving the tofu to marinate in chocolate, I walked around the counter and headed for a chair. She intercepted me. Towering over me in her five-inch platform shoes, she repeated herself: "I've made an appointment with Family Planning. I want you to take me. But if you don't want to, Josh will."

In my stocking feet, I had no advantage here. I was slipping and sliding inside, looking for solid footing. I wanted to sit down. I really wanted her to sit down. I wanted a mother/daughter, heart-to-heart talk. I slid an inch closer to the dining table, hoping to coax her in my direction. She stood firm. She had delivered her ultimatum. She peered down at me, waiting for my answer.

I squiggled by her, collapsed onto the chair, and without looking at her asked, "Are you sure?"

She sat down with me. I could feel her looking straight at the top of my head, shameless. "This is the only time in my life I'll be able to have unprotected sex with no fear of AIDS." Her answer came out well rehearsed. No doubt she had anticipated this question. Quite likely, she had asked herself the same question. And in all probability, her girlfriends had prepared her for this question, both grilling and tutoring her.

I'd heard the unspoken message: We're already sexually active. Josh was a virgin. We need the pill. I'll be safe.

Sara had fallen for Josh when she was in eighth grade. At the time, he was a sophomore in high school, a straight-A, Ivy League–bound jock with only a fleeting interest in arousing the admiration of a prematurely hot-looking junior high school girl. By the time Sara reached her sophomore year, Josh's attention span had lengthened.

Six months, maybe more, had passed since I first walked in on them. Josh had leaned against one arm of the full-size family room couch, his legs sprawled over the cushions. Propped up by the opposite arm, Sara sat with her legs draped over his. The talk was soft, obviously too intimate for a mother to join in. I made myself scarce. I felt a motherly twinge—

sweet happiness of knowing my Sara had crept her way into the heart of a boy she thought she'd never reach, combined with the sad certainty of her newfound vulnerability.

When I heard the door shut and Josh's car rumble down the driveway, I ventured toward the family room. Sara intercepted me en route. Glowing from her girlish conquest, she gave her mini–victory speech. "Mom, you can expect Josh to be spending a lot more time here."

My mind raced for a response that would not result in the immediate rolling of her eyes. How does a mother who entered high school in 1960 ask the relationship question? Are you going steady? No. That was passé by 1962. Are you together? No. No. No. That meant *sex* in 1965. Are you seeing each other? Yes. That's what Manju, her older sister, always said at the beginning of a relationship. So I asked, "Are you seeing each other?"

I had gotten the words right. No eyeballs rolling in disgust. No head shaking in disbelief. No "Oh God, Mom." She simply replied, "Well, I wouldn't say that," prompting me to wonder what I had just said. Had I asked her if they were going steady? Having sex? Going to the movies every Friday? Lying on our couch and cuddling after school? Before I could ask her what I had just asked her, she continued, "We're going to take it slow. Spend more time together. See where it goes." Her reasonableness, her maturity, and her patience impressed me. I answered, "That's good, Sweetie." I didn't realize "spending more time together" translated into "every unscheduled moment." I didn't know "taking it slow" meant they wouldn't have sex for at least five months. I didn't envision "seeing where it goes" would bring us to this moment, in the kitchen, me facing the Family Planning Ultimatum with the tofu waiting and a hot flash kicking in.

I knew I couldn't squeeze out of this predicament. "Yes. I'll take you."

She beamed at me and pronounced her judgment. "Good."

On cue, Gabrielle, her best friend, showed up at the back door. Sara stood up, all smiles, light on her height-enhanced feet. Off she trotted, leaving me in a tofu stew.

Yes, I'd take her to Family Planning. No, I didn't want Josh to take her. Yes, I knew she'd go anyway. No, I didn't want her having sex at fifteen. Yes, I knew she would anyway. No, I didn't want her taking birth control pills. Yes, I understood she could get pregnant. No, I didn't want her to get pregnant. Yes, I wanted her to understand the connection between commitment and sex. No, I didn't want her to expose herself to an early overload of potentially carcinogenic estrogens. Yes, I did want her to make responsible decisions. No, I didn't want her to get used to unprotected sex. Yes, I wanted to support her. No, I didn't want to be a permissive, indulgent mother without any balls. Yes. No. Yes. No. Yes. My mind flung itself between the sides of my skull like a ball trapped in a squash court.

It didn't help one bit when I caught Sara glowing with daughterly pride.

On the appointed Friday, she returned from school with Suzanne, a good girl whose mother teaches at the all-too-local, all-too-public school. As they flounced up the stairs, Sara called out, "Mom, I know we have our appointment. Suzanne's just picking up some books she needs."

I scurried to the bottom of the staircase, wordless. I must have looked sad, worried, pathetic, because she tilted her head and said, "Awww. Poor Mommy. What's wrong?" I don't remember saying a single word, just whimpering nonsense, "Uuuuh . . . aaaaah . . . eeeeee . . . doooooo." Slowly, with compassion, she descended the stairs, stood face-to-face with me, and stroked my head. "Mommy. You can tell me." I formulated a pitiful single sentence: "I think I'm being a bad mommy." She soothed me, "Oh, no. You're a good mommy, a very good mommy. Other girls get pregnant and have abortions and their mothers don't even know about it." I nodded, a wretched specimen of spinelessness. Sara hugged and reassured me. "Mom, I know this is hard for you. Don't worry. It's okay. Really." Then she pivoted and bounced up the stairs.

I caught a glimpse of Suzanne studying me from atop the balcony. In a flash of panic, I saw myself in my daughter's friend's eyes. Oh God! What had I become? I'm "like, the coolest mom." I don't want to be, and I never wanted to be, a "cool mom."

Sara joined Suzanne and leaned over the banister. Sara's long, "sun"-streaked hair flowed over the railing. Looking up at her long locks, I had an epiphany: The witch in *Rapunzel* is my hero. That fang-toothed captor is the good guy. I'll rush right up those stairs, push her into her room, lock the door, install a doggy door for food, sit on the balcony, and cast evil spells on any big scruffy male who wants inside.

Within five minutes, I was in the car, driving to Family Planning. It was a spring day. Of course it was a spring day. All flowers, birds, and bees. What crap. It had to be a spring day. I have no idea how I made conversation. I only remember thinking the whole episode would have been easier in a blizzard. How can a mother possibly talk her daughter out of love when the breeze smells of honeysuckle?

So we arrived in Northampton. We walked up to the Family Planning building on Gothic Street. Who do we bump into, right at the front door? Jeremy Goff.

Now and forever, Sara loves Jeremy. He's the only one of her parents' friends whom she counts among her friends. But at this moment, despite the fact that I adore Jeremy, he was the last, the absolute last person on earth I needed to see. Jeremy has AIDS.

Jeremy was thin, as in emaciated, but he glowed, as usual. After making some typically upbeat comment about the glory of the day, he asked, "So, what are you two lovelies doing on my side of the river?" Sara sang out our destination: "Mom's taking me to Family Planning." Jeremy straightened his body, tilted his head, and said, "Ooo. . . . Saraaaa. . . . congraatulaationsss."

My reaction: *pure horror*. Here's Jeremy, the personification of my worst nightmare, encouraging my daughter. No "Sara, be careful." No "Sex is a serious commitment." No safe-sex caveats. Just pure, simple, unadulterated approval! Should I say anything? Should I point out the poignancy of meeting Jeremy at this particular moment in history? No. Too insensitive. Too obvious. I just hope she got the message—the one I think God sent, not the one Jeremy delivered.

By the time we sat down in the waiting room, I had transformed from wimp-mom into mother-protector. I wasn't about to relinquish my baby to raging hormones without some strategic considerations.

A woman looking far too clinical in her burgundy suit and pageboy hair came to fetch Sara. She wanted Sara. Alone. Not with me. Miss Prissy Discount Pill Dispenser was intent on a behind-closed-curtains powwow with my child. I asserted my authority: "I want to talk about the options before you write a prescription."

This woman, definitely not a mother of a teenage girl, didn't even bother to look at me. She turned and asked Sara, "Do you want your *mother* to be a part of that discussion?" The word "mother" dripped with disdain, like motherhood was a state of dreaded contamination.

Sara's eyes drank me in sweetly. "Mom, I want you to come in after the exam."

The woman, the enabler of plague-infested semen, conceded to Sara's wishes: "All right. You can come in later." With Sara in tow, she walked past my chair. I imagined tripping her, just sticking my foot out and seeing her go *splat*, facedown, spread-eagle on the cheap linoleum. I controlled myself. I sat on a hard chair reading pro-choice propaganda and filling out financial forms. "Will I make a contribution?" Yes. I believe in birth control—for somebody else's child.

Examination and intimate confession complete, I was allowed to join Sara and her Pill-Pushing Advocate. I had concerns. Here I am, this missionary for soy, this menopausal evangelist decrying the dangers of pharmaceutical estrogen. I wasn't about to let my daughter pump megadoses into her bloodstream without taking a stand. I challenged the Advocate: "What about the increased risk of breast cancer?"

This crusader for one cause alone could have cared less. She issued standard information. "All the birth control methods we recommend contain estrogen."

I repeated, "What about the risk?"

She mounted her high horse and proselytized, "I'd be concerned about my daughter becoming pregnant."

I studied her face. No wrinkles. No sag. Not even a worried brow. I thought: Miss Negative Population Growth is speaking figuratively about her mythical offspring. Still, I gave in. "Tell me about the options."

For the first time she looked at me and I saw her thought bubble: *Lady, it's only because of your daughter's good graces that you're even in the room.* Her head snapped in Sara's direction, and she listed the options. I hated every single estrogen-saturated one. I repressed my desire to tell this woman to grow up and get a daughter. Discussion complete, I took the last word: "I want the pill with the smallest dose of estrogen." The Pill Pusher looked at Sara, who nodded in agreement. Then this too-prim, too-proper, too-closed-minded lady, turned to me and said, "It will cost *you* more." I bit my tongue and said, "That's fine."

Deed done. Home.

One year and seven months later, I was sitting in a coffee shop near Wesleyan University, proudly reading Sara's completed manuscript *Ophelia Speaks.* I turned a page and came to the pregnancy section. She'd written:

> I had to take a pregnancy test once. After purchasing the test at the drugstore, my longtime boyfriend and I waited five minutes in darkened silence. Before I sat up to look for a plus or minus sign, he told me he loved me. He tried to comfort me: "Whatever happens, it will be okay." His words did not reassure me. I looked at the result. A single horizontal line had appeared. I sighed a breath of relief, deeper than any I had ever breathed before. Silently, I wondered if anything was worth the anxiety I had just exhaled.

Sara was about to tell the world what she had never told me. The day she had made the appointment with Family Planning, she had been more responsible than I had known.

O ver and over, a daughter's adolescent quest for love and sex will place a mother naked on a razor's edge. Injury is inescapable. If we make a move, if we don't make a move, either way we bleed. We exert control and we're stabbed in the back. We give up control and we're taken for suckers. Charise Williams remembered it all. As she began writing it all down, so many bad memories came back. In the end, her story is an inspiration.

e~

THE UNEXPECTED
by A. C. Williams

My name is Charise.

My daughter is Mae.

My granddaughter is Marie.

My first husband and I divorced when our children were very small; Mae was eighteen months and our son was just six months. I became a single parent at the age of twenty-six with two small babies. I always had a good feeling about raising my children, but in the back of my mind, I was terrified of the teenage years.

I had an excellent relationship with my daughter until she reached the age of fourteen. Overnight, Mae seemed to turn from an obedient, nice little girl into a disobedient, unhappy, and miserable teenager. The relationship with her father had always been one of convenience (his). After she turned fourteen, she started to rebel. This did not sit well with her father. They had a confrontation where he got physical. Consequently, Mae did not see her father for over three years.

It was during this time that I remarried. I had been alone with my children for fourteen years. My daughter was not happy with "this situation." "This man" was moving in and taking over "her time." Mae was jealous. My new husband's heart hardened.

I dealt with Mae's rebellion alone. I had never felt so totally lonely.

If I tried to talk to my mother, I heard about all the talk shows featuring rebellious, selfish, pregnant, and unruly teenagers. I'd think, "Surely she wasn't implying that my daughter is like those kids, is she?"

If I talked to my sister, I usually felt worse rather than better. After all, her son, who was the same age, never did anything like what my daughter was doing. My sister told me once that I'd be lucky if my daughter wasn't pregnant by sixteen. Oh, what a disgrace that would be to our family.

Anyway, I didn't want to hear about someone else's outrageous teenagers or my sister's good teenage son. I wanted support. I wanted some help.

Since I couldn't find the support I needed from my family, I searched elsewhere. I found books about what other parents had gone through. I learned I wasn't the only one and felt better. I found friends who had experienced the same problem with their children and could relate to my feelings. These friends became my confidantes.

And the Lord became my best friend. I was so exasperated one day, I finally had to just pray for the Lord to take care of my daughter. I didn't know what was going to happen, but I knew that the Lord would take care of all of us. I truly learned to put my trust in God. I learned about faith. I learned to really pray.

My daughter did things that I never even imagined doing at her age.

At fourteen years old, Mae lost interest in school. She didn't do homework, couldn't concentrate, and couldn't sleep. She missed school and lied to me. Most disturbing to me was the fact that we couldn't seem to communicate anymore.

At her birth-father's recommendation, we saw a counselor. The sessions terminated when the counselor called me in to let me know that my daughter thought I was too "old-fashioned." I didn't want my daughter to date until sixteen. I'd always taught her to wait until marriage to have a sexual relationship. I'd always said, "Sex is very special and shouldn't be shared with just anyone." How dare the counselor tell my daughter that she would know when it was time to have a sexual relationship. At fourteen? I felt like this woman was giving Mae permission to make adult decisions when she was still a child. Well, I can tell you, this counselor certainly did not help our relationship.

Things didn't get any better.

I came home early from work one day to take Mae to an appointment at school. I arrived to find a truant officer at my home because Mae had missed so much school. The officer told me the authorities would "have to take action if I couldn't keep my daughter in school." I was so upset.

I just couldn't understand. Why was I being punished with such a disobedient child? I had always been a good student. I never openly disobeyed my parents. Oh sure, there were times when I might have stepped over the line, but I never got caught.

It seemed like Mae almost wanted to get caught. She did the dumbest things. Once she had one of her young friends call me to ask, "Can Mae baby-sit for me?" I didn't have a good feeling about this request. I confronted Mae. It turned out she had lied to be with a boy. Either she thought I was awfully stupid, or she was as stupid as she thought I was.

I followed Mae around and checked up on her. Of course my detective work didn't do anything to strengthen our trust in each other. But I wanted her to know that I cared about her. I had to let her know I was concerned enough to investigate. She caught me snooping a few times. But hey, if she was where she was supposed to be, then I was happy. And if she was embarrassed, I didn't really mind. After all, Mae had put me through a lot of pain and misery.

The young men she wanted to hang around with were deadbeats. They weren't in school. They smoked and drank and looked like a mother's worst nightmare. What was happening? Why was she willing to settle for the bottom of the barrel? I was so afraid for her. Would she end up on welfare somewhere? Would she have babies and divorces before twenty? Would she get AIDS? I was making myself sick just thinking about what could happen to her. Even if she didn't care, I did.

I sought more help from books, friends, and counselors. I felt I was doing the right things. I let her know I loved her, I told her and showed her. I never called her names, even though I wanted to so badly. I never talked about her negatively to our family or her father. She had a big enough burden just being fourteen or fifteen. She didn't need the negative gossiping of our families behind her back.

When Mae was sixteen, we finally found her a good counselor who helped our family doctor put her on antidepressants. Her school situation and self-esteem improved. My daughter worked on her school studies at home. She went in once a week to meet with her teacher. Eventually, Mae graduated from our local alternative school.

Mae had made it to eighteen. She finished high school. She hadn't gotten pregnant. Yes!

That summer, she decided to move to Yosemite to work for the summer. It seemed to be a good experience. For Mae, the real world was better than the school world. She made new friends. She loved the outdoors.

She came home pregnant.

I thought, "Oh no, here we go again."

This situation was embarrassing for me. While they were growing up, I had constantly reminded my children that they must take responsibility for their actions. So I let Mae tell all our relatives. My mother wanted to pull my daughter's hair out. Her birth-father said he would support her but later backed out. My sister wanted to adopt the baby. Everyone was upset with her choices and a little afraid she would be a burden to them.

The baby's father wasn't interested and provided no help. (What a surprise!)

Mae checked into adoption but decided against it.

Mae had no job and no money. She had to go on public assistance. My parents helped her get to her doctor's appointments. My family helped in small ways.

I told her I still loved her but was disappointed for her. I was the only one who believed in her. During her pregnancy, my daughter and I became close again. She was able to apologize. She told me she loved me with all her heart and wanted things to be better. She could finally see what I had been telling her and why.

My prayers were finally answered. My daughter and I had grown to be best friends.

On June 24, 1997, the most precious baby girl was born. Our family gathered at the hospital to celebrate Marie's birth. To us, she is a miracle. Because of this child's birth, our family became closer. All of the past pain was forgotten. My granddaughter brought so much joy.

Our family had lost my brother on September 24, 1996, exactly nine months before the birth of my granddaughter. Coincidence? Maybe. Maybe not. I like to think it was planned that way. We had lost someone very dear to us, but we all gained someone new to love. Marie brought a lost joy back into our family.

Marie touched all our lives in another magical way. She stayed with her great-uncle and -aunt every weekend. Marie became their little girl. She helped my sister heal from losing her baby girl, who was eight days old when she died in 1979.

Marie mended the terrible strain between my husband and my daughter. I thought my husband's hardened heart would never soften again, but through the magic of an infant, it melted. He is the most wonderful grandpa. Now Mae and my husband have a loving father/daughter relationship.

Through the birth of my granddaughter, my daughter has matured and turned into the most wonderful person. She now works full-time. She began working when Marie was nine months old. Since then she has become a very valuable employee. Our family is very proud of her accomplishments.

Sometimes when we're in the midst of deep despair, we think we're the only ones. We cannot see the forest for the trees.

What I have learned is, no matter how bad things get, don't give up on your child. There is always hope. The ending doesn't always have to turn out to be bad.

I love my daughter with all my heart. While she was growing up, I expected her to take responsibility for her actions. Consequences can be good or bad, but either way builds character. As parents, we must help our children build their character.

There is a happy ending to my story.

On October 7, 2000, we celebrated my daughter's wedding to a very nice, decent, and hardworking young man.

The wedding was held at an old nineteen-thirties two-story white mansion with a circular driveway and a Peter Rabbit fountain. The ceremony took place under an arbor on the front lawn. The reception was held on the side lawn. Mae had made table decorations, mason jars with candles and potpourri, and put them on every table. A rosy scent filled the air. The cake had layers and layers of white frosting with ribbons and roses cascading down the sides.

It was six P.M. with candles everywhere. The grounds have these large mature trees and lots of flowers. A keyboard, a flute, and a violin played lovely music. As the evening progressed, with the lights in the trees and the candles burning, it was just unbelievably gorgeous.

After so many years of pain and heartache, what a joy it was to see my granddaughter and daughter walk down the aisle in the dresses I had made.

During the ceremony, Marie sat on my lap and waited for her turn to take part. As the minister spoke, I reminded Marie to listen carefully because it was very important. About halfway through the ceremony, Marie said, "I have a daddy now. Can we go have cake?" I guess this sharp little three-year-old really understood what was going on.

When she was fourteen, there was no way I could see the blessing my daughter would become. But today I am so proud and happy for all three—my daughter, my granddaughter, and my son-in-law. I thank the Lord for giving me the faith to get us all through the trials and tribulations of adolescence.

I do have a beautiful story to tell. ◐◑

the lure of intoxication: alcohol and drugs

❧

I STOOD AT THE IRONING BOARD, IRONING THE WRINKLES OUT of a blouse, or maybe it was pants.

Sara walked past, stopped, turned, and said, "Mom, I don't think it matters what parents do. Kids are going to drink and try pot."

I put down the iron, didn't say a word, and paid attention.

She continued, "That's just the way it is: Kids do bad things. I know kids whose parents are completely straight and have all these strict rules about drinking and drugs. And other kids whose parents let them drink and smoke at home. They do alcohol and drugs just the same. No more. No less. Really. I've thought about it. Parents don't have any control."

What's a mother to say?

My fourteen-year-old daughter was speaking with authority. I wanted her observations to be purely philosophical. But even I, the most naive of mothers, knew she was talking from experience.

I froze.

Sara bounced out of the room.

What's a mother to do, if it doesn't matter what she does?

Actually, what we do does matter. According to the National Center on Addiction and Substance Abuse, families may not be able to prevent drug and alcohol abuse entirely, but we can reduce the risk. Simply eating together has influence. Teens who eat dinner often with their parents are much less likely to smoke either cigarettes or pot: 6 percent of adolescent smokers and 12 percent of pot smokers eat dinner with their parents six or seven times a week compared to 24 percent of smokers and 35 percent of pot smokers who eat dinner with parents zero to two times a week. With drinking, the positive effect of maintaining a family ritual of eating together is less: 20 percent of adolescent drinkers eat with their parents nearly every night; 35 percent of drinkers almost never eat with their parents. A strong family bond, clear rules, and involvement help reduce temptation, but they don't eradicate the lure of intoxication.

Shockingly, the most dangerous years for our daughters are when they're young, really young—twelve to thirteen years old. During that time, teens report that easy access to marijuana triples from 14 percent to 50 percent. The percentage of adolescents who know a student who sells drugs also triples, from 8 percent to 22 percent. Our thirteen-year-old daughters are three times more likely than our twelve-year-olds to know another teenager who uses acid, cocaine, or heroin. At that very moment, motherly influence wanes. The percentage of teenagers who say they rely on their parents' opinions for making important choices drops from 58 percent to 42 percent. Children most often begin using drugs at this young age.

When I've told mothers that the dangers of substance abuse sky-rocket at age twelve, they've reacted in two ways: shock and relief. Mothers who believe their girls haven't indulged in alcohol or drug use register shock, suddenly realizing that their daughters are surrounded by tempting influences. Mothers who know their daughters have experimented with alcohol and marijuana express relief. "Really? I was so worried. I thought my daughter was so young, too young. Weird, but the fact that she's not so unusual makes me feel just a bit less worried."

There's little reason for that relief. Adolescents report that alcohol is the number-one problem among teenagers. Early consumption of alcohol predicts increased risk of alcoholism and death. Eight young people a day die in alcohol-related crashes. During a typical weekend, one teenager dies each hour in a car crash. Nearly 50 percent of those crashes involve alcohol. And teenagers vastly underestimate the lethal dangers of binge drinking.

The facts about inebriation's deadly consequences—car accidents, alcohol poisoning, lifelong addiction—send mothers scurrying for answers. Our protective gears engage. We leap from blindly trusting our daughters to tight-lipped intelligence-gathering about their social scene.

A mom who wished to be anonymous wrote about the day that suspicion invaded her seaside home, the day she was driven to spy on her daughter.

SPYING WITH SOBER EYES

by Anonymous

"Drinking?" I gasped as I clung to the telephone. I felt a weight settle into my chest as I listened to the words coming through the receiver.

A well-meaning parent, trying to break the news gently, had just told me that my daughter had been drinking and shoplifting with her friends. My fourteen-year-old daughter. My baby. I sighed, tears rolling down my cheeks. The voice on the line tried to explain how sorry she was to be the bearer of such bad news: "I prayed about it all last night and this morning and decided that if it were my daughter, I'd want to know. I'm so sorry, I . . ."

What had I done wrong? I always thought my relationship with my daughter was so close. We talked about anything, everything. Whenever the subject of alcohol or drugs came up, Callie had always reassured me. "Mom, me and my friends would *never* do that." Was it all a lie? I felt so betrayed. And worse, to be told that the girls had been doing this for months. How could I have missed it? Why didn't I see what was going on?

I had known that Callie was attracted to this new group of friends. They were the wilder kids in school, a little more dangerous than the rest of her friends. But I was afraid that if I forbade these friendships, Callie would rebel and be even more drawn to them.

I had decided to include these kids in our family activities, always picking up an extra kid here or there to take to the movies, the skating rink, the mall, wherever. I thought that if I included them and they were supervised, everyone would be better off.

I thought back to all the times Callie had talked to me about the "druggies" in school. She used to tell me about all the things they got into. These were the kids who were now her friends. When did she start lying? I wondered.

I walked around the house in a fog, picking up laundry here and there. I climbed the stairs to my daughter's bedroom, stuffing dirty clothes into a basket. Then I noticed the diary on Callie's bed. It wasn't a diary, really, but rather a notebook. Callie had been writing in it for the past few weeks. I had known it was there all along. Callie always left it wide open on her bed. But I never read it out of respect for her privacy.

"To hell with her privacy," I thought.

I sat on the edge of the bed, picked up the notebook, and started reading.

Sometimes mothers have their own secrets. We are, after all, baby boomers. Many of us are recovered hippies and flower children, women who went or wanted to go to Woodstock. We sat in smoky dorm rooms under the influence, listening to "Lucy in the Sky with Diamonds," awed by the profundity of the image, whispering "Oh wow," unable to form two-syllable words. So many of us smoked, drank, got high—and maybe more. How do we tell our daughters not to do what we did? One anonymous mother confessed her confusion—an ambivalence shared by more than a few.

DO I DARE TO TELL?
A Story from Another Anonymous Mom

"I've always been so honest with my daughter. She can ask me about anything and I'll give her a straight answer. She has a brother, and their favorite story is to hear about how their mom had her first drunk on her eighteenth birthday. I swigged cheap champagne with my boyfriend, sucking a mint between my teeth to kill the taste, then spent the rest of the night throwing up in front of him—God, how mortifying!—and communing with the toilet back in my own home, much to my mother's amusement. The kids can't get enough of that story. They make me tell it over and over, savoring the gruesome details.

"Right now, my daughter's living in the land of black and white. Drinking and drugs are bad, plain and simple. People who do them are evil; case closed. She gets hysterical if she sees my husband having a beer and me having a glass of wine in a restaurant; she's convinced we're going to be driving drunk. She hasn't asked yet, but I don't quite know what I'll say when she asks me if I've ever gotten high. The truth is, I did *everything*. I don't want to lie to her, but all my friends tell me they're planning to lie to their kids. I think kids can smell a lie a mile away, and I think it'll damage our trust permanently if I don't tell them the truth.

"In reality, I don't think my pot smoking was all that horrible. I didn't do it a lot, it never affected my studies or grades, and I stopped in my twenties. I still get high now and then. I don't have all those drug horror stories, although I can certainly tell my kids about some bad experiences some friends had. The D.A.R.E. classes make it all sound like evil incarnate.

"What I really worry about is that everything today seems so much more hard-core: the crystal meth, the heroin, how easily available everything is even in middle school. I worry not so much that my daughter will get into this stuff but that she'll take a ride in a car with someone who's drunk or high. I want to prepare her, but I don't want to scare her, and I want to be honest. What it all comes down to is that I have no idea in hell of what I'm going to say, and I'm dreading this moment." ❧

Charlene Mason also considered a dreaded confrontation with her daughter. Surrounded by metropolitan sophistication, Charlene chronicled her distressed glimpses into the world of her daughter's alcohol consumption.

SCENES OF APPREHENSION
by Charlene Mason

I'm not a credible gauge of alcohol and its problems.

Ask my husband. Ask my daughters. They'll tell you: I'm too puritanical, too overreactive. I can't be trusted to measure when drinking crosses the line from normal to addiction. There's just too much alcoholism in my family.

THE PAJAMA-PARTY DISCOVERY

In the fall of Rebecca's eighth-grade year, Tom and I flew off to Paris. My sister stayed with Rebecca. Anna, Emma, and Lindy were scheduled for a sleepover. I had no doubt my sister could keep this group in line. All she had to do was stay out of their way.

I never worried about these girls. Why should I? They had known one another since first grade. They lived with wonderfully attentive parents. They were high achievers. On Fridays, they slept over at one another's houses. On Saturdays, they studied. On Sundays, they volunteered at a midtown soup kitchen.

The morning after the scheduled pajama party, I called from France. I asked my sister, "How was the sleepover?"

My sister answered with a mischievous giggle, "You said to leave them alone. I hope you like how they redecorated Rebecca's room. They found gallons of old paint and made the entire space, walls, floor, and ceiling into a Jackson Pollock installation."

I got the picture, splashed and dripped primary colors everywhere. Worried, I asked, "Did they tramp paint all over the apartment?"

My sister reassured me, "No. They kept the entire disaster inside Rebecca's room."

My next question: "Does Rebecca like it?"

My sister's reply: "Rebecca *loves* it."

My answer: "Fine. It's her room."

By summer, Rebecca hated the unsightly mess. As she left for camp, I asked, "Do you want me to paint your room?"

Her round blue eyes registered undying gratitude. "Would you? Would you paint it white? I don't know what came over us that night."

Days later, I learned what had come over them.

I went searching for off-white paint. Vaguely remembering leaving a container in Rebecca's room, I ventured into her overstuffed closet. Behind the stacks of clothes, piles of shoes, and forgotten board games, I found a distillery—half-empty bottles and bottles of hard booze.

I crouched in my daughter's closet, my knees pulled up to my chest, my hands over my mouth, numbed by disbelief.

Slowly, feeling every beat of my heart, I stood. Looking around my daughter's paint-splashed space, for the first time I noticed the evidence of a forbidden reality: a Budweiser baseball cap hung over a light, a Heineken mug on her desk, an Amstel logo propped against her glass of pens, a Coors label taped to her computer. This room, my daughter's room, was a shrine to alcohol.

I sat at her desk and studied the hundreds of photographs glued together into a collage above it. I drank in the details: New York's finest girls dancing, hugging, laughing, lying with their heads together. Their eyes were too often glazed, their movements too uninhibited. These photographs paid tribute to their drunken abandon. I felt like a simpleton, too starry-eyed to see the glaring evidence of my daughter's dereliction.

A month later, Rebecca arrived home from camp. Her dad and I stood together, confronted her with the evidence: a blue recycling bin, eighteen inches deep, one foot wide, and two feet long, full of emptied booze bottles. With no trace of defensiveness, she confessed, "We drank last fall and winter. It's over now. It was a phase, a stupid phase. Don't worry. I won't do it again."

Without prompting, Rebecca threw out the icons of alcohol and moved back into her newly off-white room. Satisfied, reassured, I breathed relief.

TENTH GRADE: UNDER THE INFLUENCE

Seth seemed a good influence. Certainly, he was arrogant, practically insufferable, but he had reason. He was, after all, a straight-A student with 1500 SAT scores, an Ivy League–bound Merit Scholar. For a sopho-more girl, this senior was a catch.

Rebecca loved Seth. She adored him with every inch of her soft teenage heart.

Her dad and I liked the influence he had on her grades. When Seth and Rebecca began dating, Rebecca became a compulsively serious stu-dent. She played less and studied more. How could we, how could any parents, do anything but trust this relationship?

Then one night, I woke to the sound of deadweight being dragged down the hall. Ears opened, I heard Seth's whispers and Rebecca's slurred responses. Under my blanket, keeping quiet, I listened. Seth closed Rebecca's door with uncharacteristic care. On tiptoe, he retraced his steps, locked the entry-hall door, and escaped down the elevator. I waited, hop-ing Rebecca would follow her usual affectionate routine. This night, how-ever, she did not come up the stairs to our bedroom, walk to my side, lean down to kiss my forehead, and say, "I'm home. I love you, Mommy."

I walked into her room to check her condition, to be sure she could talk, to be certain she was breathing normally, to stay close enough, long enough, to know she wasn't on the verge of unconsciousness.

The next day, we talked. I tried my best not to be Hysterical Mom. I wanted to be the thoughtful messenger who delivers words too logical to be refuted.

Rebecca blamed the boys she was with. "I was with Seth and his friends. They drank. I drank. They didn't get drunk. I did." She groaned, "My head hurts. My body aches. I feel like shit. Do we have to talk now?"

"Yes," I snapped. Frankly, I was glad she felt awful. I hoped her head throbbed, her stomach heaved, and everything about her escapade repulsed her. "Rebecca, you know better. You're not a mindless idiot. You weigh what—105 pounds? Seth weighs how much—180? Think about it."

Having expelled my anger at her stupidity, I delved deeper into my worries. I told cautionary tales she had never heard—the alcoholic his-tory of my side of her extended family.

My grandmother, her insides scalded from years of gulping brandy straight from the bottle, sat propped up in her hospital bed. The majority of her stomach had been surgically removed. Her liver was deteriorating. Yet the diminished size of her stomach only temporarily interrupted my grandmother's secret rendezvous with her cherished schnapps.

My cousin Judith, just two years older than I, died from sclerosis of the liver. She left four children behind.

I told Rebecca stories about only two relatives, chosen from many. One, two, three uncles—unrepentant alcoholics. One, two, three, four, five, six, perhaps more of my cousins addicted to alcohol. In her generation, who knows? Who can count? Their parents don't volunteer the information.

Rebecca listened. My litany of the bloodline dangers and alcohol's dehumanizing reverberations seemed to make an impression. She said, "I didn't know about our family. I do know that alcoholism is a hereditary disease."

I wasn't finished. "If you get drunk again, I'm sending you to an AA meeting."

No need. For the next two years, I saw no problem.

FRESHMAN YEAR: THE CALL FROM THE UNIVERSITY

The phone call came at an unexpected moment. In words spoken slowly, devoid of Rebecca's usual lilt, she confessed, "I was in the emergency room last night. I went to a party. I drank. I think someone put something in my drink. I passed out. My friends got me to the hospital. I was unconscious, my blood alcohol levels were too high, but my heart was racing—225 beats per minute."

I understood. Rebecca had been poisoned. Now, with her body aching and her spirit flattened, she needed to hear the soft, soothing tones of her mother's voice. I did not judge. I volunteered to go to her, to take care of her, to bring her home.

"No. It's okay, Mommy. My friends are taking good care of me."

Rebecca's dorm mates had rallied around, making her tea and bringing her gifts. I hung up the phone, more worried about the mysterious additive to Rebecca's drink than her drinking. Was my beautiful baby in danger? Were young men intent on raping her unconscious body? What sleazy dangers were lurking behind her school's prestigious reputation?

Later I found out.

Rebecca had consumed a near-lethal dose of alcohol. She needed no help from the antihistamine some zealous student bartender had popped into her drink. She poisoned herself. True, if Rebecca had been left to her own appetite for booze, her heart wouldn't have speeded into heart-attack zone. Left alone, the beats of her heart would have slowed, perhaps to a stop.

Yet even when I heard the alcohol level of her blood, I chose denial. I thought, "Maybe, just maybe, Rebecca has, might have, an alcohol problem. Yet maybe not. Probably not."

JUNIOR YEAR: MY MYSTERIOUS BEAUTY

Rebecca's older sister, Samantha, was about to make her New York stage debut.

I walked through the white hallway, attracted to an elegant statue of a ballerina. My attention veered right, attracted to a more exquisite figure: a young woman stood framed by a doorway, her willowy body dressed in black with just a touch of red, her straight blond hair draped over bare shoulders. Neon words flashed through my mind: "What a beautiful girl." Then came recognition: "Rebecca. My daughter."

For a moment, I hadn't recognized my younger child.

Now my pace quickened with delight. I hugged her, felt the softness of her once chubby cheeks melt into my face. My heart leaping with mother-joy, I settled into chatting. I barely took note of new boyfriend Jeffrey, her sweet and constant companion. As she spoke about their trouble arriving on time, the three-hour traffic jam, I saw the pallor behind her makeup and blush. Rebecca's voice was devoid of its usual scintillating charm, and she looked drawn.

She did her sisterly duty and sat through the final act. She declared Samantha's performance "Incredible, amazing," forced some polite conversation, then made an early getaway.

Why had my younger child, my social butterfly, been so anxious to escape?

Her dad offered a clue. "Jeffrey said they partied last night. Midterm exams were over. The pressure was off. They got a little tipsy. Rebecca got more than a little tipsy."

Had Rebecca been drunk? Again?

That night, I tossed and turned, revisiting the moment when I hadn't recognized Rebecca. A mystery haunted me: How well do I know my daughter? What secrets cling to her, hidden beneath the gorgeous exterior of this accomplished young woman? Was there a reason I was unable to sleep and heartsick? Was I simply paranoid? I dragged my troubled body out of bed. In my study, I wrote to Rebecca, detailing every suspicion-provoking incident.

THE REACTION

Rebecca received my ten-page brief. She phoned.

"Mom, I'm really mad. Why didn't you talk to me? I know you. You get all weird. You spin out of control. Next time, I don't care if it's three o'clock in the morning, call me.

"Mom. Now listen to me. You have nothing to worry about. I don't have an alcohol problem.

"I admit to those incidents in the past. I'm embarrassed. I was immature and stupid. The last time I got drunk was more than two years ago. Mom, I've grown up.

"I wasn't hungover at Samantha's debut. I was exhausted from exams. I was irritated about the traffic. I was starving because I hadn't eaten all day. I still had one paper to write. Jeffrey's parents had flown in for Parents' Weekend. They expected us to have breakfast with them. I felt pressured. I needed to get back to school.

"I kicked Jeffrey when he told Dad I had been woozy. My boyfriend thinks it's the cutest joke if I get the slightest bit tipsy. Mom, I hardly ever drink. I drink less than any of my friends."

As Rebecca spoke, my mind examined the evidence. Since her last bout with alcohol, I had spent twenty-four hours a day for weekends, weeks, even months with my Rebecca. She never drank. Her exasperated tone reassured me.

"Mom. Are you listening to me? I am so good. I am so responsible. I've got a three-point-eight grade point average. I work. I pay my bills. I'm not like a teenager anymore. I don't do bad things anymore. Don't worry."

MY UNREASONABLE FEAR

My uncle Jerry died last month. He was nearly a saint, that man. He spent his entire life ministering to the poor. His final prayer, "Dear God. Let me die before my daughter."

His prayer was granted. His daughter, my cousin Ruth, the smartest of all my cousins, stopped drinking to spare her father the pain of seeing her die.

Then Uncle Jerry died and Ruth drank again.

My aunt called last night. Ruth had died. Her death was no surprise. Her liver had stopped functioning. Her heart was barely beating. No operation could save her. No family's devotion could resurrect her.

It's true. About alcohol, I don't know what's normal. ✑

Sometimes one alcohol incident follows another in quick succession. Instead of years between binges, there might be only days. Instead of weekend partying, there's weekday indulging.

Jodie's daughter was in high school when the facts emerged. Her daughter had a problem. Jodie sent her message from a little town tucked in the mountains.

HAPPY AND SANE
A Message from Jodie Noble

"They said Ally was an alcoholic. Maybe she was. I don't know. Maybe she is. But now it doesn't seem like it. Now she's in a much better place. She drinks, but it doesn't become a problem. Personally, I think she was really depressed and she self-medicated.

"Ally was driven to perfection. By the time she was twelve, she was driven. Always. Always driven. She sat at the dining table for hours, drawing. I watched in awe. She totally focused, creating this intricate work of art. Then she ripped the paper out of the notebook and tore it to shreds. I screamed, 'What are you doing? All that work. Gone. It was so beautiful.' She said, 'It was shit.' She was so frustrated. She had this compulsive obsession with perfection.

"In high school, she drank. She got Cs and Ds. She was bored and unhappy.

"This kid got a 780 on her verbal SAT. When the scores came in, the school didn't believe it.

"Senior year, she showed up at school incredibly drunk. The police were called to remove her. She managed to get through. She graduated. A college on the other side of the country took her. She settled in. Then a man broke into her room and attacked her.

"Ally called, told me she was drinking a lot and needed help. I called the school to ask them to help her. They said, 'She's eighteen, she has to ask for herself.'

"She wasn't in any shape to reach out. I had to figure it out. I searched for a really good drug rehab program. I found this highly recommended rehab way out in the middle of nowhere. This place takes kids for a month. Parents have to participate at the end of the program.

"In the parent groups—that's the place I found the most support for everything I had been through. And tears. It was a comfort to know other parents were in the same boat. We cried—lots of tears. We shared our stories, looked at our parenting, tried to find answers. I spent lots of time searching for what I had done wrong, for the faults in what I had done. I went through all this remorse about a million things I should have done differently. Other parents had done those things differently, and their kids still had drug or alcohol problems. By the time I left this retreat, I stopped blaming myself. The guilt was wiped away.

"Women blame themselves. I was always looking for what I did wrong. After the retreat I felt that the cards fall. Kids just travel different paths and you have to be there to say 'I love you.' It's all you can do.

"Back at home, she went into therapy. Now she's in a small school. She's happy, nurtured.

"She phoned me and said, 'Mom, I painted this ancient oak tree.'

"I asked her, 'Do you like it?'

"Ally said, 'Mom. It's really good.'

"That's the first time. The first time she ever liked one of her own drawings.

"I went through years of feeling like my daughter was lost. I felt helpless. Other mothers didn't want to talk to me. When my daughter was in trouble, drinking in school and hanging around without a purpose, women kept their distance. So I thought if I speak out, if I tell other mothers what I went through, maybe I'll help in my own little way. I wanted to talk because I wanted to give other mothers hope. I figure that's the one thing I can offer—hope.

"My kid returned to me. She came back happy and sane." ⌒

The alcohol stories go on. In the United States, an estimated one third of all children grow up exposed to family alcohol dependency or abuse. Yet the National Center on Addiction and Substance Abuse reports that 2.6 million teenagers don't know that a person can die from an alcohol overdose.

Neither do mothers. Two of my friends have been college doctors at two small, prestigious women's colleges. Both have confided that each weekend, several young women often end up in the emergency room in danger of cadiac arrest. The girls who are most endangered are those who are living away from home for the first time and have little to no experience with drinking, who drink too much, too fast, just for fun. Sharon Spellman detailed her nightmare.

⌒

THE TALE OF THE CAUTIOUS CHILD
by Sharon Spellman

Calls at four o'clock in the morning seldom bring good news.

My husband's sudden lurch toward the telephone woke me. I pried my earplugs out and heard the worry in his voice: "Is Naomi okay?"

At the sound of our daughter's name, I bolted upright. I strained to hear Paul's words over the sound of my heart pounding. "Where is she?

The hospital. Should we come right now? In the morning. Okay. Chelsea, wait. You're a good friend. Thanks so much for calling."

As Paul set the receiver down, he related the details in composed order. "Don't worry. Naomi's been hospitalized for acute alcohol poisoning, but she'll be fine. I'll tell you exactly what Chelsea told me. Chelsea met Naomi in the quad late last night. Naomi was headed for a party—some all-school bash or another. At first Naomi seemed fine—a little tipsy, talkative, happy. Then she changed. Her legs got rubbery. She collapsed. Chelsea managed to take her back to her dorm room. Then she really became worried. Naomi's eyes started rolling up into her head. She was passing out and hardly breathing. Chelsea called security. The security guard carried her to the infirmary. Naomi was rushed to the hospital. In the emergency room, they resuscitated her and put her on an IV. Now they've got her on an EKG to make certain her heart remains steady. Chelsea said she's okay now. Still a little inebriated." I had no room for thought, only information and relief.

Before sunrise, I awoke with an irrepressible need to see my daughter. I kissed Paul on the forehead, filled a mug with tea, and drove down a deserted highway. I sang and prayed and meditated along the route. I needed this time to center and to prepare myself to be with Naomi.

I swung into the hospital parking lot, ready to see my baby hooked to an EKG, tethered to an IV, in a baby-blue dressing gown, on a regulation hospital bed, but inside, a nurse told me she'd already been sent back to school.

I sped through town, reached the school parking lot, slammed on the brake, and jumped out of the car. As I rushed toward Naomi's dorm, I caught myself. I was in danger of falling into that "Mom's lost it" place. I instructed myself: Breathe. Be still. Be with her. Nothing more. Nothing less. Just still.

I opened her dorm door slowly, so as not to disturb. The covers rustled atop her futon. Her pretty little face peeked up at me. My baby girl. Delicate. Disoriented. She said, nearly in a whisper, "Mom. What happened?"

I sat down on her bed, touched her cheek, and retold Chelsea's story. I chose each word slowly, trying to keep my voice low and my tone soothing. Yet with every sentence, I saw fear flow through her. By the time the tale ended, she lay limp.

"Mom, I don't remember anything. That's the scariest part. A piece of my life went missing."

Listening to her, I was gently released from the grip of my own fears. I thought, "My baby's okay."

I asked, "How do you feel?"

She answered, "Like shit."

I suggested she nap. I reached for her hand, and we both drifted off.

When she rustled, I woke up. "Mom, will you get me some water?" she asked. I fetched water and returned.

She noticed little blue tags taped to her body. "What are these things? Something from the hospital. What did they do to me there?"

Moving her fingers quickly from one to the next, she pulled them off and threw them across the room. Reminded again of her trip into the void, she asked me, "Mom, can you find out?"

Just then, a tall, gangly boy peeked in. He rushed to kneel at Naomi's bedside. Hugging her, he burst into an apology. "Naomi. I'm so sorry. I feel like such a jerk. I'm so awful. Nathan had to be sent to the emergency room, too. But then he wasn't as . . . well . . . as unconscious as you. Oh God. Naomi . . ."

Suddenly his head turned and registered my presence. "Uh-oh. Your mother's here." He swiveled to face me.

"I'm Ezra. You must think I'm such a terrible person. I got your daughter drunk. I hurt people. I'm actually nice. I really am. But you don't know that. I'm sorry. I'm really sorry."

Feeling quite maternal toward this overwrought youth, I assured him, "I know. I can tell. You're a good person."

Relieved, he turned back to Naomi.

At my daughter's request, I set off to the infirmary to gather more information.

A salty old nurse read me a precise description of Naomi's condition from her chart: "Naomi Spellman was brought into the infirmary at . . . She was unconscious . . . Only responding to deep pain . . ." They must have been slapping my baby's limp body. "Her breathing periodically stopped . . ." Oh my God. "Her heartbeat was . . ." Dangerously, nearly fatally, slow. The critical details sobered me. A delayed reaction: Fear kicked in. I had almost lost my child.

A few days later, Naomi came home. Like the little boy in *Where the Wild Things Are*, she wanted to be where she "was loved best of all."

That weekend, we went to Allan and Kathy's for Passover. Kathy greeted Naomi at the door, hugged her, and gushed, "Naomi. I'm so pleased you're home. I love looking at you, seeing this mature young woman. You're different from my wild sons. They think they're immortal. But you, you're so careful."

Accepting the compliment, Naomi unveiled the essence of her near-deadly bout with alcohol poisoning. "I've been feeling my mortality lately." Volunteering nothing more, she looked in my direction. She held my eyes as though to say, "Don't worry, Mom. It will never happen again." ⌇

N ot every mother's story ends happily. But every story I heard ends with love.

Alcohol may be the deadliest drug, but heroin is the scariest. Heroin addicts have a name—"junkies"—as though a person who inhales or injects that drug becomes a disposable piece of garbage. What could be scarier to a mother?

Yet Karen Margulies Green's poetry isn't steeped in fear. It's saturated with unconditional acceptance.

MARCH 12, 1994
by Karen Margulies Green

I respond to your telephone call.
"I want to go to the hospital, now tonight.
I'm scared, the guys in the building say they want to be my
    friend, but they lie.
They're harassing me. My boyfriend's gone. I'm alone."
"Are you sure this time?"
"I swear. Please."

I drive to your part of town.
You greet me at the corner Exxon
wearing an old navy jacket, thin sweater, torn jeans.
"Come on in while I get my bag. It's okay."
Approaching Meridian Hill, we pass two muscular men on
    lookout.
You wave. "This is a friend. This is my mom."

Your words grant protection.
We keep walking, past cars, parked and double-parked.
Your building is gray stone.

As we climb the iron steps, you point down to the basement
   apartment.
"They found a suicide yesterday.
"There, see—the window's closed."

"The lock doesn't hold." You push against a sturdy oak door
and we edge our way past aluminum tables, four stacked
   wooden
chairs, a tan couch, tufts of stuffing ooze out of slashes, a black
   dresser, broken—no drawers, bookshelves with orange
   peeling paint. Near the sink—scattered dishes, a toaster,
   flashlights, two stand-up lamps without bulbs. I recognize
   the portable radio I gave you last birthday, and my travel
   clock.

"It's really big, isn't it?"

"What's this?" I notice three dark green garbage bags
Scotch-taped to an army blanket on the wall.
"Those cover the place where the windows were.
Keeps the cold out. The landlords don't give us much heat."
"Is that why people just leave all this furniture? To pay for
   broken windows?"
"Whatever. People get arrested. The cops take their stuff, store
   it here."

We drive to the emergency room, settle into waiting, but you
jump up from your seat, scrounge around in the sand ashtrays.
"Need a smoke," you say, hopping from left foot to right.
"Need a smoke," as if everyone looks for cigarette butts in
   public ashtrays.
"Got a light?" you ask a man in a brown coat and get one.
"Must be my smile." You grin, returning with two long
   cigarettes.

The doctor invites me into the curtained-off dressing room.
Within your hospital gown, you shiver—can't hide dark
   blotches,
red scratches, sores, sagging thin breasts, all as foreign as your
   rough hands,
torn jeans, dirty sneakers, holes in your socks, vacancies

everywhere but here. The doctor says, "Sorry. We can't admit
  your daughter.
She's uninsured. It has to be a matter of life and death."

Regulations. Rules. We don't know these rules.
"But she's eighteen and indigent," I argue.
"Try D.C. General."

You dress. When we reach
the night air, you look at me and laugh.
With a thief's delight, you reveal a handful of Diabetic 10s.
"Look what I stole! The fools. They leave a drug addict alone
in a hospital examining room with an open container of
  needles!"

Driving back, I become confused. "Which way?"
Always levelheaded and much better at directions than I,
you set me straight. "Make a U-turn, then a left."
I pause at the yield sign
then proceed with care.

WONDERLAND/WANDERLUST
by Karen Margulies Green

Six months of the year, Demeter
  searches for
her daughter, Persephone.
I do not search for my daughter
Yet I find her.
I find her portrait in
  a photo essay book on the
  homeless.

She telephones me collect. West
  Coast to East Coast.
"You can find me on the inner
  fold,
And on the first page after the
  title,
And I'm on page 99,
That's my birthday, 9/9."
Like me, she believes in magic.
"Oh! And I've adopted a stray
  dog.
He's part pit bull and real sweet!"

I go to Borders Bookstore and find
  the black paperbound book—
"Proceeds go to AIDS victims,"
  reads the sticker,

I break the plastic cover—and
    turn the pages
And there she stands
    "Allison Wonderland"
reads the title across from the
    picture on page 99.

"We didn't mean to end up like
    this,
    we had everything—jobs,
    apartment—
    but we like living on the edge."
Eighteen and nineteen, she and
    her boyfriend left home to
    follow the Grateful Dead.
At first they danced and whirled
    in clusters of loyal
    Deadheads
Later found LSD, speed, cocaine,
    crack, heroin.

I look at her portrait, hardly
    recognizing her.
There she stands, fierce—light
    blond against the
    dark backdrop of the
    photographer's cloth.
A warrior—a Valkyrie in a San
    Francisco park.
Eyes illuminated through the
    sunlight
She stands three-quarters
    straight. An extra
    jacket flows
    over her thin wrists.
Five feet tall, not more than
    ninety pounds.
The portrait, unsettling, asks
    questions of the viewer and
    gives no answers.

This heroine is a heroin addict—
    she looks out to a vision only
    she sees.

Dawn to dusk, day after day.
    my daughter and her
    boyfriend live and sleep in
    the open air, among loners,
    drifters, and danglers.
    Deviant and disenfranchised,
    their only protection the two
    stone lions in repose that
    guard the entrance to the
    park.

After five years, I empty her room
    at home
    of her posters, possessions,
    photos, and notes
I ask a friend to repaint the room
    as a guest room
    perhaps.
She works as if the room were a
    theater set
With sea sponge, feather, and
    brush
Until the ceiling becomes a light
    blue-green sky with white
    clouds
The walls, a delicate purple-gray
    sunset.
When my daughter returns, I will
    offer her peace, nature,
    stillness.
With the still quiet leap of a deer
    she will cross back to my side.

❧

I read her poems and phoned Karen Margulies Green.
My first question: "How's your daughter?"
Karen's answer: "Still alive."

Living in the moment has a whole different meaning when addiction hangs over your daughter's life like the precariously mounted blade of a guillotine.

"My daughter makes me laugh. I make her laugh. My daughter is a politically active human being who cares deeply. Her eyes are open to terrible things. She bonds with people in a special way. Everyone in her world says, 'We just love Allison.' She always finds someone to take care of her. She's in an outpatient methadone program. Even when she slips up, they treat her decently. She's chosen that life. I hope her journey ends in some good way.

"Still, it's easier for me when Allison's away. We can talk. Laugh. I don't have to see the little red dots all over her legs."

the edges of emotion: depression and eating disorders

༄

WHEN DAUGHTERS REACH ADOLESCENCE, THEY COME TO THE edge of an emotional precipice. From the time they're twelve until they're twenty, our girls walk blindfolded along a narrow path. On one side, there's solid ground; on the other side, a precipitous plunge into psychological danger. Sudden hormonal gusts, winds of insecurity, storms of rejection all threaten to send them toppling head over heels into self-destruction. Depression and eating disorders rise up from the abyss, ready to snatch and devour our children.

Mothers walk alongside their daughters, never sure how to keep a safe distance. Too close and we push them toward the edge. Too far and we leave them vulnerable. We fear a misstep in either direction will drive our daughters into despair and self-destruction. No one's immune.

Mothers watch their daughters and find reason to worry. For one mom, it's the moods. "My daughter has such emotional extremes. I know teenagers have moods, but sometimes hers just don't seem normal. She gets so happy, giddy, high. Then she gets so down, so down. There's nothing I can do to reach her."

Another woman listened to her daughter confess, "Sometimes I think I might do something to myself." The mother talked about her own reaction: "All I could do was love her. All I could do was hold on to her and be strong for both of us. But when I was alone—I had to find places to be alone—I'd scream. I'd scream out all my despair."

Judy worried that she had bequeathed a legacy of despondency. "I tell my daughter, 'It's the genes. I take medication. My sister takes medication. My mother takes medication. It helps. Take medication.' But she doesn't listen to me. She doesn't believe in drugs. I can't influence her. I can just stay close and worry."

An anonymous mom described her closely guarded concern. "She tries so hard to be perfect. She's so good and so smart.

She works so hard. Before a test, she stays up all night. She practically shivers from nervous tension. Then she aces it. But it doesn't give her any joy. That frightens me."

And finally, Marsha, a psychotherapist, admitted with embarrassment, "My daughter's counselor called. She said, 'Do you know your daughter's severely depressed?' I didn't. I didn't know. I didn't see it. Now she is on medication. I can see it helps." Marsha was not so different from me.

Devoted to Denial

I put a smiley-face on all the signs of my own daughter's despair. Sara went through her depression alone. And I still feel guilty.

Sara had been a socially dependent creature since age two. Five minutes after her friends left, she would complain, "I'm bored."

At age sixteen, she changed. She chose to be alone. She drove to quiet coffee shops, sat at tables for one, read her favorite authors, and wrote in her journal. I didn't know whether to be worried or relieved. Was she isolated or independent? Engulfed in loneliness or claiming her personal strength?

She reassured me, "I enjoy my alone time."

Comforted by her response, I indulged in pride. "Sara's stronger. More independent. Finding joy in solitude."

Day after day after day, Sara came home directly from school to watch *General Hospital.* Then she would fall fast asleep until dinner.

My husband worried about his little girl but deferred to me, the psychologist, the expert mother. "Do you think Sara's depressed?"

"No," I reassured him. "She's fine. Her grades are soaring. She might be working too hard. She just needs downtime."

So I did nothing except join her TV addiction. Each afternoon, I sat on the couch and we bonded. For the first time in my life, I became engulfed in the melodramas of soap stars.

Then, in the middle of one night, I had wandered down the stairs blurry-eyed, aiming for the bathroom, when I tripped over Sara. She was on the landing, curled up in the fetal position. She sobbed from the stinging attack of pains in her stomach. I held her and rubbed her tummy. The physical pain in her belly forced me to concede: Something was wrong.

The next day, we were at the health center, talking to a female physician. This youngish doctor ordered a slew of tests. But even as she wrote out the forms, she voiced a certain skepticism. "We may not find anything wrong. Sometimes with girls this age, the problem is emotional. Have you thought about a referral for counseling?"

I hadn't. I didn't. I looked at my daughter and saw the picture of emotional health, a beautiful young woman with stellar grades, high-achieving friends, and a portfolio of extracurricular honors. No. This girl of mine was not depressed. This girl was simply ill. And if all the tests failed to find the cause, the tests would be at fault. A week later, the tests did fail to find a cause. And I did assume the tests were at fault. I did nothing, just waited for her body to heal itself.

A year later, Sara asked me to read the first draft of her book. She handed me the manuscript with instructions: "Don't change a word. If you have any comments, write them in the margins." I read her carefully selected words:

> The worst night of my life, I envisioned my own funeral, my death by suicide . . . writing here is only the third time I've confessed those deathly images. The next day, I tearfully told my tenth-grade boyfriend. Later, I confided in my journal. Now I tell you . . . Virginia Woolf, Maya Angelou, and Alice Walker became my most trusted companions. . . . Alone, nameless to others, I concentrated on my own self-healing. . . .

In the margin, I wrote: "I love you, sweetheart." ◦◦

I had maintained denial. Now I mourn the loneliness Sara endured. Other mothers don't have the luxury of pretending. Depression enters like a monster from another world, grabs their daughters, pulling them toward a dark and inaccessible reality.

When Remi Beth Langum's daughter turned thirteen, the demons of depression entered their lovely Maryland home.

LITTLE GIRL LOST AND FOUND
by Remi Beth Langum

I looked across the kitchen table at my daughter, God's greatest and dearest blessing in my life. She had taught me so much in her brief thirteen years. With her growth came a burgeoning love, fierce and unconditional, different from any other love I have ever felt. I would do anything to protect her.

I looked across the table at my daughter, defiant and desolate; at the sullen face, the weighted-down shoulders, the rageful mouth, the intractable presence. Everything about her screamed of suffering, challenging me to love her as she retreated behind the fortress of anger. Suddenly, precipitously, everything had changed.

I looked across the kitchen table at my daughter and vowed to love her through *this*, to be her support and strength when she needed it, whether or not she wanted it. I promised to take care of her. I vowed to work with her to find a new way to be, to come through *this* together, stronger, healthier, wiser, and closer.

Today I was meeting my daughter as though for the first time. I felt intimidated by the strength, the palpable force of her inward fury. I was terrified of her. That fear was visceral; a twist of the stomach, a tightening of the heart. I grieved at the loss of our easy closeness. Now she repudiated the should-be-taken-for-granted love. What was given freely now had to be tested and proved. She now questioned my love as she doubted her own ability to be loved. I felt inexpressible sadness for her pain and for our estrangement. That grief came to reside in my marrow like a permanent part of my being, felt with every movement.

I have read books that say such adolescent metamorphosis doesn't occur overnight. With us, it did. The difference from one day to the next was startling, stark, like a picture to its negative.

One day my child was happy and life was easy. The next day her world was dark, and life was bleak. One day my world was intact; the next day, shattered. Without any instructions on how to reconstruct a new whole, I relied on the strengths that had gotten my daughter and me this far—love, instinct, and determination.

Elizabeth was suffering from depression, an unfortunate, nonreturnable genetic gift from both her parents. My husband, his mother, and my mother all suffered from depression. And I've certainly sparred with my own demons on an all-too-regular basis.

Our journey through Elizabeth's depression, complicated by puberty, lasted for two years. For much of the time, I was suffocating. My spirit felt as battered and ragged as my body had once been after a forceful ocean's wave struck and pulled me under in one deft movement, sweeping me over its jagged floor before spewing me out.

When I was most frazzled, I wondered if I would ever be able to breathe again; to sleep or feel rested; to feel sane; to assuage my raging fears; to find the best way to care for my daughter; to remember my husband; to figure out how or even whether we would survive. During desperate times, I often found myself sitting at the kitchen table, staring out a large window. The view gave me a wonderful sense of openness, space, and possibility. I saw our backyard filled with life—with trees, ivy, flowers, rabbits, squirrels, and birds at the feeder. When I was rooted to that spot, I felt connected with nature and reconnected with my spirit. As I sat in my spot, staring out the window, my mind would calm, and eventually, from somewhere within, I found what I needed to continue.

I was driven to act, to do for my daughter. I overcame my insecurities, my concern about being judged a bad mother, and my inveterate reticence to ask for help. I contacted a wonderful friend and talented psychologist from back home—a thousand miles and a lifetime away. I talked with the faculty, administration, and visiting nurse at my daughter's middle school. Together we would weave a strong safety net for Elizabeth.

I remember a meeting Elizabeth attended. At one point, she began writing on and coloring her hands and arms. My sweet, hurting daughter used her body as a canvas, her pain palette in shades of black and blue. I took the pens and kissed her hands. I felt so scared. I hoped and prayed I would be the mother Elizabeth needed and deserved.

I met with my boss to arrange for time off under the Family and Medical Leave Act. During the three months that I stayed at home, I walked my daughter to and from school. At first, Elizabeth made it clear that she resented my presence, my intrusion. But I believe that in addition to the anger, she was glad I was with her. Sometimes we talked. Sometimes we shared silence. Eventually, Elizabeth began to open up, to reestablish her connection by talking. Tenuous initially, the connection grew in strength. Our closeness was essential in getting us through the pain and challenges yet to come.

In the summer between eighth and ninth grades, things were going much better for Elizabeth. I asked my daughter why she rebelled so vehemently against me as opposed to her father. She looked at me with sympathy, as though I were a simpleton. She smiled and explained with great patience. Since we were so close, it was only natural that I receive the brunt of her rebellion. Besides, she was changing.

She informed me, "No one at school is close to their mothers. It just isn't cool."

I stifled a desire to screech, wring her neck, laugh hysterically, or blurt out some smart-ass comment. I said, "You didn't have to go from being close one day to surgically removing me from your life the next."

She laughed and said she missed me.

Toward the end of my daughter's freshman year, she began to unravel again. Whatever the reason, she engaged in high-risk behaviors. She became school-phobic and lost interest in everything, most especially and poignantly herself. The pain tore at the fabric of her being. I held and rocked her, wrapping my arms and soul around her, forming a physical cocoon and emotional integument to protect her.

And I marshaled my resources for another battle.

Here was a child who had been in the gifted-and-talented program throughout grammar and middle school, who started high school with a B-plus average and who was now on the verge of failing. Elizabeth had ceased to learn. The high school became a toxic environment. I pulled her out of school. I placed her in a short-term treatment program designed to address her immediate needs.

I hired a lawyer, a caring and true advocate, to help me take on the school system and ensure the county lived up to its responsibility. I persisted. I brought her picture to meetings. I found allies in her therapist, her school counselor, the county psychologist, and the other county workers. Eventually, we won—all of us won. Elizabeth was placed in a special school at the county's expense. She received the care that she needed. She survived, as did I.

After she graduated, Elizabeth told me that at one point, she really didn't think she'd make it through her teenage years. She had come that close to the precipice. The full effect of that truth filled us. We both cried, out of relief and gratitude, I think. We hugged. She thanked me for all I had done, especially for being there, even when she made it unbearably unpleasant. To see her healthy, intact, and on her way to college, to hear her laugh; to feel her strength and her presence—my daughter a gift regiven—made my heart sing.

There had been times when I sorely missed changing dirty diapers and the smell of upchucked liquid vitamins with iron. When faced with figuring out how to love a prickly, combative daughter, I thought wryly, "God gave parents adolescence to make it easier to let go of children." I indulged in fantasies of waking up on the other side of *this*, packing her off to college, and reveling in peace, time, energy, and space for blooming in her absence.

Elizabeth is now almost twenty and a junior in college. She attends a university that is three hours away; just far enough. I don't visit impulsively, and she doesn't flee home when things get challenging. She is doing well and so am I. She has graciously invited me to be a part of her college life. I have over a dozen adopted daughters. I didn't have to carry them. Or give birth to them. Or love them through adolescence. All of them, especially Elizabeth, are wonderful young women, and the world is a better place because they are a part of it. 〜

In a lakeside village nestled in northern hills, the world appears to be a perfect place. Yet even here, daughters are diagnosed with depression. Even in this supportive community where mothers bring homemade soup to flu-stricken neighbors, girls close their bedroom doors, take out sharpened instruments, and cut themselves.

Depression sometimes dumps daughters at the edge of self-destruction, where self-inflicted wounds keep them in a never-never land between life and death. The next writer traveled with her daughter to that purgatory. She kept breathing and found a healing connection.

ON PINS

by an Anonymous Writer

It was already dark when I picked you up.

I had spent the afternoon in women's qi gong practice, working with releasing fear from my mind and body and becoming aware of body truths, those moments when my body speaks to me loudly and I often refuse to listen.

When I walk into the space where you've been rehearsing, I see you doing a girl's nails, and I imagine you're being girls together. You look tired.

Later, sitting across the table from you in the café, both of us not saying much, I keep up the talking end of a sparse conversation. In the middle of dinner, you pull from your pocket a small piece of paper, partially filled with pinholes, and a long-tipped metal pushpin.

As I watch you methodically punch holes in the paper, I feel in myself a bodily truth that presents me with the choice of shutting down or staying witness. I know I'm right in the middle of your pain with you; in the place where I see you shut down, avoid eye contact, want to sleep more—a place of anger, I wonder?—the place where you seemingly slip from my grasp; where you won't let me in; where, most important, I usually go into a total state of fear, fear related not so much to your pain but to my own mother-panic.

And you have just let me in. I am in the middle of your pain and I'm present. I breathe and watch and I do a spontaneous form of tonglen—

breathe in my pain, breathe out spaciousness, breathe in my fear, breathe out spaciousness . . .

After a minute, you look up and smile. Then you put your things away. Neither of us has spoken. ❦

Meredith and Jenny, big and little sister, had made a show of hating each other when they were children. Now, with both fighting adolescent growing pains, they had become allies. Gena Harris, their mom, confessed her gratitude for their belated friendship.

"Meredith wanted to talk about her sister. 'Mom, you have to promise. You can never tell. I mean it. Never. Jen can't know I told you.' I swore silence and she continued, 'Jen's cutting herself.' My heart stopped midbeat. Signals raced through my mind. Long sleeves in summer. No swimming at the pool. No eye contact. Finally, I breathed: 'Thank God she has a sister.'"

Some daughters don't inflict pain upon themselves in methodical increments. For some, the pain drives them right to the edge of suicide.

I tore open a white envelope and read:

A TIME FOR WORDS
by Katie

Some days maybe I was better off being numb. At least then I didn't realize the magnitude of my problems. I didn't know the magnitude of my daughter's pain. Nor did I know the magnitude of mine. I was numb until the ton of bricks fell on my head. I don't think I will ever forget the pit in my stomach. I thought I would vomit. I only wanted to fix everything. I wanted to make it go away, to be back where I was just a few minutes ago, to be ignorant of the real trouble. My daughter was frightened and I was terrified. My child wanted to kill herself. She had decided today was the day.

What to do, how to keep her from "doing it"—chasing her around the house, feeling helpless—calling hotlines, psychologists, anyone who could offer a solution—I felt so helpless. Finally, a calm reassuring voice: "Here are the choices. If she will go for assessment, take her to the psychiatric hospital."

There was no way I could be prepared for what happened next or for the shock. I couldn't imagine leaving "my baby" in this place. But there was no choice.

For the first, very first, time in my entire life, I could not control the situation. I ceased to function. I could not speak without crying. I stared, could not sleep, could not move without pain. I was in shock.

What had happened? Where did I go wrong? It was all a blur. My life was suddenly even more on automatic than it normally was. While I was busy with my career, my child, right under my eyes, had reached the bottom. Was this the result of being numb? Did I think if I ignored the situation, it would disappear? I didn't know the answers. But I really felt guilty. How could I have let my daughter become so desperate?

Helpless, I had no idea what to do. There isn't a parenting class on earth that can prepare you for how it feels to try and stop your baby from killing herself. There was no way I could understand what had driven her to this point. I was sure it didn't seem as overwhelming to me as it was to her, but then again, I was numb. Or did I just want to ignore how I felt and hope and pray for the pain to go away?

Confrontation was always very difficult for me. As a young person, I always hid from it. Anything to keep the peace. "No yelling. Please, no yelling." The surest way to get what you wanted from me was to confront me in an angry manner. That meant you did not love me; I must have been bad.

My lack of boundaries, my inability to confront my problems, had put me in a very dark, depressed place. When this started, all I wanted was to save my daughter. By the time it ended, I had learned that to save her, I had to save myself. Now I'm helping myself, and when I do, I help her. ⬅∘

What do you say to a mother whose daughter attempted suicide? I dialed Katie's number. I thanked her for writing, for being so generous with her story. I heard the soft tones of compassion in her delicate voice.

"When all this happened, it drove me into the core of my own issues. I was raised by an emotionally absent mom. She was completely shut down, locked inside herself. She had no interaction with me. None. I grew up numb. I've worked out a relationship with my mother. I've worked through being a frightened little girl. I'm more balanced and open and true to myself. Now I can talk. Now my daughter can talk to me.

"Partway through our healing, in the middle of our rebuilding period, my daughter and I decided to do anything we could to help other mothers and daughters. If any one piece of information helps another mother to see the early signs, some good will come out of our ordeal.

If telling our story helps one mother and daughter survive, all this pain will come to some good.

"Silence nearly killed my daughter.

"Speaking saved both of us. Without fabulous therapists and without the support of other women, we would not have made it.

"All this anguish happened for a reason. We were given an opportunity to change our lives."

Mothers watch their daughters' self-loathing take many forms of self-destruction. Depression, eating disorders, self-mutilation, and suicide are related. All find their noxious power in self-judgment. Bulimia and anorexia wield self-control like a weapon targeted at its owner, designed to lay life itself to waste.

Marianne Peel Forman, a gifted writer from the Midwest, wrote two poems that captured her helplessness as she stood by a daughter grappling with bulimia. Now, with eating disorders in her past, Marianne's daughter wrote a note granting permission to publish the poems.

FAR TOO LONG
by Marianne Peel Forman

She was gone too long,
my daughter.

Wrapped in Calvin Kleins
that showed how flat
her stomach really was.
I watched her eat
all the fettuccine,
even slurping the noodles
and nodding approval at me,
letting me know I could
cook this supper again.

Not like the time she
negated the rosemary chicken,
throwing out the jar of
rosemary

right in the middle of
dinner—
her guarantee that I would not
cook that poultry again.

But she was gone too long,
my daughter,
And I knew that the meal
she savored
was being purged
from her seemingly satisfied
gut.

That she had
once again
decided to expel the calories,
the nutrition—

acid them up
through a throat that must
by now
be scarred
and bruised.

Later
I would find the vomit
on places she wouldn't suspect—
under the rim of the toilet seat
where she forgot
to wipe off the evidence.

And I watch her grow thin,
collarbone catching necklaces
in absurd angles,
eyes that sink deeper into her face,
too tired to even accuse anymore.

Until I no longer
recognize this child,
my daughter,
who has been gone
far too long.

SPARROW HOSPITAL, 11 P.M.
by Marianne Peel Forman

I offer to hold her down
to sit on her stomach
and pin her to the gurney
with my own hands.

She is hollow,
collarbone like chicken wings
protruding,
pulsing at me
as she tells me
no needles
not needles.

I show her my arm,
prick it at the bend of my elbow,
show her how easy
blood flows.

She curls away from the dripping
     vein
fetuses up on me
with her sallow face

to the wall.
I notice she needs
a belt now
to hold up her jeans.

She wears a size two
and there are still spaces
between her sunken hips
and the denim.

The emergency staff
tells me
she cannot be forced
to give blood.
She's a minor
and they force only
drug addicts or DWIs to give
unwillingly.

She tells me
that if I force the needle

into her arm she will continue to
go in the bathroom,
vomit whatever she has
crammed in her mouth,
make herself sick,
and it will be
all my fault.

I pull the curtain
between us,
creak it slowly across the track,
and watch my own blood
trickle down my arm
and out of my hand.

◆⊃

None of our daughters, not one, slides with perfect ease into a universal model of adolescent perfection. Yet too often, the craving to achieve some impossible vision drives a compulsion to squeeze their bodies into ill-fitting proportions.

Sarena Neyman wrote about her daughter's quest to leave her genetic roots, to trade her God-given body for one with media-approved measurements.

OUR THIGHS
by Sarena Neyman

The first thing that I noticed after pushing out what felt like a series of greased-up balloons was that my newborn daughter had my thighs. Exactly my shape, exactly my proportion—muscular, not plump or fat, but rather with bulging quadriceps, almost like a little wrestler. And rather than bemoan her genetic legacy, I was suddenly filled with a sense of enormous relief. I realized that I, too, had been born with these thighs, and there was not much that dieting or targeted leg lifts were ever going to do to reduce them. They were what they were and had always been and would always be, a gift from some ancestor from millennia gone by, and that was that.

For a long time, I was very much at peace with my legs, and they even became a source of self-satisfaction approaching vanity. I could bench-press impressive weights with them and run miles and miles every day on my sturdy columns. I smiled to myself when I overheard, on more than several occasions, lesbians admiring my muscular endowments.

As my young daughter grew up, I watched my reflections on her little body with pride, even though they were far from the sleek, sinewy loins that sold magazines to men.

Then one day I noticed my daughter, now a beautiful and exotic, curly-haired teenager, standing on legs I did not recognize. They were very thin, reedlike, fitting into jeans marked size three, or sometimes even size one. I heard there was even a size zero for those who had nearly disappeared. How could that be? The same daughter I could have sworn had been born with my solid thighs had become a waif so quickly I didn't even notice.

When the middle school guidance counselor called, I had an answer to my query. Was I aware, he asked, that my daughter had told her friends she was throwing up on a regular basis? No. I was not. Of course—how else could a legacy so strong have disappeared except by a force that went against all nature?

My daughter and I departed from discussions of the body to more intimate depths of the spirit and the soul. And since they were not my spirit or soul, I cannot tell you the story. I do not know what happened beyond the facts. After going through half a dozen well-meaning and expensive psychotherapists, all coincidentally thin as rails, one young insightful and quiet woman succeeded in breaking through the daunting armor of secrecy and shame. And then, over a year later, there they were again. My daughter's thighs—the thighs I knew as well as my own—returned.

I think it was sometime last summer. I was lying on the beach, feeling cool wind on my skin, after a long, vigorous swim in the ocean. From behind me I heard my daughter say, "Oh my God, Mom. I just realized I have your thighs."

And in that voice I heard a sigh of relief and resignation. A realization that there was no sense fighting biological destiny. These thighs were ours for the keeping. ⋘⊙⊃

I imagine our daughters feel a gap between where they are and where they are supposed to be. It's as though they are perched at the edge of a fault line. Adolescence comes, the earth shakes, and the crack widens.

Some girls try to leap over the abyss, using this thought as their parachute: "If I change myself, I will land on the other side, perfectly accepted." To make the change, they turn dissatisfaction on themselves. These sensitive daughters diet, or vomit, or study compulsively, or alter their personalities, or abandon their values.

Others girls make that leap imagining they can change the world, that they will create a personal utopia. These courageous children rebel—pierce and tattoo their bodies, confront authority, hold tight to their difference.

Either way, girls are assaulted by the message that they are not okay as they are.

The sensitive ones endure judgment that attacks from within. The courageous ones face judgment from all around: peers, other parents, teachers, strangers. Leaning in one direction or the other, girls are in danger of falling into depression.

When daughters are lesbian, the danger of being engulfed in depression is so much greater. Gay and lesbian adolescents are two to six times more likely to attempt suicide than other teenagers. Prejudice accounts for the pressure: 97 percent of public high school students report hearing homophobic remarks from other students. The typical adolescent hears twenty-five antigay slurs a day. If lesbian daughters remain closeted, they feel shamed by their own secrecy and self-denial. If they come out, they risk bigotry, name-calling, exclusion, even violence: 80 percent of gay and lesbian youth report verbal abuse, 44 percent report threats of attack, 33 percent report having objects thrown at them, and 30 percent report being chased or followed.

Mothers can't make the world safe for their lesbian daughters.

Alma's daughter, Meg, endured spirit-breaking onslaughts when she publicly acknowledged her sexual orientation.

ENDANGERED BY COURAGE
Alma MacDougal's Story

"When Meg was fifteen, entering her sophomore year of high school, she announced to her father and me that she was gay.

"Both our girls had gay and straight friends in and out of our house all the time. Sometimes I felt something was a little off, but I never guessed.

"I think Meg had known she was a lesbian for a while. She said she felt different when she was eight or nine. That really bothers me: how long she felt alone. I wanted her to be in a hugging home.

"After the initial shock, waves of fear shot through me. I envisioned the hardships my daughter might possibly face. We went to several PFLAG (Parents for Lesbians and Gays) meetings and got support.

"One of my favorite memories is when Meg and I attended a PFLAG conference. I volunteered in the 'hugging' room. Many young people came in just to talk and get a hug. These kids weren't safe in their own homes. It broke my heart. I realized then that the best gift I had given Meg was a safe place to grow. So many other young people missed that safety. Something as simple as a hug was so important to them.

"Meg became the president of the Safe Schools Club. She was verbally and physically abused. She even got death threats. One day, she came home from school after someone smashed in the side mirrors of her car. She reported incidents to the principal, but these hateful things continued. There'd be no consequences. The principal didn't seem able to do anything.

"Meg was so *out*. Not in your face, but so open. She wasn't going to hide. I just couldn't convince her to hide. Her honesty made her a target.

"It was terrible to watch. I was anxious, always scared for her to go out the door. Meg wouldn't tell me when things happened to her. Except now and then. I'd go ballistic.

"Then the depression came on. Strange sleeping habits. She'd never slept well, but she started sleeping less and less. She didn't eat. She had problems concentrating. I suffer from depression myself, so I could see it. I worried.

"I had switched to a female primary-care physician when the girls reached puberty. I made appointments for Meg. I couldn't go along, and I knew Meg wouldn't say anything. So I called the doctor and told her what was going on. This woman doctor is a really warm person. Finally, Meg opened up to her.

"Meg was diagnosed as suffering from depression. This was a personal blow to me. I had trouble separating her suffering from mine. Still, I tried to teach her what she had to do to cope. Her case was severe. She started to take medication, but she wouldn't stick with it. She went through a tough time.

"One day, a guidance counselor from school called. Meg was having blackouts, and she was receiving hate mail in her locker at school.

"My brother-in-law had been very ill and died. On the day of his wake, Meg tried to hang herself.

"We hospitalized Meg. She was placed on a suicide watch. When I saw her in the hospital, I saw myself. I had been hospitalized for drinking. I knew what it was like to be in a psychiatric institution.

"I spent time with Meg, sitting through evaluations by psychiatrists, school boards, and therapists. Meg was gifted, a talented writer and artist, but she had to graduate from psychiatric placement. I worried: Was she going to find a way out of this? I could share my experiences, but Meg had to find her own way.

"I've watched her suffer, then persevere through obstacles and become a strong young woman. Meg's fearless. I admire her. I think all she's been through has given her a strength and depth very few people have at her age. She has so much maturity and compassion. I still feel protective. I'll feel protective when she's fifty.

"Today Meg attends college in a northeastern city. She's doing so well. Meg found out she's more than a lesbian. She's active in Amnesty International and People for the Ethical Treatment of Animals. She's learned to meditate. She's just happier in a more liberal environment. Freshman year, she had kidney stones. She dealt with them all by herself. I worry so much about her being so far from home. Then I think, 'She handled kidney stones by herself. Meg can handle anything.'"

Depression forces some mothers and daughters to endure repeated episodes of debilitating discouragement. Judy Pohl worries that her daughter's sincere efforts will never be rewarded with stable happiness.

FINDING AND LOSING HOPE
A Story from Judy Pohl

"On the surface, Catherine's all bouncy. She makes jokes, says, 'I was born into a bad gene pool.' It's humor with a truthful edge. Depression runs through our family. Underneath, there are these currents, these dark moods.

"Something happened in Catherine's senior year. I don't know what it was. Up until Christmas, everything was fine. She had a close group of friends. Her grades were good. Then she got sullen, and the friends seemed to drop away.

"One day, I get this call from her school. The person on the other end says, 'Your daughter's not going to graduate.'

"What do you say to that?

"Catherine had failed. It was over. She dropped out.

"She worked at these minimum-wage jobs for a while. She saw she had no future. She decided to go back to school and get her diploma.

"Everyone said, 'Just get your GED.'

"But she was insistent. She wanted a real graduation, a regular diploma. It meant something to her. I understood. My daughter was so glad I understood. Somehow, knowing I believed in her gave her strength.

"She found a program in a special school designed for kids who had dropped out. She worked really hard, studying and holding down a job. She succeeded. She was going to graduate.

"My husband and I were sitting in the audience. The program had this pretty graduation ceremony.

"Catherine didn't show up.

"We walked out to the parking lot. There she was. She'd overslept and missed it. She cried and cried. I held her. I tried to comfort her. All I could say was 'You worked so hard. You wanted to graduate so much.' She sobbed and told me, 'Mom. You're the only one who understands.'

"Catherine was down, but she rallied. She got that regular diploma in July. Two weeks later, she was off to the Navy. She got accepted to this high-level training program. She was excited. I was thrilled. I thought, 'Now she'll be okay. Her life will be on track.'

"By the end of August, she was home. The Navy couldn't keep her. She was too depressed.

"Every time she gets up, something from inside her knocks her down.

"I can't influence her. I try. I tell her going into therapy and taking medication can help. I'm on medication. But Catherine won't listen.

"Her older sister, Anna: She's my best hope.

"Anna called and said, 'Send Catherine to stay with me.'

"I said, 'Why do you want this surly child?'

"Anna just wants to help her little sister. I can't rescue Catherine right now. She won't let me. I've always told my daughters, 'Stick together. I'm going to kick the bucket someday. You'll only have each other.'" ⟿

In the middle of hopelessness, help comes from unpredictable sources. Amanda Ornstein spoke and wrote about emerging from hard times.

ℓ⟿

LEARNING A NEW MANTRA
A Story from Amanda Ornstein

"It was as though a dark cloud descended upon our home. My happy-go-lucky girl metamorphosed into a dark, depressed, angry, troubled human being. She suffered from major identity issues that led to shifting friends, music, grades, and dress. She exhibited extreme fluctuations in mood.

"Emily began to live behind the closed door of her bedroom. I tried to stay a part of her life, but she just pushed me out. There was lying, sneaking, self-destructive behavior.

"When she wasn't in the house, I'd cross the forbidden threshold. I'd walk into her room, stand there, just studying her space, wondering, 'What's she doing?'

"I felt helpless. What could I do?

"I attempted to talk to her. We'd have these almost nonsensical discussions that never resolved anything.

"I spent nights without sleep, repeating my mantra: 'Let it go. Give it up to a higher power.' I held tight to the thought, 'Inside this ugly person is my wonderful daughter. She's going to come back.' I had to believe.

"Eventually, she went into therapy.

"The psychologist called to say Emily was depressed and recommended medication.

"The school year ended. She graduated and announced she was driving west. She said, 'I'm going. I need to purge myself of the Midwest. And there's nothing you can do about it.'

"She was seventeen, barely seventeen, but in the eyes of the law, she was an adult. I let her go and I prayed.

"This girl who had sequestered herself in her room and refused to speak to me called every night to say 'Mom, I love you.' By the time she got to the Oregon coast, she had found her spirituality. Freedom and nature had reawakened her to herself. And maybe the medication kicked in, too.

"Now she's off to college. I feel like I'm waking up from a coma. For the first time in years, I'm taking an interest in myself. My spiritual life is reawakening. I'm taking a yoga class. I've found a synagogue that supports mixed marriages. I tell myself, 'Some good will come from this.'"

A week or so after my conversation with Amanda, I received a note from her: "After we talked, I found myself feeling hopeful and blessed. I began to realize that every time my daughter seemed to be at an abyss, and I was beginning to lose hope, something miraculously and unpredictably shifted. She ended up being okay.

"Last night, I received an incredibly warm, insightful, intelligent e-mail from Emily—the most positive and reassuring communication I've had from her in years." ✐

minding the body: illness and disease

ALL MOTHERS SHARED ONE NIGHTMARE, A BOLT-UPRIGHT-IN-BED horror—that our daughters will be harmed. Stephanie Palladino confessed that fear to her daughter.

IN MY DREAM
by Stephanie B. Palladino

In my dream last night, I was pulling wads of your hair out of a bathtub drain. Each time I thought I had reached the end, more hair appeared. At first I wasn't startled, but at some point, that changed as I realized how much of your hair had been shed. Then you appeared and proudly showed off your new haircut. Thin wisps of straight hair fell just above your shoulders in a pageboy style—your broad grin surprised me. Was this some grotesque joke you were playing on me? I was stunned when I saw that your scalp was now visible beneath the thin strands of hair that barely covered it.

All day, I have tried to forget this dream. I am disturbed and puzzled by it. Why did my unconscious conjure up such a damaged image of you, my child? In reality, your hair is so beautiful—thick black curls fall in ringlets to your midback. Was this dream an expression of my anxiety about your safety while you travel so far from home? Most likely. For the next three weeks until your return, I will harness all the positive energy I possess and send it in your direction so that not a single strand of your beloved hair comes to harm.

Sometimes anxiety combines with guilt. Not shame over a misspoken word or mistaken deed, but uncontrollable guilt, fear of diseases born of genes. Jeanie French wrestles with the fear that her daughter is destined to relive her history. In the shadow of her genetic legacy, Jeanie's motherly devotion turns into vigilant attention to her daughter's body.

179

MIRROR IMAGE
by Jean L. French

Genetics—it's a funny thing.

My son looks just like me, except for his nose. The nose, his voice, his laugh: all like my brother's, drawn from my gene bank. There's little of his father in my boy.

My daughter, on the other hand, looks more like her dad's family. Amy's eyes are deep-set, the hazel color of her dad's. Her mouth is like his mother's. The exception, bless her, she got my brother's nose.

So it always gives Amy and me the giggles when people say, "Oh, Amy, you look so much like your mother." We really look very little alike.

Amy's beautiful, although she doesn't think so. She thinks I'm pretty, and she wishes she looked more like me.

Now Amy's probably wishing I hadn't passed on any of my genes.

I have scoliosis, a curvature of the spine. When I was twelve, I underwent surgery, a spinal fusion. That was in the nineteen-sixties.

In 1981 I married and had a child, a son. In 1984 I had my daughter, Amy. I believed neither of my children would be affected by the disease that had twisted my spine, contorted my torso into the shape of a question mark, and left its scars upon my body and psyche. Basking in my misconception, I wrote a poem about my relief: My children would not be twisted by this disease.

When Amy was three, I learned the truth about scoliosis. Genetic research had come a long way since my childhood. Scoliosis proved to be genetically transmitted. I began to watch my little girl like the proverbial hawk.

"Stand up straight for Mommy, with your feet together and your arms loose at your sides. Now bend over and let your arms hang down in front of you."

Every couple of weeks, I did a visual scoliosis test. I'd check the line of her spine, the smooth skin of her sweet little shoulders, hoping not to find telltale signs of curvature.

It was just a game for Amy until shortly after her sixth birthday. I discovered a slight curve. I took her to the doctor immediately. The X rays showed she had developed a curvature of six degrees.

"Six degrees isn't a significant curve," the doctor told me. "We don't usually do anything until the curve reaches eighteen degrees. Most girls don't develop the disease until sometime around puberty."

I was upset. I'd been diagnosed with scoliosis when I was seven. For the next five years, doctors just watched my curve worsen until I had a fifty-eight-degree curve, too advanced for a brace. Surgery, then nine months in a body cast, was the only option for me. The treatment straightened my body thirteen degrees, stretched my skeleton to five feet four inches, pared my weight down to seventy-two pounds, and left me, at thirteen years old, with a forty-five-degree curve, a permanently disfigured torso, an angry red thirteen-inch scar down the middle of my back, and a deep-seated belief that my body was ugly. Deformed. Bad.

I would not let this happen to my daughter.

Encouraging Amy's strength, taking her to gymnastics three times a week, didn't assuage my nagging guilt. I confessed to a friend how awful I felt about passing this disease on to my daughter, how afraid I was that Amy would be like me.

My friend looked at me oddly. "Jeanie, you're one of the strongest people I know. How'd you get that way?"

"Well, I had a lot to overcome—" I broke off. I knew what she was getting at.

Then she asked me another question, one that was a lot harder to answer. "If you had known that you could pass this disease on to your children, would you still have had them?"

I thought about this question for a long time. The answer was clear. "Yes, I still would have had children."

I wanted children very much. I knew I'd be a good mother. And as much pain as scoliosis has caused me, I've always recognized that it had a huge role in shaping not only my body but my character. I had struggled, emotionally and physically, but I liked who I'd become. And if one of my children had to face that battle, I'd be there to help. Several years passed. Amy's curve progressed to nine degrees. She continued in gymnastics. By the time she was eleven, the X ray showed her curve had decreased three degrees—normal variance.

But I knew, and the doctor knew, and by this time Amy knew that we weren't out of the woods. Amy hadn't reached puberty, when scoliosis most commonly shows itself. I continued to keep watch.

After eight years of gymnastics, Amy was tired of the sport. She wanted to play basketball and volleyball at her school. When she was twelve, I finally said yes.

Amy became a star in volleyball—tall for her age, strong, well conditioned, and able to jump higher than anyone else. But something else was happening.

Amy turned thirteen; she started her period, and the scoliosis came back.

"Ten degrees," the doctor said. "Bring her back in a year."

"Six months," I said.

"No, a year's fine. Bring her in sooner if you notice some dramatic change."

Eight months after that checkup, Amy's curvature was more noticeable, more visible in photos than in the flesh. I knew what I was seeing. And so did Amy. After all, she'd been seeing it right in front of her, on her own mother, all her life.

Amy's right shoulder was now higher than her left, and her right breast sat higher on her chest than the left one. When I traced her spine with my finger, I felt the curve. When she bent from the waist, I saw where the twisting of the spine pushed out her right shoulder blade.

I wanted to scream. "Amy is beginning to look like me. I don't want her to look like me."

I phoned the doctor and scheduled another exam.

I thought back to that long-ago conversation I had with my friend, to the question she asked: Would I have had children if I'd known? I didn't know if I'd give the same answer this time.

I can't imagine my life without my children, can't imagine life without my daughter—my wonderful daughter who has so much to give the world, so much to be and do in the life ahead of her. But I never imagined how hard it would be to see her becoming like me.

As a teenager, there was a part of me that resented my mom for allowing doctors to watch me become more and more deformed before they finally did something about my disease. I knew that my mother did the best she could for me, but still . . . I guess when you're thirteen and fourteen and fifteen and feeling like the ugliest girl in the world, it helps to have someone to blame. Just a little. Just in the secret place in your heart that you seldom acknowledge even to yourself.

I needed to give my daughter the chance to tell me how she felt, even to tell me that she was angry with me for giving her this disease. I told her how I felt about my mom, and I asked her to tell me what she was feeling.

"Yes, I'm a little angry," Amy admitted, "even though I know there was nothing you could have done about it. Except not to have had me. And it would be stupid to be mad that I was born!"

I asked her the question my friend had put to me. As I had, she thought for a while. "I don't know. Scoliosis isn't usually life-threatening these days, right? And I know you think you're deformed, Mom, but honestly, how many people actually notice? I don't think anybody's thinking, 'Oh, how gross!' even when they do notice. Besides, maybe by the time I'm ready to have kids, scientists will have figured out how to fix the gene. I'm not sure I even want to have kids anyway."

Amy's so levelheaded yet optimistic. Sometimes it almost scares me.

The news from the exam was good. Despite the evidence before our eyes, the new X rays showed an upper curve of six degrees and a lower curve of three degrees. The upper curve, the one we were most concerned with, had actually decreased. The slight distortion we can see in her upper torso probably won't get worse. We'll wait and see. But Amy will be sixteen in less than two months. When she stops growing, the twisting of her spine should stop as well.

Amy's five feet nine inches. She doesn't think she has a pretty face. I just tell her she's beautiful. If she becomes adamant about her unattractiveness, I agree with her in a Roseanne sort of way. "Yeah, you're ugly all right. You're so ugly it's a wonder the mirror doesn't crack when you look into it. And how come all your friends haven't asked you to wear a paper bag over your head when you go out?" I always get a shamefaced laugh out of Amy. God bless Roseanne.

Amy and I have a mutual admiration society. She tells me, "You're so confident, Mom. I want to be confident like you." I tell her that it took me years and much conscious hard work to develop confidence in myself, my skills, my mind, and yes, my own unique physical attractiveness.

But Amy has a physical confidence I've never had. She's tall and slim, with long, gorgeous legs. She knows her body is strong and healthy. She feels in command. She isn't worried about how much more her spine will curve. Even if she has to wear a brace, she won't give up volleyball. It's her passion; playing keeps her in shape. Recently, she told me, "Well, I may not be pretty, but I do like my body."

Pretty amazing.

Maybe living with someone whose body is so far from normal has been good for my daughter's body image, bad genes and all.

So Amy's not stressing over her scoliosis.

But Amy's not the mother. I am. ❧

Some mothers live with anxiety that the rest of us can hardly imagine: Serious illness threatens their daughters' lives.

I can't pretend to know how it feels to travel from day to day with a menacing shadow hovering over my children. I only know when a fleeting vision of their falling seriously ill or being injured passes through me, I feel my heart ripping, my face suddenly flush, my body on the verge of paralysis.

For Catherine Hellmann and Gail Parker, my momentary illusion has been their constant reality. These mothers have stood up to the unjust hand that nature dealt their daughters. They have not been struck immobile; rather, they have mustered strength in the service of love.

MY LITTLE TROUPER
Thoughts from Catherine Hellmann

My conversation with Catherine had been light, sprinkled with giggles, bordering on girlish pleasure. Catherine skipped from topic to topic— boys, school, grandmothers, siblings, discipline, ex-husbands. We paused on ex-husbands.

I asked, "So how do you manage to share Emily so smoothly when you and her father have such different styles?"

For the first time, Catherine's bubbling banter stopped. She took a long breath and told this story at a slower pace.

"Emily was born with holes in her heart. They had to be fixed. She had open-heart surgery twice: the first when she was five, and the second when she was six. Her father and I were already divorced. Our differences didn't matter; we had to get along for Emily's sake.

"Emily was little, kindergarten age: My ex-husband and I fly with her to Boston Children's Hospital. She's in surgery. We're waiting in the hallway. He hears this 'code blue' alert. He tells me, 'I think that's for Emily.' He goes off to ask the primary-care nurse. Just as he sees this nurse, she starts running. Emily's jugular vein got punctured.

"Months later, we were back in Boston for the second surgery. That wasn't such an adventure.

"Now Emily's thirteen. My little trouper doesn't hide her war wounds. She's not self-conscious. She's got this enormous scar down her chest, and she wears these little tiny bathing suits. People notice. She gets asked, 'Is that from open-heart surgery?' She doesn't mind. She's got this confidence about her body."

Catherine Hellmann had described a daughter with a spirit as indomitable as her own. Emily's gigantic mark made by scalpel and stitches left an indelible impression. Catherine is forever grateful for whatever normal turbulence her daughter's adolescence brings. ✁

The threat to Gail Parker's daughter lurked undetected through her childhood. The fatal possibility suddenly intruded when Carolyn hit her teenage years. Gail worried her daughter's life might be tragically shortened. Not so for her daughter Carolyn. Something completely different tipped her perfect emotional equilibrium.

LIFE-THREATENING LOSS
by Gail Parker

It turns out that my thirteen-year-old daughter and I cry about different things.

Carolyn lies in the hospital with a collapsed lung, the result, apparently, of a congenital defect. A week of no improvement brings tears to my eyes each day. I wonder what the next day will bring. No change. The lung does not mend. Each day the same. Pain with every breath for my daughter and sleepless nights for us both. But strangely—bravely—there are no tears in her eyes.

And then comes the dreaded pronouncement from the doctor that surgery is the only option now. Perhaps he can do it thorascopically, with only three or four one-inch incisions along her side. But perhaps this lung will require a thoracotomy, a five-inch incision from front to back, moving her ribs.

I cry at the thought of saying yes to this surgery, of having to make this decision for my daughter, wincing at this new pain she will undergo. But I dry my tears and call on God's strength and face my daughter to tell her the news.

She is calm. "What will the surgery be like?" she asks.

I explain the two options.

She thinks for a moment. Then she asks quietly, "Could I die?"

Somehow I do not flinch.

"Well, this is not really life-or-death surgery," I tell her. "You have one very healthy, very good lung already working hard for you. So it's not likely that you would die."

Carolyn mulls this over. She is at rest, propped up in her bed.

Silence.

Then, "When will I go back to school?"

I breathe a sigh of relief. She is so brave! She is ready to tackle this hard thing and get beyond it. "You'll be in the hospital one more week and then at home for a week after that."

As soon as I tell her the recovery schedule, she bursts into tears. "That long? Two *weeks*? I'll be out of school fourteen days! I won't see my friends *forever!* I'll miss my friends." She sobs, wiping the tears off her flushed cheeks, trying to catch her breath. "I'm missing *everything!* I'm missing my *whole life*." ❧

For Catherine and Gail, their daughters' life-threatening diseases came and went. Carolyn Lewis lives with no expectation of resolution. The challenges of chronic disease will span her daughter's adolescence. Her twelve-year-old suffers from arthritis and fibromyalgia. Labels, good and bad, have attached themselves to her child. Carolyn's commitment: to never allow those labels to limit her daughter.

A GOAL WITHOUT COMPROMISE
Thoughts from Carolyn J. Lewis

Some days I have the strength to tackle the gods and win. Some days I could stay in bed under the sheet and pray that we get one good thing out of the day.

Self-esteem? We deal with it. Beads, bangles, painted fingernails? She's not the type.

When is it that one gets past the idea that one's child is not, and never will be, average? Every day.

How do you get your daughter over shyness so extreme that private schools have turned her down because of it? We work with love and compassion.

Anger? She's got a ton of it.

But a graceful, willowy child with a heart of gold? She's that, too.

What is our goal? An intelligent, useful, compassionate life. ❧

From a rural community drenched in loveliness came a contribution from another mom, Jinny Savolainen, a gifted writer who navigates her daughter through the hardships of illness and the awkwardness of adolescence. Jinny described herself and her daughter ever so briefly: "I am the mother of two children, a thirteen-year-old daughter and a ten-year-old son. My daughter has spina bifida (and a host of other related medical problems). She has had many surgeries in her lifetime and went from using a walker to a wheelchair when she was about seven. She has an amazing spirit—full of love and compassion and indescribable strength. She also has a lot of anger, frustration, and sadness about her situation. In some ways, she is quite balanced. She is in many ways like a very typical teenager."

Jinny's story, like many, speaks directly to her daughter, embracing her child with gentle thoughts while allowing us to enter their intimate relationship.

THE TENDERNESS OF NEW LIGHT
by Jinny Savolainen

Light is pouring through your bedroom window. Your room is cloaked in amber—beaded, sparkling, warm light. It is deceiving—tricking us into thinking it's warm outside, or that there is warmth between us at this moment.

You are a teenager. I forget, I remember. I forget, I remember. I remember to tell myself that your actions and reactions are not necessarily a reflection of who I am as a mother, as a woman, as a friend, as a "used to be" little girl.

It is early morning and we barely speak. We are tired and taking care of the mundane task of getting ready for school. I watch you getting dressed. One breast is clearly larger than the other (and continually growing). I wonder if you see this imbalance. I know you feel the imbalance of your changing body, changing hormones. You are putting on your bra, but you have already grown out of it. I watch you try and make your breasts fit. You push them down inside and they slip out the bottom. You tuck them back in underneath and they creep out the top. Your bra does not fit—but I'll bet you're thinking that your breasts do not fit. I wonder how many things do not fit for you any longer. I wonder about the feeling in your heart when you think about relationships that don't fit anymore, or capabilities or desires or motivation or anything that used to fit before you became a teenager.

Now I am remembering again that seventh grade has found you happier than you've been in years. What do I make of this? Is it your ideal tutor/companion in the middle school? Is it coming to terms with who you are? Is it feeling the glory of your budding womanhood?

These days you hug me more. You say "I'm sorry," you smile, and you participate more. I give you more space. And I give you more undivided attention. I trust you more.

So now, as the light continues to pour in, it also pours through me. I am remembering that there is a warmth between us. We are bathed in the pearly light of each other's company.

You break the silence by saying good morning again—and you lay your head on my lap. ❧

When Grace Wozniak faced breast cancer, she worried about how her illness would affect her daughter. She discovered that the experience gave her daughter a chance to grow in a way she never could have anticipated.

"DON'T WORRY, MOM, I'M RIGHT HERE"
by Grace Wozniak

The diagnosis was a complete surprise. During a routine breast exam, my ob/gyn said, "Hmmm. I'm not sure I like the feel of this." I could tell by my doctor's face—she's a friend—that she was worried. I was scheduled to have a routine mammogram in a few weeks anyway, but I called the radiologist and made them take me right away. The mammogram was fine. They said, "Great. Go home." I said, "No, my doctor's worried. I want a sonogram." The ultrasound showed this very, very small mass (what a lovely word that is). The radiologist, also a friend of mine, said, "I'm sure it's nothing—just a dried-up milk duct." I asked, "How do you know?" He said, "I'll wash your car naked at midnight if it's malignant." So I said, "Great, but how do you know?" He said the only way to know for sure was a biopsy. He told me to come back in six months; I wasn't going to wait even twenty-four hours. I had the biopsy on New Year's Eve, 1998—everyone's favorite time to be in surgery. The surgeon took it out and told me the margins were clear, it was very small, but she was still concerned. That was when I started to entertain the possibility that I might become a statistic on the other side of the percentages. It would take four days to get the full pathology report. My husband and eighteen-year-old twins, Lily and Dan, were with me during the biopsy. We were all convinced that everything would be fine.

On January 4, 2000, the doctor called. "I want you to come over to my office." I knew it wasn't going to be pretty, so I rounded up the whole family. This doctor is very soft-spoken, very calming. She told me I had stage-one "garden-variety, vanilla" breast cancer: "the best cancer you could have." I was stunned.

I hadn't known anyone close to me who had breast cancer. None of my friends, relatives, kids, friends, parents—nobody. We left the office after four hours. Nobody had any definitive answer about what I should do next, except I was supposed to have another surgery to remove my lymph nodes. Before this started, I had been in the hospital only to have the kids. We went straight from the doctor's office to a bookstore. Every family member was going to look for a certain kind of book.

Information was going to be our courage. We came home with twenty books and tapes. This was going to be how I'd handle my medical illiteracy. I wasn't going to tell anyone or ask anyone for anything.

I'd bought a journal along with all those textbooks. That night, Lily started writing me notes. They were the most dear, supportive, positive, encouraging blessings I could ever have. "Don't worry, Mom, I'm right here." "We'll get through this together." "You're the best." "You're so brave about this." Everything from sappy clichés to remembrances of special times she and I had shared. She wrote them on stickies with brightly colored ink and happy, cute drawings. She'd slap them down on my planner so I would wake up and find them. They became our little communication system. I got her a pretty journal, and I started writing her back. I pasted her notes into my journal, and she put my notes into hers. It was the things that were almost too important to say out loud that we could express in writing.

I had the second surgery. The kids got out of school so they could be at my side with my husband. The whole gang went to every appointment with every oncologist I interviewed. There were no secrets.

The second pathology report came in. I was going to need chemo-therapy and radiation. I was just flattened. I was three months away from a launch of a statewide program I'd developed, plus I was finishing a major writing project and waiting for the kids' college acceptances. I decided I'd treat it more like I'd broken my arm; it was an inconvenience, but once the cast came off, I'd be fine.

I asked Lily how she felt about it. She and I didn't talk about how frightening it was but about how lucky we were. As odd as it may seem, my overwhelming emotion was gratitude. I was so grateful for catching it early, for having great doctors, for having a diagnosis with a definitive treatment, and most of all, for having work I love and great kids and a husband who were so loving and positive.

Dan wanted to tell his teachers about it, but Lily was adamant. She didn't want anyone to know. She said she didn't want anyone to feel sorry for her or treat her differently because her mom was going through this. That was exactly what I was thinking. I was 90 percent denial, 10 percent "I am Woman, Hear Me Roar." "I'm the same me that everyone always knew; I just have this little broken-arm problem." I refused even to use the language of the disease—words like "survivor"—it just made no sense to me.

I started the chemo. I decided I was going to be the only person on the planet who took these chemo drugs and wouldn't lose her hair. Lily and I went to the "Wig Lady," just in case. She and I were just howling at the modus operandi that the Wig Lady used to encourage us to get a particular wig. I had so much hair you couldn't put a wig on me, so we tried the wigs on Lily. It was like she was a little girl again, playing dress-up. We actually had a lot of fun there because it was just so unreal; her attitude and mine protected us from the reality of the situation. Of course, two or three weeks later, my hair started to fall out. I bought some extra-heavy-duty Aqua Net and sprayed my hair into this horrible, matted, ratty helmet, just glued it to my head. I went out looking like that; I really thought I was pulling it off. One night, Lily came over to me and said, "Mom, I have to tell you something. We've got to talk about the hair." "Yeah, isn't it great?" I enthused. She said, "It's not good, Mom." "What do you mean?" "Things could have died in there and we wouldn't know. I think it's time for the wig."

Without even questioning her, I just said okay. We drove right over to the guy who does her hair. She sat with me the whole time the hair came off. She stayed until the last strand was gone. I thought it was a real heroic effort on her part; I don't know if I could have done that for someone else. After that, I wore the wig, but always backward, just for humor. Even at my presentation in front of fifteen hundred people. It was my rebellious spirit.

The whole time, Lily and I were keeping my illness a state secret. We were going to get through this together, as a family, but damn if we were going to ask for support from anyone else.

Spring was coming. When Lily got accepted at her college of choice, what took me by surprise wasn't so much the trauma of her going far away, but knowing that she wasn't going to the same school as her brother. They had never really been separated. They'd never gone to different camps or even on different class trips. The thought of them living on their own was really surprisingly devastating to me. It was a real insight into my own unconscious agenda; I hadn't realized that I found so much comfort in the fact that they had each other. It had been a relief to be able to worry less about how they were handling my illness, knowing they had each other so close. Now that would change. But Lily was so happy about her college, I knew I had to come to terms with my own emotions. And my other fear—that she would turn down her college of choice to stay close to home with me—didn't materialize.

I was also dealing with the empty-nest syndrome; it's just so hard when your two children leave home at the same time. Interestingly, the research on my major project centered on just that subject, and it was enormously helpful to me. I was literally proving the veracity of my own work. My big fear about my separation was that I wouldn't be finished with my treatment and strong enough to help Lily move. I wanted the experience for her to be as normal as possible. The radiation treatments were finished in July. Two weeks later, she had to ship out all her stuff. She and her brother started school the same day; my husband took Dan, and I went with Lily.

I checked the mirror before we left. I had barely any hair, my face was totally washed out, and since I'd gotten lymphedema, my left arm was wrapped in this weird bandage. I was so worried that I was going to embarrass her. Of course, Lily was still adamant that she didn't want to tell her new roommates or their mothers about my illness. I respected her privacy, but that was the most emotionally challenging thing for me, because I really wanted to be able to explain away this pallid face, the wrapped arm, the really short hair, my fatigue.

The notes continued, even through college. Lily and I would save up a week's worth, then send them off to each other. When I needed to make sense of what had happened, I'd go back and reread them. They're a great tribute to the eighteen years Lily and I connected before the diagnosis.

We related on a whole new level. If she'd say, "Oh, I look so fat in these jeans," or "I can't do anything with my hair," or "What is this zit now?," all I would have to do is look at her, maybe say, "Hello?," and she'd say, "I know, I know, it's not that big a deal." So we had a new bar by which to judge problems. And that has continued to this day.

For the first semester of her sophomore year, Lily had a women's studies class, and she had to do a final project designed to make a difference in the community. For the past five or six years, before my diagnosis, we'd walked together in Race for the Cure. She e-mailed me and told me that a major tennis star's mother and sister had been diagnosed with breast cancer. She came up with this thought: She was going to put together a tennis tournament to raise money for women with breast cancer. She was even thinking of asking this star if he'd play in it or endorse it in some way.

I had such conflicting emotions. I was thrilled that she'd found ways to make her experience empowering instead of destructive. I truly believe it has changed her for the better, just as it has changed me for the better. But I was wishing that she didn't have to have this personal connection to this whole world of illness and pain and trauma and tragedy. The mother in me just wanted to protect her from it all and keep her in this Pollyanna state. But I knew it was too late for that.

What really floored me was the speech Lily gave to her classmates, which she e-mailed to me: "Two years ago, my mother was diagnosed with breast cancer. I was scared. I didn't know what it meant. I didn't know anything about the disease. Neither did my mom. We both learned together. By being proactive and getting the support you need medically and emotionally and intellectually, you can help turn your fear into confidence." There it was. She'd never verbalized her fear before. It was the first time I realized that she had deliberately shielded me, that she had prioritized our feelings and put mine first, that she was there to support me. For the first time, I saw her as an adult.

As parents, it's very easy for us to be stuck in that role of not only doing for others but shrugging off offers of help. "Oh, don't worry about me. I'll be fine." I had such a strong model from my own mother: Keep all your problems inside, help everyone else with theirs, but don't you dare share yours. Lily and I talked a lot about that. It was so hard for me to ask for help, to appear needy. Not anymore! I don't want her to be that way, either. When she needs me to be there for her at college, I'm going to depend on her to tell me, particularly now that she's so far away. We made a deal on that. We're there to help each other. ⌒

part three

Tied in
Family Knots

I sat in a hotel conference room on one of those red velvet fake French Provincial chairs, the kind that look silly and feel uncomfortable. Surrounded by colleagues at this "for licensed psychologists only" affair, I waited for the speaker to step up to the podium. Nearly a football field away, a dynamic woman with an enormous reputation began speaking. Within minutes, she was analyzing the interpersonal dynamics of the typical family. Actually, she was pointing out their dysfunction.

"The mother in this family is the switchboard."

The speaker paused and stared at the audience, waiting for a knowing chuckle to ripple through the audience. I began to squirm. I glanced at the suited men on either side of me. They grinned. Their heads bobbed in agreement. I hunched over, scribbled notes, and prepared to duck. I knew the next comment would hit close to home.

"All messages go through her."

Oooo . . . direct hit. That hurts. The speaker went on to explain that the mother places herself in the middle of every conversation, attempting to elevate her stature within the family by acting as the all-important conduit but in fact inhibiting direct communication between other family members. The implication was that the meddling, self-important mother was the source of the family's dysfunction. I cringed, thinking of my own family. Guilty as charged.

Now, looking back, I think, "So? Mothers *are* the switchboard. We do connect the members of our family to one another. We listen carefully to messages, process them, try to sort out the shrill and the hurtful, and translate them into love. We feel the responsibility of the conduit role. To our husbands, we are both wives and the mothers of their children. To our children, we are mothers as well as their fathers' partners. We are the mother to more than one child. We are our mothers' daughters and the mothers of their grandchildren. We connect everyone, and it ties us in knots."

In this section of *Ophelia's Mom,* mothers talk for themselves about the fun, folly, and frustration of being in the middle.

fathers and husbands

e∽

THE MILLERS—LISA AND JEDD, THEIR FOURTEEN-YEAR-OLD daughter, Jenna, and their seventeen-year-old son, Elijah—live on Summer Street. Lovingly tended flower gardens surround their nineteenth-century farmhouse. Their home looks as quiet as framed embroidery. But it's not. Inside, dogs bark, music blares, people squeal and shout.

Even Lisa, a mom whose vivacious goodness explodes in song, finds her home "a bit too noisy sometimes, especially when Jenna and Jedd play. My husband and daughter can be raucous. They still play—squeal and scream and chase each other around. I feel like I've got two kids romping through the house. But just as I'm about to scream at them to be quiet and settle down, I'm overcome by this warm, fuzzy feeling. I treasure their relationship. Jedd doesn't get caught in her attitude."

Lisa is an exception. Most mothers talk about how adolescence complicates their husbands' relationships with their girls. As daughters take on a womanly form, a new awkwardness enters the father/daughter relationship. Dads as well as daughters pull back from kisses, hugs, and cuddles. Girls look for affection from boys, and dads suspiciously listen to see if the boys' voices have dropped yet. Fathers feel more alienated when their daughters become possessed by hormonal demons. It's harder for them to relate; it's outside of their experience. They can't believe the irritation, the rejection, the outbursts aren't personal. And the pads and tampons and blood make them downright squeamish. A distance normally comes between daughters and fathers during adolescence. Mothers work, sometimes very hard, to keep them connected. Gloria Vera watched the discomfort looming between her daughter and husband and recalled how her own father had dealt with the situation.

NAVEL GAZING
by Gloria Vera

My mom had given me this tube top/overshirt combination for my fifteenth birthday. It was gorgeous but tummy-baring, and it took me a while to screw up my courage to wear it to a party. I'd fussed and primped for an hour, tentatively convinced myself that I bore a passing resemblance to foxy Maria Muldauer on the album cover of *Midnight at the Oasis,* and was ready to head out to the proving grounds. Just one problem: To get out the front door, I'd have to walk by my dad, who was reading in the living room.

This was a man who pulled no punches in expressing his opinions about my appearance: My hair was raggedy. My clothes were sloppy. Once, when I'd applied the merest trace of eye shadow to the very edge of my lids, he cornered me at the breakfast table and put his foot down: "I won't have you going outside looking like a clown."

I felt insecure enough; I knew I wouldn't be able to handle any criticism, so I decided I needed a little camouflage. I scooped up the family cat, clutching her to my bare midriff. I was halfway across the hall with Fluffy when he snapped down his newspaper.

"Where are you going?"

"Out. To a party. Mom said it was okay."

"What are you doing with that cat?"

"Nothing."

There was a long pause, then the order: "Put the cat down."

Fluffy ran for cover as I stood there, navel bared. My dad gaped at me. For the first time since I'd known him, he seemed at a complete loss for words. I felt my cheeks burning; I might as well have been standing there completely naked, I felt so exposed. Finally, Dad just snapped his newspaper back in front of his face, which I took as my dismissal. I fled for the door.

Clearly, he'd seen that I was no longer the little girl who rode him piggyback or wound her arms around his neck as he dove deeper, deeper into the pool at the YMCA. From that day on, if I ran into his arms, he'd push me away after the most minimal contact. I missed his burly arms, the smell of his English Leather cologne, the scratchy feel of his favorite bum-around-the-house sweatshirt. I still miss those wholehearted hugs he used to give me.

I look at the relationship between my husband and our daughter, Ariel. They're a mutual admiration society, and they still have this easy physical closeness. She still slips between us in bed for a cuddle first thing in the morning, plops herself unceremoniously into his lap, flings her arms around him when he gets home from work. Ariel doesn't even have boobs yet, but there's something about the way she dances unself-consciously around the house, shaking her fanny, shimmying her hips, that's definitely . . . sexy. My husband has turned to me and admitted, a little nervously, "You know, she's already got a body on her."

I know he's proud of what a beautiful young woman she's becoming. I know he's worried about when she's going to start dating (it scares the hell out of me, too). But I don't want him to pull away from her the way my dad pulled away from me, the way I see other dads pulling away from their daughters. What are dads so afraid of?

If I see it happening, I'm going to tell him, "Okay, she's got a body. Deal with it. If you feel self-conscious about touching her, get over it. She's your daughter, and a daughter really needs her dad's hugs."

Eva Wallace wished her husband and daughter would both grow up. Eva, like many women, felt that her daughter's puberty had re-awakened her husband's adolescent irrationality. I listened to her words coming slowly through the telephone.

LOSING DAD
Thoughts from Eva Wallace

"I'm only going to tell you this because you're writing a book."

Eva had a story, a private story: the kind you keep to yourself but might tell a stranger on a bus; the kind you hide from neighbors but confide to a faceless woman calling you from halfway across the country.

"Shirlene by herself, I have no problem. Shirlene and her dad. Now, there I have a problem.

"Robert. I love the man. He's a good husband. His heart's the size of a truck. He's kind and generous to everybody. Everybody. Except Shirlene.

"With her, he regresses. He's not the dad. He's like another sib—like her big brother. He reacts. He calls her names. Berates her. Criticizes. Generalizes.

"And Shirlene. Actually, she's so, so much like Robert: a bigger-than-life personality, a devoted, forgiving friend with an out-of-control need to be in charge. He gives orders. She overreacts. And now, like most teenagers, she's hostile. At least I think most teenagers are hostile.

"Anyway, Shirlene is. She's one hostile little lady. But don't think she saves her hostility for Robert. No. She distributes it equally to the entire family, to her little sisters, to me, and to him.

"With me: I ask her something once, then a second time. She freaks out, screams—probably believes—'You've asked me that fifty times.'

"This girl prowls the house, eyes narrowed, looking for confrontation.

"When Robert and Shirlene face off, it's fireworks.

"Usually, not always, but usually, it's about her clothes. Robert's the high school principal. So he feels it reflects badly on him if she looks anything but sweet. Naturally, of course, she's going through this hippie-revival look—beads, peasant blouses, tight jeans, a ton of earrings—everything short of body piercing and tattoos.

"During Christmas vacation, we went to Disney World. Mostly for the younger girls, but Shirlene was up for the ride.

"The first morning: Robert, my two younger daughters, and I are eating breakfast in the hotel. Shirlene walks into the restaurant late, her hair twisted into dreadlocks. Robert turns purple.

"Before Shirlene can sit down, Robert stands up and commands, 'Young lady, you go right back to that room and turn that rat's nest back into hair. No daughter of mine is looking like a dope-smoking Rastafarian.'

"Shirlene shakes her head wildly. The dreads make her look like a wild woman. She taunts him, 'It's vacation, Dad. What do you think? The chairman of the school board is going to see your savage daughter and send us back to Africa? Loosen up. Get a life.'

"Robert leaps straight into 'I'm your father and you'll do what I say.'

"She comes back, '*Really!* You think I respect your ridiculous power trip?'

"In minutes, they're screaming at one another. It's embarrassing. She runs out the door, full tilt down the street. I beg him to stay put, assure him I'll work it out. Then I run after her.

"I'm running down this street in Orlando yelling, 'Shirlene. Shirlene. Wait!' She keeps running until I say, 'Dad won't come.' Then she stops. I feel awful. I have to assure my daughter that her father will stay away from her.

"We sit down. Right there. On the sidewalk.

"I let her cry and scream and rant on. Just sit there nodding my head. She calms down in three minutes. Then I explain her dad to her. 'He's rational. If you stay calm and logical, if you explain things to him, he'll respond well. He'll be generous and loving. He'll try to understand you. But if you so much as raise your voice, or say something a little hostile, he'll pounce.'

"Just when I'm beginning to get through, Robert shows up. He couldn't stay away.

"By now, Shirlene has her head on my shoulder. She's holding my hand. I'm stroking her cheek.

"The sight of our affection throws Robert into a paranoid state. He attacks, starts mocking me, pointing to his chest then to me, and obsessively repeating, 'Bad parent. Good parent. Bad parent. Good parent.'

"I understand. It's hard for him. He wants to be loved. To tell you the truth, he's usually so emotionally controlled, it did my heart good to see him irrational.

"I take in his concern. I vow, 'I won't run after Shirlene the next time she takes flight.'

"I don't have to wait long to test my new resolve. A week later, we're home. It's a Saturday night. Robert and I rent a movie and settle in with a tub of micowave popcorn. Shirlene bounces through the family room in a too-tight, too-low-cut tank top. Robert shouts, 'Where, young lady, do you think you're headed dressed in that slut uniform?'

"Now, I certainly don't approve of his choice of words. But I do have sympathy with the sentiment. I keep my promise. I stay out of their fight.

"I watch the battle rage, biting my lip the entire time.

"She barks at him, defending her right to wear whatever she wants.

"Then he begins with the insults. 'You look like a whore. You have no dignity. You're just a crowd pleaser.' Then he goes on to the generalizations. 'You always need approval from the wrong kind of people. You'll never make anything of yourself with that attitude of yours.'

"She screams back her version of his insults. 'You're an old-fashioned prude. You're a middle-class wannabe who's forsaken his roots.' Then she launches into her generalizations. 'You always want to control me. You never see my point of view. You always judge.'

"You can imagine: Robert doesn't take this well. He retorts, 'You're a spoiled brat who'll never appreciate what you have.'

"I say nothing. I wait out the storm.

"Later, she's out of the house. The younger ones are in bed. We've watched the movie. I bring up the fight. I confess, 'I'm still so angry.'

"Robert nods. 'Yeah, Shirlene was so outrageous.'

"I tell him, 'No. It's not Shirlene. It's your behavior that I'm angry about.' He stops, looks at me, and says, 'Oh.'

"So I've made three rules: No hostility. No insults. No generalizations. Trouble is, all three rules apply to both my husband and my daughter.

"Still, I'm enforcing the rules gently. I say, 'Gee, doesn't that sound a bit hostile?' Or 'Isn't that an insult?' Or 'Would you call that a generalization?' Who can argue with me? I'm just asking questions.

"But you know what really bothers me? He's losing out. The time for him to be her dad is running out. He'll never have another chance.

"And Shirlene, I'm afraid for her. Afraid she'll be like me. Spend the next ten years of her life involved with men too old for her, looking for a dad to love her."

Eva had told her story, stripping layer after layer until she revealed her most vulnerable place. Yes, she hated her husband's and daughter's arguments. Yes, she felt pressured by the role of referee. Yes, she took pride in her insight and skill. But underneath it all, Eva fears for her husband and daughter. Will the chasm between the two people she most loves leave an insatiable hole within each of them? ⟨∞⟩

J udy Pohl once had reason to harbor similar worries. Time has dispelled those concerns.

With four adolescent daughters and a headstrong husband, Judy never underestimated the challenge. She made certain her love glued them all together.

Judy sat in her two-story home by the water's edge. The boat had been put away for the winter, the girls were off and about, her husband was settled in somewhere. Finally, Judy had time to chat.

ℯ⌒

RUNNING THE STAIRS
Thoughts from Judy Pohl

"My husband: He calls my oldest daughter 'the Feminazi.' Don't gasp. It's okay. They laugh about it. They love each other. But when she was in high school, they couldn't stay in the same room.

"Here's some background: My husband's confrontational. He'll get in your face. He'll argue you down. But if you stand up to him, he'll back off. He's always been that way. He's like that with everybody. I wanted all my daughters to have his strength. They do. They can stand up to anyone.

"Still, I have to say: Anna, my oldest one, and my husband, they were hard to live with.

"One night they got into this argument. My daughter was in the kitchen bawling her eyes out. My husband was in our bedroom fuming.

"I put a pad of paper in front of that girl and stuck a pen in her hand. I ordered her, 'Write it down. Write down everything that you want to say to him. Now. While you're hysterical. While you remember it.'

"Anna grabbed the pen and wrote furiously. She filled up six pages.

"I took the notepad up to my husband. I said, 'Sit down! Read.' He read one sentence and objected, 'No. That's not true.' I cut him off and said, 'Be quiet. I don't want to hear it. Just read. Read the whole thing.' It was hard for him, but he read it.

"Then I told him, 'Now. You. Write down what you feel.' He did. He wrote and wrote and wrote.

"I went down to the kitchen and delivered his message to Anna. She started reading and saying, 'No. It's not true.' I wouldn't listen to a word of it. I ordered her, 'Anna. Sit down. Just read. Don't talk to me. I don't want to hear it.' She read quietly, then wrote him another note. I went back and forth, up and down stairs, delivering messages.

"I felt drained, limp, pulled between them. But it worked. They got the messages and respected each other.

"Whenever those two are together, they have this way of 'agreeing violently' without listening to each other. They still do better when they pass written messages. Now they write e-mails to each other. They communicate and I'm not stuck in the middle.

"My husband says, 'I'm glad we didn't have a boy. He'd be just like me. By the time he was five, one of us would have to move out. And I own the house.'" ❧

Gerry DiGesu did have boys, two sons, both adopted. After fourteen years of marriage, she gave birth to her daughter, Nancy.

By then, Gerry's boys and husband had bonded. Later, Nancy felt locked out of that bond. She felt like she was the adopted child, the one who didn't belong. Gerry found herself cast in the role of her daughter's sole defender, and later, blamed for Nancy's drug use.

NANCY
by Gerry Rita DiGesu

My daughter called me into her bedroom for a chat. "Nice," I thought, "we haven't had a talk in a while." Now seventeen and a senior in high school, she was busy with friends and school activities.

"Mom, I'm using drugs."

I stared at her angry face, steadied myself, and sat down on her bed. I was ashamed of my first thought: "I can't let this make me sick."

I have chronic fatigue syndrome, a severe immune disorder that keeps me in a constant state of severe fatigue, depression, and pain. I'd had it for five years, and my health had continued on a steady downhill slide. I wondered how I could stay strong enough to deal with this horrible news.

While Nancy was speaking, I looked around the room and saw pictures of myself taken at a party a couple of weeks ago. I saw how awful I looked; I was afraid I was going to die. "I'm so sorry, Mom. I didn't mean to . . ." Nancy fell into my lap, sobbing. "I stopped, and I promise I'll never use them again."

My daughter didn't know why she started to use drugs. She professed that she had used them only during the past few months, but in large doses and on a daily basis. The high school parking lot was a distribution center for any student who wanted a quick fix. The drugs were cheap and abundant.

Head spinning and heart pounding, I held her close to me so I could think.

"Don't tell Daddy or the boys, please, Mom," she begged.

"I have to tell Daddy, honey, or together we can't help you."

"But not the boys," she cried.

Her brothers, twenty-three and twenty-five, would be devastated. She couldn't face them. I promised not to tell.

After supper, I told my husband. Unbelievably, he said he wasn't surprised. I wanted to hit him. How could he say such a thing?

"She's been hanging out with new kids, been out too late on weekends, and looks sick," he yelled.

He was right, but I always had to defend Nancy against her dad's anger and disapproval. No matter how hard she tried to please him, she felt she had never been able to win his acceptance. He didn't see it that way. He loved her like crazy but resented our close relationship. We were best friends who shared our feelings and laughed and cried together. Like so many other men, he was never truly emotionally available.

As I cringed, looking ahead to the long battle between the two of us over how to handle this horrible problem, he confronted me. "You always think you have all the answers, so go ahead and do what you want. You will anyway. But you have to get her help right away."

I pleaded, "Why me, what about *us* getting her help?"

"You always like to take charge. You think you know everything, so go ahead," he challenged.

I sobbed as I cleared the table. How could I do this? How did we get to today? What did I do wrong? How had I failed her?

Since Nancy had been in seventh grade, there were many times when she just didn't make sense. She was a wonderful kid in every way. Attractive and bubbly, she had lots of friends, and the boys constantly asked her out on dates. She participated in school sports, was active in Girl Scouts, baby-sat, and did odd jobs in the neighborhood for spending money. She was a good, reliable kid. Yet she experienced mood swings and would go from being her cheery self to a brooding, nasty adolescent within hours. I knew all teens experienced some of this behavior, but her reactions seemed extreme.

Although a marvelous athlete, Nancy was often sick and had been tested for mononucleosis repeatedly during her teen years. An honor roll student, she would start projects enthusiastically and then not complete them. A gifted artist, she scattered her art supplies all over the basement with a few wonderful, half-completed watercolors languishing on the table. Her dad said she should "shape up and get her act together," but I knew it was more than that. She was hurting inside, but I couldn't tell why. Maybe I shouldn't have been so protective. Maybe I should have made her "shape up." Maybe then she wouldn't have turned to drugs.

I knew our local hospital had a drug counseling center. I didn't want to go there. I didn't want anyone to know Nancy's problem. Then, ashamed of my feelings of denial, I checked the number, called, and got an appointment for the following day.

I told Nancy when she got home from school.

"Not me. I'm not going there. I don't need any stupid drug counselor. I stopped using. I'll get stronger by myself," she screamed.

"We have to find out why you used drugs, Nan, and make sure you stop for good," I reasoned.

"I hate you," she yelled and ran from the room.

We entered the counseling office the next day, Nancy ahead of me, head hunched down into her jacket. I prayed I wouldn't see anyone I knew, because the questions I always heard when a teen used drugs were "Where were the parents? Didn't they see what was right in front of them? How could they be in such denial?" Where had I been? What had I missed? Her moods and behavior had always been erratic. I hadn't seen a major change in her personality.

Nancy answered the counselor's request, listing the drugs she took. When I heard "hallucinogens," I felt sick and weak and turned away from her. The room spun. Dear God. How had I failed her so deeply that she had to run away into this horrible world of fantasy and destruction? Did she do permanent damage to her brain?

The counselor wanted Nancy to come as an outpatient to their clinic every afternoon after going to her morning high school classes.

"I'll never come here. I'm no druggie. You guys don't know what you're doing. The kids at school who come here just laugh at their half-day off and keep using. I won't come!"

She ran out of the office and I started crying.

Who had my child become?

"I'm sorry. Thanks for your time and help. I'll have to call you," I told the counselor.

I ran out of the office, relieved that there was no one in the waiting room.

Nancy was leaning on the car, crying, punching the door. I grabbed her arms and held her against me until she quieted down. By then, I needed her to hold me up. I was too weak. I couldn't do this. We got in the car and I screamed at her all the way home.

"Who are you? How could you do this to us? Why didn't you care about yourself or your family?"

Nancy sat motionless, not speaking until I parked in our driveway.

"Wait, Mom. I'll go back to Dr. Louis. I can help myself. I can do this. I know I can. That program at the clinic is terrible. They don't help anybody. I'll go back to Dr. Louis and talk to him."

Why hadn't I thought of Dr. Louis? Nancy had seen this psychologist sporadically since her early teens when she seemed severely depressed. They had a good rapport, and I was thrilled that she was eager to talk to him. Still, I questioned her.

"Why can't you talk to me, Nan? We always share everything."

"I just can't, Mom. I can't."

Numb, I went into the house.

Nancy didn't eat supper with us. I told my husband and sons about our appointment with Dr. Louis, how Nancy wasn't herself and needed help.

"I know she's a good kid," said my older son. "But you know, Mom, you always favor her and let her get away with everything we couldn't do. Now look what happens."

I couldn't believe it.

My other son chimed in and agreed. "We've been telling you she's spoiled, just like Dad always says. She does whatever she wants. You never let us have the freedom she has. You sure messed her up this time."

My husband nodded in agreement.

Furious, I screamed at them. "It's always me you blame. I'm the one who has to keep everybody happy, has to keep the peace, watch out for your feelings. 'We can't make Daddy mad. Don't make waves.' I'm sick of all of you. I need your help so much, and this is what you give me. Go to hell."

I could hardly get up from my chair. My brain was fuzzy, my legs felt like lead, and the fatigue was unbearable. Halfway up the steps to see Nancy, I stopped. Maybe the boys were right. Since she was nine and I had become ill, I had always asked Nancy to help me clean up after her father and brothers. They worked all day and I was so tired. She protested that they made their mess and should clean it up. I made her do it anyway, to keep the peace, to not make Daddy mad. That's how I had been raised—to be a good girl, to keep quiet, to make everybody happy. And I had never become me. Now, without realizing it, I had done the same thing to Nancy.

Nancy started therapy with Dr. Louis. After three visits, he called me in and said she needed medication for severe depression. He recommended a psychiatrist who could help her.

"I'm not taking any damn pills," she cried. "I'm strong. I'm getting better. I don't want them."

A week later I dragged her into the psychiatrist's office. After her evaluation, she stalked past me out the door.

"Please fill this prescription as soon as possible," said the doctor. "Call me if you notice any of the side effects listed." And he was gone.

Nancy suffered severe reactions to the first three medications she tried, and it took a few months to find the right one. When I saw the diagnosis "manic depressive disorder" listed on the psychiatrist's bill, I wouldn't believe it. Not my daughter. He was the crazy one. But could he be right?

Ever so slowly, the pills seemed to help. Nancy smiled more, started completing school assignments, and began playing on the varsity softball team. She told me she had taken drugs "because they made me feel good, feel happy. I forgot who I was and where I was. I could be me. I didn't think how mad I made Daddy all the time. I didn't care. It just felt good and made the pain go away."

Dear God. By providing a horrible role model and not letting my vivacious and quirky daughter be herself, I had stripped Nancy of self-esteem. She had turned to drugs for peace and joy. She said she had stopped. Could I trust her as I always had before this happened?

Finally we got to June, high school graduation. Nancy was being awarded the Gold Award, the highest award in Girl Scouts, equal to that of Eagle Scout for the Boy Scouts. We were tremendously proud.

Before the award dinner, Nancy had an appointment with Dr. Louis. I waited in the car and relaxed in the warm afternoon sun. When she came out, she had a strange look on her face.

"I told him, Mom."

"Told him what?"

"I finally told Dr. Louis I took drugs."

"You didn't tell him all these months?"

"I couldn't, Mom. I just couldn't have him so disappointed in me."

Dear God. Again, the daughter I trusted. Who is she?

"But, Mom, tonight I'm getting the Gold Award. I couldn't stand up there knowing I had lied to Dr. Louis. I'm finally starting to know I'm okay the way I am. Who I am. And I want to be proud of myself."

I couldn't answer. I was afraid to say the wrong thing. She had made tremendous progress. I didn't want to spoil it. But I felt like a failure. I didn't really know her.

The award dinner was wonderful. The next evening was high school graduation. As I watched her march into the auditorium with her classmates, a prayer of thanks and of hope for her future filled my heart.

My husband and Nancy are becoming closer all the time as they communicate, love, and learn to accept each other. Life is good. We keep learning and loving and growing. ❦

While Eva, Geri, and Judy felt like a living firewall between their husbands and daughters, Jenny Talbot wished she could ignite some fatherly involvement. Sitting in a rural farmhouse surrounded by her favorite companions, her pets, she summed up her situation.

A MARRIED SINGLE PARENT
Thoughts from Jenny Talbot

"I was a married single parent.

"My husband and I always had different parenting styles. Brian never initiates. I always take charge. From the moment Caitlin was born, he adored her. But he didn't have a clue about what to do with her. He just didn't think about it. Like I'd ask him to change her diapers. He was willing to change them. He just never thought of it all by himself.

"I accepted the difference until Caitlin hit adolescence. Then his passivity got harder for me to take. Every time there was a crisis about drinking or boys or school, Brian just looked at me and said, 'God, honey. What are you going to do?' He never, not for a moment, considered what *he* was going to do, or what we might do together. The whole concept of actually making a parenting decision never entered his mind.

"Then, when Caitlin hit Mrs. Hicks, that's when the shit hit the fan.

"We were packing for a family vacation. Getting ready to escape to a cottage on a wilderness lake. Before leaving civilization, Caitlin took a quick run to the grocery store.

"She hopped in her car and drove down Main Street. Mrs. Hicks, this eccentric little old lady, was riding her bike, going in the same direction. Suddenly, without warning, Mrs. Hicks swerved in front of Caitlin's car. Caitlin slammed on the brakes. Too late. Mrs. Hicks was lying on the ground unconscious. Caitlin ran into the nearest house, called 911 and me.

"Caitlin and I followed the ambulance to the hospital. We hung around the emergency room. We were frantic to find out everything we could, desperate to do something, anything, to help. The nurses, doctors, and police kept saying, 'She'll be fine, absolutely fine. There's nothing you can do. Just go on your vacation.'

"Caitlin hadn't said a word. We walked out the hospital door and through the parking lot. When we got to the car, she looked at me and said, 'Mrs. Hicks is going to die.' I tried to reassure her: 'The doctors and nurses said she'll be fine.' Caitlin couldn't be convinced. She shook her head, unconvinced, and said, 'They always say that.'

"We left for vacation that afternoon. We were in this remote cabin. The nearest telephone was an hour's boat ride away. We settled in.

"Next day, I sent Brian across the lake to call about Mrs. Hicks. I met him at the dock. He told me, 'Mrs. Hicks died.' Then he left. He just took off. He was gone. I was alone.

"Everything came crashing down on me. All the years of parenting, his lack of support, culminated in that moment.

"I went into therapy. I wanted to save my marriage. The therapist was a man-hater. She'd say, 'You don't need this guy. You can do it all on your own.' Everyone who saw this woman got divorced.

"Strange, in the process, hearing her berate him, I realized I loved Brian. I found more compassion for him. He had been abused, emotionally neglected. His mother: I have to tell you, this woman is such a bitch. She never gave him anything good, never a birthday present, never any affection, never a kind word, never a fun treat to eat, nothing.

"As a father, he repeated his mother's neglect without a trace of her malicious edge. You see, Brian's actually a kind man. But when Caitlin was little, I'd have to say to him, 'Hug her. Just go over to her and hug her.' He didn't know how. He'd never been hugged.

"After therapy, I decided to accept him. I learned to tolerate his well-meaning ineptitude. Our styles are different. I initiate and he follows. That's just the way it is.

"Caitlin has learned to accept him, too. For years, she'd yelled at him, 'I hate you, Dad.' Now that she has her own boyfriend, she sees her father's good qualities. Brian can fix anything. He keeps the cars, the appliances, the garden, everything, up and running. Caitlin's boyfriend isn't handy. This kid can't change a lightbulb. Caitlin sees the difference. She sees that everyone has strengths and weaknesses, even her dad.

"When Brian took off in that boat, leaving me to deal with my own emotions and Caitlin's guilt, he didn't mean to abandon us. Brian was in grief, too. He couldn't reach out. He had to be alone."

Sifting through the ashes of tragedy, Jenny had found enough compassion to embrace both her daughter and her husband. ◁∘▷

daughters and sisters

WHEN I WAS A YOUNG WOMAN, I HAD CONFIDENCE IN JOHN Locke's declaration "All men are created equal." I also believed its psychological corollary, that every human is born as a blank slate. I had no doubt that the nuances of personality were engraved on individuals by family and environment. Then I had two daughters and reassessed my faith: "Blank slate? That's surely a theory concocted by men."

Every mother who's given birth to more than one child knows children come into the world with inborn differences. Asked about the differences between two daughters, the women I contacted reviewed how the recognition of those contrasts changed their mothering. Most felt the pressure to be a perfect mom more keenly with a first child. "I thought, 'My God. She's so perfect. I could ruin this child.'" Then, with the birth of a second daughter, came an epiphany: "She's so different from my older one." A sigh of relief followed: "I didn't do anything to make her different. She just is." Somehow the contrast between our children frees us from the delusion that we're the primary creators of their personalities.

Most of us are more relaxed with second children. We've matured from having our first and know the limits of our power. We realize we're responsible for protecting personality, not creating it. Poor Manju, my older daughter. I swear that child couldn't turn over without my picking her up and nursing her. I didn't let her sleep through the night until she was three years old. By the time Sara was born, seven years later, I saw that Manju had flourished despite all my overanxious, well-intended mistakes. I didn't overburden Sara by trying so hard. Stories from mothers with adolescent daughters followed the same theme.

THE REFEREE ROLE
Thoughts from Helen Carter

"In utero, my girls were opposites. And they've played out their differences. They've made me believe there's something unique and separate about them, something that persists totally apart from any-thing I do, anything that society does."

Helen spoke to me from an enviable climate in an equally enviable neighborhood. We compared notes. As she spoke, I nodded my head in knowing agreement. I could have been speaking. Almost any mother of two adolescent daughters could have empathized.

"Janine, the older one, she slept in my womb. She came into the world docile. She was so easy, except that she wanted to be carried all the time. Everywhere. All the time. She didn't walk until fifteen months. She talked before she walked. At three years old, she used words like 'assimilate,' and she used them correctly. One fall, in preschool, the teacher took me aside and said, 'When we go outside, all the other children run around and play. Janine goes directly to the big oak, lies down, covers herself with fallen leaves, and stays there meditating.' That's the way she was, and that's the way she still is. She's independent, not constrained by the group. She's a tomboy—dresses in baggy clothes, likes hanging out with boys, and could care less about her appearance. I respect her. I trust her judgment.

"Kimberly, the younger one, she started life in constant motion. She bounced around in my womb. Every part of my body got bruised. She was born screaming. She cried continually. When I tried to change her diaper, she kicked and squirmed. I'd have to pin her to the table. She walked at eleven months. She's been on the go ever since. She's a girly girl who seems to think she's Britney Spears, a 'hair-flipper' with lots of friends.

"Janine tells me nothing. Kimberly tells me everything. I honor their differences. I talk to each of them separately. It's a challenge to let them both know I love them, especially when they fight."

With that, the topic turned to sibling conflict, another theme famil-iar to all mothers of more than one child.

"I try to open them up to talking. Mostly I comment and validate feelings. I'm working on teaching them elementary respect for one an-other. I give them really complicated messages like 'Say good-bye to your sister, not just to Mommy.'

"It's a triangle. I'm at the apex. I know I have to make rules and set guidelines. But it's lonely at the top."

Helen's voice faded into soft sadness as she described her desire to be close to both her children, to be their confidante instead of their referee.

Like Helen, I found myself being a referee to my two daughters. I hated the role.

Manju had always, and in every way, been a reasonable person. Then, at thirteen, in arguments with her six-year-old sister, Manju turned into an immature child.

I confronted Manju. "Why do you behave like a six-year-old when you fight with Sara?"

She responded with irrefutable logic. "Sara can't come up to my level. I have to go down to hers."

Okay. Makes sense. But what do I do?

Mostly, I sent them to one of their rooms with an order: "Stay in there until you work it out." With a little time and isolation, Manju invariably rediscovered her maturity and cut a deal.

One day, I was the one to regress. I was in the kitchen, cooking. Manju and Sara were in the adjoining family room, watching TV and drawing with a set of one hundred and fifty Magic Markers. They bickered continually over the TV and the markers. I continued stirring my pot of stew, telling myself, "It's okay. Let them work it out. They're just learning to compromise and negotiate." Somewhere between adding the carrots and chopping the onions, I couldn't take the sound of their whining for one more instant.

I stomped into the family room, picked up the metal box of neatly lined-up markers, and threw it upside down on the floor. The metal crashed. All one hundred and fifty markers flew, scattering extravagantly. I stood tall and ordered my daughters, "Now. Pick them up. Both of you. Together."

I guess that was my spontaneous idea for a cooperative activity.

Manju and Sara looked at each other. They bonded instantaneously over an identical thought: "Mom's lost it."

My daughters said nothing. I left the room, went back to my stew. They picked up the markers, nicely, quietly, in harmony, together.

By the time Manju left for college, this incident had become the stock joke of many a family dinner: "Remember the time Mom lost it and threw all the markers on the floor?"

Sande Boritz Berger employed subtler skills as she looked for ways to restore peace to her home. Sandy lives with her two daughters in a landscape filled with skyscrapers. For most of her girls' childhood, she idealized their compatibility. Then came adolescence.

e~

TWO FLAVORS
by Sande Boritz Berger

Sometimes—but never to their faces—I call them my chocolate and vanilla girls: My blond, blue-eyed older daughter is a clone of me, and my dark-skinned, curly-haired younger daughter the image of her father. Our Russian/German heritages combine in a mysterious way to make them what I always wished I had—*sisters*.

They share a special language: subtle nuances, weird observations, in-jokes that send them hiccuping in hysterics, making me feel a little bit excluded. But mostly, I am thrilled by the powerful magnetism that draws them together. I find comfort knowing they're a team, that they can depend on each other.

When they leaped over the threshold into their teenage years, I was reminded of a sudden gust of wind slamming a door shut. The cozy calm I once knew was shattered as the desire to be separate human beings became evident. Although this transformation has made life more interesting, it becomes harder to be their mother. A response or suggestion used successfully when parenting one daughter can fail horribly when applied to the other.

Overnight, they developed varied interests, chose different friends, expressed opposing opinions, usually in aggressive ways. I thought the strong magnetic pull would stay with them forever. I believed in the notion that opposites attract.

At thirteen and fifteen, Jennifer (there are at least five Jennifers in her class) and Bari (she likes and hates her name on alternate weeks) have both everything and nothing in common.

The everything is their shared obsession with the smoothness of their hair and the never-ending search for the highest-wattage blow dryer in America. And I can't forget the ten-foot yellow plastic appendage they grow from their shoulders known as the telephone cord. We keep the yellow princess phone in "Switzerland," which is what we call a small patch of occupied hallway just outside their bedrooms. Whenever the phone rings, their doors open simultaneously as they make a jackknife dive for the receiver. The quicker of the two, at that moment, yanks the phone into her room to talk in PRIVACY PLEASE!

The nothing is their totally different tastes in music. Jennifer has tried out for *Annie*, as in Orphan Annie, and she had the lead in a camp production of *Annie Get Your Gun*. Bari prefers acid rock and groups that end their concerts by blowing themselves up onstage. Her clothes, often an eclectic mix of plaids and stripes, remind me of the colorful swatches my father used to peddle as an upholstery salesman. Jennifer prefers whatever's in vogue or hanging off the skeletal mannequins in the local mall. Or in others' closets.

They shared a bedroom until their constant bickering turned to screaming and screaming turned to bleeding. "It was just a little mole I scratched off her, Mom. No big deal. It would have been removed anyway."

Too often, the dining room chandelier trembles, leaving me to expect, at any moment, a fluffy-slippered foot to protrude through the plaster ceiling. Hadn't I suffered enough growing up in a household with two rowdy younger brothers? What happened to my two pigtailed pixies in matching Healthtex overalls? Finally, I decided it wasn't too big a price, really, to give up my writing room so they could have separate bedrooms. There's a closet right off the laundry room with my name on it. I'll have privacy one day, I'm sure, perhaps when I'm seventy.

Now in separate rooms, Bari spends hours working on craft projects, reading books, and writing stories; Jennifer is usually on the telephone, mediating some major fracas that occurred between friends that day at school. Their bedrooms become different forks in the road with bold *No Trespassing* signs. ❧

All mothers hope our children will find a way to complement one another. Even more, we hope our homes will always be a shelter from the meanness of the outside world. But that meanness invaded the relationship between Jan Marin Tramontano's daughters.

INFILTRATING THE FAMILY
by Jan Marin Tramontano

Peer pressure infiltrating the family: what a nightmare. My daughters are in their early teens. They always had different styles. But who would ever think they'd grow to hate each other? Especially now, right at a time in their lives when they need to be cut some slack somewhere. Safety: Isn't that what home should be about?

Tess is fifteen and has always lived on the fringe. She's teased at school, has befriended those who would have her. Her younger sister, Laurel, has many friends and is in that "popular group" that always made Tess miserable.

The other night, Tess described a scene at school. She decided to join a club. When she walked into the room, the girls stopped talking. One of them asked, "What are *you* doing here?" I could just hear their tone. They inspected her and made her feel like a misfit.

I listened, stunned by their cruelty, but Laurel got the picture right away. She is totally unsympathetic to her sister's misery. She looked straight at Tess and said, "Well, what do you expect? You go to school looking like a garbage bag. Why don't you try going to school looking normal instead of like a weirdo? Maybe you won't scare everybody away. You want to borrow some of my clothes?"

Tess hissed back, "I hate you. You're a shallow jerk, just like them. And I wouldn't be caught dead looking like you."

I'm almost ashamed to admit it. I could see both sides. What you wear is shorthand for who you are. Tess dresses in black, big baggy shirts, wide-legged jeans dragging on the ground. She likes the way she dresses. It suits her. But it doesn't attract the people she wants to be with. I respect her right to be herself, to dress any way she pleases. But sometimes, for her sake, I wish she'd compromise, wear something in between. Make her life a little easier.

Laurel doesn't have to compromise. She enjoys wearing trendy fashions and finds the path easier. That doesn't seem right.

I don't really understand the importance of clothes for this generation. The need for certain brands, the friendships formed around a style of dress. But what pains me the most is the mind-set that's brought into our house. After all, isn't that supposed to be the place where children learn their values, form their relationships, and learn how to negotiate in the world? ∞

I n time, most sisters outgrow their adolescent insensitivity. Inevitable eruptions of rivalry burst and heal. Then sisters look at one another and, like their mothers, see beauty.

Cindy Hamilton found herself placed in an awkward position by her older daughter's nurturing impulse.

℮

A CONSPIRACY OF ADMIRATION
by Cindy Hamilton

Mimi, my big girl, my oldest, my nineteen-year-old, and I met for lunch. She pulls me into the quietest corner of this cute little café and whispers, "Mom, what are we going to do about Zoë?" What am I supposed to say?

Zoë is my baby, my youngest, my fifteen-year-old. As soon as Zoë was born, Mimi looked at me and decided I wasn't up to the task of mothering her little sister. She always behaved like the mom in charge. As far as she was concerned, I needed constant monitoring. She instructed me on proper diapering, diet, and discipline. I tried my best to relieve her of the responsibility. I told her repeatedly, 'I'm Zoë's mom.' Somehow the biological fact never translated into competence in Mimi's mind. She's continued to inform me of my motherly duty at Zoë's every milestone.

So in the café, listening to Mimi, my mind has two voices tugging for attention. One says, "Tell Mimi she's not Zoë's mom and you can handle it." The other is saying, "What is Mimi talking about? What's wrong with Zoë? Find out what she knows."

While I'm bouncing around in the land of "What do I say next?", Mimi's launched into her speech. "Zoë's interested in this new guy. Mom, he's worse than the last one. He's, like, so dorky. It's unbelievable. He's, like, sort of weird-looking and he can barely carry on a conversation. At school, he's following her around like a puppy dog. Mimi thinks he's sweet, sensitive, kind of cute. Mom? Mom! Say something."

How could I say something? Mimi hadn't paused for a breath. Now she glares at me. I say, "Gee. I liked Zoë's last boyfriend."

Wrong answer. Mimi turns blue-faced before berating me. "Mom! How can you say that! The boy was so much below her. Zoë is so beautiful, so smart, so talented. Compared to her, that kid was such a loser. Mom, you have to face facts. Zoë has a self-esteem problem. She settles. She needs to have higher standards. Look at the people she hangs out with. Her entire group of friends is, like, computer nerds with no social skills. She has to get out more."

By now, my head is spinning. Actually, Mimi had a point or two. Zoë is shy. She does underestimate her beauty, her intelligence, and her musical talent. She spends hours and hours buried under books. Her friends and boyfriends do tend to be a bit bumbling. I know she can fall into a sad, self-conscious place. I do worry that she isn't demanding enough from her relationships. Instead of calling attention to my concerns, I've always bathed her in unconditional approval. Instead of belittling her friends and boyfriends, I've always welcomed them into our home. Now here was my older daughter, her sister, trying to cheerlead me into some proactive mother/daughter pep talk.

On considering Mimi's viewpoint, I reject any change in my mothering. I explain, "Your sister is fine. Actually, she's great. Any suggestion that she be more like you—more popular, more stylish, and more attracted to hunk material—will only make her feel like there's something wrong with her. Zoë is perfect the way she is. If she settles, it's okay. As long as boys treat her well, she's golden. I'll worry and I'll say something if I feel she's being mistreated. Otherwise, her attractions are her decisions."

Mimi stares straight at me and slumps. "Mom. I don't judge Zoë. I adore her. I just want her to love herself as much as I love her."

I hear Mimi. I see her loving intention. Still, I feel guilty for even talking with her about her sister. I tell her, "If Zoë knew you were talking to me about her, she'd feel betrayed. She'd feel like we were gossiping behind her back. Mimi, you're not your sister's mother. I am." ∞

Sooner or later, the older sister leaves home. Mothers are left to parent—to cuddle and discipline and guide—without the firstborn peering over their shoulder. When that time came for Stephanie Palladino, she took a verbal snapshot. She sat down in front of a blank page and offered a memory to her eighteen-year-old.

THREE SISTERS: A NOTE TO MY OLDEST DAUGHTER
by Stephanie B. Palladino

When I walked in the door from work this afternoon, all three of you greeted me hello—each one munching on a snack, flashing me a smile. Instantly, I knew it was a moment to engrave in my memory for future recall.

First I heard Celeste's voice from the kitchen table. She was relaxing with the local newspaper, just home from her second day as a high-schooler.

Next my eye climbed the staircase to find you standing beside your eight-year-old sister: oldest and youngest side by side, munching snacks, and smiling in my direction. You, Lenore, at eighteen, glancing back at yourself in Simone's reflection.

Now I begin to feel the impact of your leaving home for college. All summer I put off this ache. A safety zone of months has somehow turned into a mere handful of days. Earlier today you stood by me in the kitchen. I placed my fingers on your shoulders and gently massaged them. Your two best friends have just left for college. You complained of restlessness. My fingers lingered, as if I might hold you here by my caress. What else could I do?

Next Tuesday your father and I will accompany you to Chicago and deliver you to your future. Once home, I will wait here in this kitchen for your handful of visits each year. I will clutch the pieces of my heart each time I watch you leave me, your father, and your two sisters again. ✦

When the oldest daughter does leave, mothers console themselves with the presence of younger ones. At least that's the way it was for me.

Our whole family drove to Vermont, four of us in two cars. Manju's led the procession. Her well-worn silver-blue Honda Civic station wagon buzzed along, packed tight and piled high with her possessions, leaving just enough space for her ten-year-old sister to travel by her side. Michael and I followed, Manju's overflow crammed into the trunk and backseat. Winding our way through green mountains, we leaf-peeped at the colors of a few trees previewing the change of seasons. We veered right at the Bennington College sign, arrived at our destination, and parked in front of Swan House. Then all four of us emptied the cars and filled Manju's dorm room. Back and forth, back and forth, again and again passing the view, layers and layers of mountains beyond the college, the vista Bennington students had forever called the End of the World.

The task was completed. The time had come. Michael hugged Manju. I held her tight, whimpering, "I love you, sweetie." Sara clung to her sister. Michael and I peeled her free and deposited her on the backseat of Michael's sedan. Making a U-turn, we waved as we inched our way off campus.

As soon as that Bennington College sign appeared in the rearview mirror, a pitiful shriek rose from the backseat. Sara threw her tear-soaked face into a pillow, but there was no muffling her nearly asthmatic gasps. By the time we reached the edge of town, I had crawled into the backseat. As we drove through the mountains, I sat with Sara's head on a sodden pillow in my lap, her body convulsing with grief. Her sister was gone. The life she had lived since birth had ended. Now she was a sister alone. Sara cried for two hours without stop. We pulled into our driveway. My first child had officially left home. Mercifully, I had no time to dwell on my loss. I had to comfort her inconsolable sister.

While Lillian Mason's daughters lived at home, she worked to mediate their differences, to find common ground and keep the peace. Once they left, she stopped thinking about how they got along with each other. She started thinking about how she got along with them and how they treated her.

Lillian's two daughters were now both in school, one three hours to the east, the other two hours to the south. At first she chatted with me about the obvious differences between her daughters: one introverted, the other outgoing; one intellectual, the other practical; one intense, the other easygoing; one her taskmaster, the other her rock. With the last comparison, Lillian had stepped into a more private realm. She began disclosing the feelings she kept behind a shroud.

MY ROCK AND MY TASKMASTER
A Conversation with Lillian Mason

"When both girls were still at home, I felt trapped in an 'I love you both equally, just differently' quagmire. I knew my daughters needed to be totally, unconditionally accepted by me. Any smidgen of variable affection was misinterpreted as favoritism. I could see that even the suspicion of inequity inflicted insecurity. I feel differently about myself when I'm with each of them.

"I'm more challenged by my older one, Tess. She's in my face, doesn't let me slack off or deceive myself. Tess is my taskmaster.

"I'm more comfortable with my younger daughter, Ginny. She accepts and supports me. Ginny's my rock.

"Tess feeds my growth, but I feel more nurtured by Ginny.

"Temperamentally, they're just like that: Ginny so soft; Tess so strong. But truthfully, I think I accentuated that difference by the way I brought them up.

"Tess was born first. I fell absolutely, completely in love with her. I couldn't take my eyes off of her. Poor baby. I fussed with her every minute. If she as much as hiccuped, I nursed her. I was a nervous wreck. I thought for sure if I let her complain for thirty seconds, I'd ruin her for life.

"My hovering continued throughout her whole life. I flutter around her wondering if something's wrong, trying to figure out what to do. No wonder I feel like she's always watching me, scrutinizing my behavior. I'm always watching her. We're just mirroring each other in different roles. I'm the trying-too-hard mother. She's still the trying-to-be-free adolescent daughter. She has to be my taskmaster so she can be free of me. I need her to be my taskmaster so I can be free of my mother role.

"Ginny came second. Sometimes I think I was so focused on Tess, I had no time to keep my eyes glued on Ginny. I was more relaxed with her, more detached. I gave her more space. She thrived on my relative neglect. She matured without all my angst niggling at her. I didn't watch her every move. Now she doesn't have to watch mine. She hasn't had to push me away because I was never smotheringly close. She can just settle in with me, reassure me when I'm down, laugh at me when I'm neurotic. I'm grateful for the ease of our connection.

"That's how they are for me. Both essential: Tess, to my growth; Ginny, to my self-acceptance.

"But you know, I think if I explained the difference to them, they'd both feel bad. Tess would feel like I love Ginny more. Ginny would feel like I value Tess more. I keep my feelings to myself." ⟨∞⟩

For many mothers, polishing the dust off of self-reflection forces us to face guilt. Alone with countless well-intentioned mistakes, we look straight at the truth: We messed up. With one daughter, we mucked up in one way. With another daughter, we mucked up in another way.

With her two daughters launched, Sandy Carter, a psychotherapist living in a small midwestern community, gives guidance to women on journeys of self-discovery. She wrote, examining her own metaphorical rearview mirror.

TO LIVE FOR
by Sandra K. Carter

Last fall I gave notice. I'm leaving my practice April 30, 2002. I had a strong intuitive feeling that it was necessary for me to create space to allow something new to emerge into my life. To facilitate this transition, I've been exploring and expanding my creativity.

In a writing workshop, I was asked a question: "What is it you can't live without?" The instructions were to begin writing immediately for thirty minutes. With that kind of assignment, you write from your heart. That's the why and how of it.

What is it I can't live without?

I gave the question some quick reflection, scanning my life from the vantage point of fifty.

What is it I can't live without?

I used to think there were lots of things I couldn't live without. I lived my life in continuous fear. I was fearful of losing what I had. I was fearful of not getting what I thought I needed. My biggest fears involved my two daughters: the dread that I would lose them through any number of imagined evils. I worried I would end up being disconnected from them, physically or emotionally or both. I imagined the terror of this separation. This fantasy drove me to focus obsessively on being the best mother possible.

I never bonded with my own mother. We lived in the same house, but I was emotionally severed from her. The hurt was unbearable. I somehow got it into my mind that I could prevent history from repeating itself by being completely available to my children. I committed myself: My daughters would never question my devotion. I imagined that through this "perfect" connection, they would gain great self-esteem. My daughters would never feel helpless, or hopeless, or small, or pathetic. My children would never experience the coldness of feeling unloved, or the shame of feeling unlovable, or the guilt of feeling responsible, or the isolation of feeling abandoned. I imagined my love would cloak them in a protective bubble. My daughters wouldn't or couldn't be penetrated by anything or anybody. How very naive I was.

I loved my two daughters desperately, from a very broken heart.

My oldest daughter felt smothered by my total commitment, my obsessive interest in her life. She constantly pushed me away, leaving me feeling hurt and angry. I was reliving my mother/child rejection. I thought my life with my daughter would be a fresh start. I thought I would have more control. This time around, I was the mother. My idealistic commitment left my real-life daughter angry and guilty.

Repeatedly, we fought. I wanted her close. She felt intruded upon. She had to push me away very hard so I could hear her. Later, when her anger dissipated, she felt guilty. We had no way to talk about these incidents. My childhood cycle spun around and around. In this generation, the roles reversed.

With my youngest daughter, a different scenario played on the same theme. Different but not better. My youngest daughter soaked up my attention. I lavished her with devotion. When I turned away to pay attention to something or someone else, she became jealous and demanding. With her, I felt so burdened. At times, I rejected her to get space for myself. I made her feel betrayed. I had promised to be connected always. She believed she needed to be tied to me. She had no power. When I distanced myself from her, she felt abandoned by me. My youngest looked to other relationships for power. She was at their mercy.

Again, rejection, another variation of my childhood mother/daughter theme. Two daughters: one side of my emotional inheritance organized around each. I played out the hurt child with my oldest. I played out the burdened mother with my youngest. In my mind, mothers and daughters just couldn't seem to have loving, solid connections. That was in my history. It went back generations.

Disturbed, I saw my daughters getting into relationships with males and females, repeating variations of the family cycle. I had reasoned: "If I love them more than myself, they will seek relationships with people who are completely devoted to them." Instead, both were getting into relationships where they were devoted to others. My girls were hurt and unhappy. The devotion wasn't reciprocated with the same enthusiasm.

By now you may wonder what all this has to do with what I can't live without.

It is precisely from the above experiences with my daughters that I came to discover and understand the answer.

I can't live without a total commitment to and a strong love of *myself*.

When the lightbulb went on, the obvious was right in front of my eyes. I refocused and started to examine my broken heart, my guilt and shame, my wounded, abandoned child. Slowly, more and more, I could see, love, and accept this inner part of myself. With my emerging vision, a magical thing began to happen. My daughters became more empowered.

As I learned to differentiate and separate who they were from who I was, we all gained a greater sense of self. I started modeling solid self-care and self-respect. They saw me getting stronger. They risked having honest discussions with me. They saw I had confidence in myself and in them. They watched as I started trusting my gut feelings. In short, they felt me opening up. We began to learn more and more from one another. Our relationships became more fluid. The roles of mother/daughter, teacher/student, leader/follower began to shift. Life moved from black and white to shades of multicolor.

Now, when I fly on an airplane and hear the flight attendant instruct passengers, "In the event of an emergency, if oxygen is needed, adults should place the mask on their own faces before assisting their children," I think of this simple instruction as a great life metaphor. Straightforward, clear; no one can argue with that logic. ◁◦

broken homes

THIS ROAD
by Janis Greve

We are
practiced travelers,
parting the waves of
   farmland with the
   shark's nose
of this car.

I'm bringing my daughter
to her father
down this road we know
like the dirt floor
of our own names:
sudden, unyielding, true,
the sure thud of our impact
   against the spinning world.

Packed hard
by the padding feet
of love and duty,
pummeled into the silt

seed of itself
by sun and tires
working their daily beat,

this road creases
the palm of my hand,
lodges in our rattled
spines and stays.

I grip the wheel and
turn the corner.
We hang on.
Now we meet him halfway
between two worlds
at the preappointed spot.

Now we make
the swift exchange
of your flesh.

For mothers who spoke or wrote about divorce, their daughters' adolescence was a particularly hurtful, threatening, and fractious time.

A number of women compared a daughter's adolescent distancing to an ex-husband's rejection. They relived the pain and complications that led to a daughter's life being divided between two homes. "I feel like I'm going through the divorce all over again. Only this time, it's my daughter who wants me out of her life."

Some divorced or divorcing mothers tremble at the phrase "out of my life." They worry their daughters will choose their former husbands over them. For women whose husbands tend toward laissez-faire parenting, this threat looms particularly large. "What my daughter wants most is total freedom. My ex will give that to her. He has no interest in making rules. He thinks I'm as uptight as she does."

Others fear their daughters' adolescent rebellion fuels their ex-husbands' impulse to reinvade their lives. "Suddenly, she has purple hair and he has new ammunition for what an ineffective parent I am." These women fear their husbands will contact the school authorities and therapists to rally support for a more regressive regime, or worse, to have their daughters taken away from their mothers.

And some women worry that the tenuous ties between their daughters and ex-husbands will be totally severed. They see fathers looking for excuses to withdraw, hunting for a way to expunge the children as well as the failed marriage from their new lives. They see how precariously their daughters are perched. Moms fear their ex-husband's abandonment will send their girls into free fall.

The scarring inflicted by divorce doesn't end when daughters move into womanhood.

THE SECOND TIME AROUND
A Conversation with Rebecca

Rebecca was about to talk about her divorce. She made certain her daughter Becky was in her bedroom, the door shut, out of earshot. Then she blurted out her uncensored assessment of her former husband's remarriage.

"My first husband, Becky's dad, he went for the quiet type the second time around. She's a mouse. I walk in the room, she crawls into a corner and begins to twitch. I scare the crap out of her.

"I mean, that woman deserves to be intimidated. She had an affair with my husband. Now she gets to be Becky's stepmother, and I've got to pretend she's not wicked.

"Behind her back, I have these evil names for her: 'Kimmy-Poo' and 'Bimbette.' But I've never let Becky hear me berate her. Around my daughter, I keep my malice about the 'Bimbette' to myself. I tell you, I'm vigilant.

"One day an old friend came over. In front of Becky, he asked, 'So how's the Bimbette?' I glared at him. I made that 'I'll cut your throat motion' with my hand. He got the message and shut up immediately.

"Becky has to go back and forth between our house and theirs. She's with my ex and his Kimmy-Poo every other weekend, summer, and vacation. Already she bounces between our different styles. At our house, we're loose, informal, laughing about everything. At his house, he's into manners. He's, like, serious, strict. Becky has to adjust, love us both. I'm just glad I never have to spend more than twenty minutes with that stuffed shirt."

Rebecca caught her breath. In a split second, she had an epiphany. "Hey, maybe Kimmy-Poo did me a favor. I should be *thanking* the Bimbette!" ⍟

While Rebecca had managed to keep her hurt from spilling over and poisoning her daughter's relationship with her former husband, Felicia Blasi hasn't been able to keep up a front. Felicia's husband's infidelity had laid her bare, emotions exposed, unable to hide, even from her daughter. Once her daughter reached adolescence, Felicia found the strength to write this confession, asking for her daughter's forgiveness.

THIS PHOTO OF YOU
by Felicia Blasi

When I look at this photo of you, I am filled with shame and regret. There you are in the white resin lawn chair, staring out at Lake Michigan. You are singularly alone. I had to take the picture from behind you, at a distance, because without words, you announced you needed to be by yourself outside. All you needed was someone to place the chair on the edge for you.

You are sitting more upright than you would have three weeks earlier. And you are far more still. Your eyes are fixed on something, but I can tell you're not just gazing at the lake. You're sifting, weighing, figuring. Already I can tell that the lake is no longer "the sea" to you. In your eight-and-a-half-year-ness, you are old. And I know I forced this premature maturity on you.

I know that right now, in this picture, your incision still throbs as it runs horizontally around you from your back, cutting through your side, ending above your navel. The staples are gone, but you are left with fresh Frankenstein-like red scars in their place. You have known more pain in one month than I have known in a lifetime. I am sure of this. And I wonder if you are thinking about that, the pain, the waking up from kidney surgery, mumbling about the catheter as I stood over you in the recovery room. You half cried, half whimpered, not much sound, given all that pain. You looked so small in that big hospital bed, and I wanted to take that pain away from you somehow. Instead, I inflicted more.

I did the right thing by living in your hospital room with you, playing endless rounds of Memory and the rhyming game during those three weeks. But I also did the wrong thing when I hated your father in your presence. And that's what made the deeper tear in you, one that won't heal. I was so angry with Dan and humiliated by Nancy's presence. He could never just come see you by himself; she was always in tow, even after I'd asked him not to bring her.

Most often I left your room when they came in, wordlessly forcing you to make a choice: your father or me. Once when they'd walked down the hall with you, I left a note pinned to your pillowcase telling Dan where he could find me when he and Nancy left. I didn't want you to be alone in that room, not even for five minutes, but I couldn't be in there for one minute with them. That night Nancy had given you the "glitter" Spirograph set, and I could not find one decent word for the occasion. But you knew and kept your joy to yourself. I demanded this goodness of you, and I was selfish. Terribly greedy, gobbling up your affection for me. Only me. I pretended I'd been wholly good. I hadn't said anything aloud to implicate your father. I didn't say, "We're not even divorced yet. Don't hurt me by bringing *her* here with you like she's a member of our family, you son of a bitch." And I didn't say, "You can't visit Liz because you and Nancy have a fucking art class?" And I didn't say, "I'm the real parent, but you get to be the frosting, flitting in and out a couple of times a week with a damn milk shake in your hand." I didn't say, "You've hurt me so deeply, and my only revenge is ownership of this child, whom I will possess and you will not."

But I might as well have. And so when you wanted to be happy about your dad's visits, you hid your happiness so I would feel good. You had to bury your honesty deep inside of you. You had to pretend you really didn't like the Spirograph. But I know you did. You could no longer mention your father aloud because of me. You survived by locking away your eight-year-old self and her feelings, desires, sadness, and pain. In her place was a girl, but she owned secrets and fear like an adult.

So now you sit and look out at Lake Michigan, figuring out, I suspect, what to make of your new self. And I know now that I no longer possess you, if I ever did. You are locked up tight. This photo always gives me pause. Always forces me to remember that goodness I required of you then, and how that robbed you of your eight-year-old spontaneity and censored your joys and pain.

At fifteen, you are still quiet, especially for a teenager. Once you locked yourself up, you swallowed the key I forged for you. And I am ashamed. And you are still far too silent. ⟨∘⟩

Like Felicia, Helena Pitziak had felt the pain of her husband's rejection. Still, Helena considered hers a good divorce—good because her first husband continued to care about their daughter. Even though Helena would sooner have severed ties, sharing a child kept her intermittently glued to her former husband. Weekends, holidays, vacations: At these times, connections had to be made. In time, Helena remarried and moved east. Logistics became a sticky business. With a chasm between lifestyles and half a country between daughter and dad, the complications threatened to decimate the last of Helena's remaining "for the sake of our daughter" resolutions. Helena found herself tempted to sever all ties. A humor-driven woman, she launched into a story.

HIGH COUNTRY TOWN
A Story from Helena Pitziak

"Then there was the day my little pot head forgot to come home from her dad's. Just missed the date. Forgot the flight."

Helena backtracked, filling in details. Actually, the story didn't begin when Mya missed her flight. The tale didn't really belong to Mya, at least not entirely. No. This scheduling misadventure was merely one episode in a long-running drama shared by three characters: Helena, the mother; Mya, the child; and, Eric, the father, also known as "Golden Feather." Oh, and Dr. Charles, new husband and stepfather: He played a supporting role.

Helena lives in the East. Golden Feather, in the West. Mya was an airplane-savvy traveler. She spent fall, winter, and spring in New England. She summered in the Colorado hills. The arrangement cycled around year after year without a glitch until Mya turned thirteen. At the end of August, Mya returned from her mountain-man dad with budding breasts and a full-blown attitude. Helena continued from there.

"My misgivings sprouted approximately one hour and twenty minutes after Mya came home. That's when she exposed her newly pierced belly button.

"High Mountain Town. My daughter goes to High Mountain Town every summer. I send my child into a drug-infused time warp. All these middle-aged Rip van Winkles with beards down to their ankles, grooving on 'like, the sky, man.' 'Ya. Wow.' 'And, like, the mountains.'"

Just thinking about it sent Helena's eyeballs wobbling. She settled her gaze on me. "Have you ever been to High Mountain Town?"

I had been to the old-time logging community tucked between mountain ranges, sleeping quietly in an evergreen forest. Walking its streets felt like a retro dream: the sixties' throwbacks hanging out in a state of permanent vacuous ecstasy. Strolling in the dry, sweltering heat, I did encounter the new generation. A youth clad from neck to toe in shiny black leather sat stiffly on a rough wooden bench. Silver bangles and studs protruded from every visible patch of skin: his eyebrows, lips, nose, and ears. His gelled black hair, meticulously twisted into spikes, mirrored his cow-skin clothing. This picturesque creature kept a companion: a girl dressed in matching garb, augmented with a collar, leash, and mittens. This adolescent child, some mother's daughter, crouched on the hard ground. Her face rested on her woolen paws. Her studded collar ringed her neck tightly. Her pubescent master held her chain taut. "Now, this," I'd thought, "is a reaction to feminism."

Seeing this duo had left me hankering for familiar surroundings, for a comfortable place, like a bookstore. I yearned to read *The New York Times.* Short of that epitome of down-to-earth East Coast civility, I'd gladly have settled into Gail Sheehy's latest tome. I walked up to a tie-dye-costumed lad and asked, "Where's the local bookstore?" His clear-as-crystal baby-blue eyes registered vacancy. I asked again. He signaled confusion. He repeated the word "bookstore." The concept—a store filled with books—seemed to elude him. Again, he intoned the word. His dilated pupils moved up and down, back and forth, searching for meaning. Then he nodded—actually he rocked,—and said, "Ya. Ya. I think I've got it. I think there's one of those over in Boulder."

I understood why Helena might feel just a wee bit uncomfortable about Mya's summers in High Mountain Town. Helena continued her saga.

"When Mya came home, her head was in LaLa Land. Should a girl really spend the summer with a man who left his watch and calendar in 1970? A man who's taken up permanent residence in the Land of No Responsibility? She spent her entire summer with Eric, excuse me, Golden Feather, 'just hanging out,' 'going with the flow,' 'doing what comes naturally.' Well, next summer she'll be fourteen, and doing what comes naturally could just land her in a pile of shit. Drugs. Sex. Eric could care. To him, it's all part of the unfolding universe."

Helena paused. Her tone turned self-reflective.

"Of course, Eric may have his reservations about sending her back to me each fall. I'm the one who abandoned my principles, sold out to the East Coast establishment, married a doctor. I'm the one infusing her with toxic materialism. He's right, you know. I changed. He didn't."

By that winter, Mya had been reminding Helena more and more of Eric. She blossomed into a raven-haired beanpole of a girl. Curly locks. Alabaster skin. Like her dad. But really, it wasn't the physical resemblance, or even Mya's Eric-like mannerisms, that distressed Helena. No. The most disturbing part was the pain Mya's surly adolescent disrespect had rekindled.

"Let me tell you. Mya hitting adolescence: It was like the divorce. It hurt. Some days, I'd say, 'Let's eat fudge sundaes for dinner,' and she'd be furiously annoyed with my childishness. Couldn't say anything right. Ouch! Expressing affection was like loading her gun. She aimed it straight at my heart. The rejection. The losing her. It was like Eric all over again."

By that spring, Charles, Helena's second husband, stopped playing "Hands off Helena's Former Marriage." He sat Helena down, held her hand, and lectured softly, "No matter what you think of Eric, he's Mya's dad. You can't sever the connection. Don't try."

So summer came and Mya flew to California on the appointed day at the end of August, at the scheduled time—you know what happened, but here's how Helena completed her saga:

"I stood in a crowd at Logan Airport, joshing with the other passenger-picker-uppers: 'My kid will be the one with the pink hair.' I craned my neck wistfully, wanting to get a gander of her new 'mountain girl in summer' look. I stretched on tiptoes. I bounced up and down. I nearly climbed onto a counter. All just to get a glimpse of her, to see her from afar, to drink her in before she started pushing me away.

"A parade of passengers pushed through the swinging metal doors. Welcomed, hugged and kissed, one by one they walked down the exit ramp and disappeared. I stood alone, keeping my anxiety under wraps. The doors swung open again. My heart gave a little leap. The pilot and crew walked past me.

"No pink-hairdo kid. No pager telling me to pick up the white courtesy phone. No air in my lungs.

"I made my first hysterical phone call to Charles, who told me: 'No word here. Try not to worry.'

"I made my next frantic call to Eric: 'Flight? Today? Really? Guess she missed it.'

"I confirmed his conclusion. 'Yes, Eric. She missed it.'

"The next day, when I drove back to the airport, no apology. Not even a little one.

"But now, four years later, Mya is extremely nice to me. She likes me. She even misses me. When I call, she screams in delight, yells to her roommates, 'Hey, guys, my mom's on the phone.'"

Helena knows beyond all doubt: Mya isn't Eric in disguise. Mya is Mya. And Mya is still Helena's daughter. Nothing has permanently poisoned their relationship. ⬤

Such stories don't always have such happy outcomes. The tug-of-war for a daughter's affection can rub raw the relationship between mothers and adolescent daughters.

Sue Lutz felt sure the move would be fine, just fine. She had done everything right. When her job was in jeopardy, she sent out her résumé. Opportunities knocked, but not from next door. She would have to relocate. She explained it all to Jamie, her sixteen-year-old daughter, who had been in her sole custody since age two. Jamie seemed accepting.

Sue and Jamie flew to interviews together. Narrowed down the possibilities together. Chose their new hometown together. Then, after the decision was made, after Sue had signed a contract on a new home, Jamie announced, "No. I'm not leaving."

Jamie moved into her dad's home. Sue moved to a distant city, started her job, and lived alone. The gulf between mother and daughter turned turbulent. Only under Sue's loving duress did her daughter finally visit. After meeting her daughter after a long separation, Sue wrote:

A DIFFERENT WALK
by Susan K. Lutz

I hardly recognized her when she got off the plane. Her hair was a little longer than she had been wearing it, and it had been stripped of its natural bronze beauty to a brassy bleached blond. Makeup was more heavily applied than I had ever seen it.

But the real reason my brain didn't connect was because I wasn't searching faces or looking at clothes. My eyes assessed each female passenger by the way she carried herself. I was searching for the jaunty cheerleader walk, the bounce in the step that would say, "I'm here and I'm revved up and anxious to see you." It was gone. Replaced by a teenage shuffle on platform shoes and an "I don't care" attitude.

Minutes later, in the car, she handed me her memory book. I leafed through snapshots of a life I am losing touch with. Teachers I don't recognize. School dances in dresses I didn't help pick out. Boys, lots of boys I know a little bit about by name but who had been faceless in my mind.

I could feel my eyes begin to tear. I had to turn my head to regain control of my breathing. At that instant came the recognition: This person in the backseat, my daughter, had become a stranger to me. ⚭

Time passed; the estrangement persisted. With phone and e-mail communication strained, Jamie wrote Sue a caustic note. Sue tried to see the tenderness hidden behind her daughter's anger. She responded:

I LOVE YOU, TOO

DEAR JAMIE,

I received your e-mail yesterday. It hurt, just as you intended. The poison that oozed out choked my heart. You'll never need a gun or a knife to protect yourself. You can inflict body-shattering damage with your words. As the pain began to numb some, I was able to acknowledge that at least you had reached out to communicate with me. So it was a step.

In your letter, the one you did not write to me, you said you were angry with me. You felt as though you had been abandoned when I moved. You said that phone calls, cards, and e-mails were not the same as hugging your mom good night. You said that photographs weren't the same as renting a movie and sitting on the couch to watch it together. You said that there were times, like when you went to the prom last year, that you weren't sure what kind of bra to wear with the cut of the dress—and you couldn't ask your dad about it. Or when boyfriends did something infuriating, it didn't feel right to ask your dad if all guys are this way.

In the letter that you didn't write, you let me know that you miss me and love me just as I miss and love you.

MOM ⚭

Sue Lutz is not alone. For many divorced mothers, estranged fathers lurk in the background. With adolescence, daughters need to pull away from mothers. When the strain becomes too much, these ex-husbands emerge from the shadows with open arms. Like Sue, Margaret Bayley also grieved over the loss of her daughter.

GRIEVING FOR CAITLIN
by Margaret Bayley

Growing up, Caitlin was a perfect little girl. She got straight As and was picked for special projects. She had nice friends who rated high on the academic level. I never had to tell Caitlin to do her homework or pick up her room. She was proud of how well she did. Caitlin collected things, like erasers or pencils, and kept them in little containers. When she was seven, she bought a guinea pig with her own money. She kept the animal in her room and was its sole provider, which included the feedings and cleaning of the cage. When she was eight, she wrote a prayer called the "Promise Prayer." That Christmas, I made copies of her prayer, had them matted and framed for family gifts. Caitlin was very thoughtful and considerate of others' feelings. Mementos became important to her. I was Caitlin's mom and so proud of that. I couldn't imagine my life without her.

When Caitlin was thirteen, her father and I separated. She seemed fine with the new living arrangement. I relied on her.

Caitlin and I were alone a lot and became buddies. We went to the mall. I was available to take her wherever she needed to go. During my sad moments, she was there for me. But she was also involved with her friends. It was easy for her to leave me alone on a Saturday night.

I started casual dating. In the spring, I met Phil. We got along great and had a lot in common. He had qualities I had always dreamed a mate should have. He also had custody of his eight-year-old daughter. I knew he was a caring father.

Phil and I announced we were getting married in April of the following year. When I told Caitlin, she slammed her bedroom door in my face. I included her when looking for a wedding gown. I wanted to share my excitement about my important day with her. I thought that she would come around. She started having outbursts to show me how upset she was with me. She admitted she was jealous. She was holding on to the last stable thing in her life. She knew I loved and cared for her, but her selfishness got in the way.

Caitlin had more outbursts. She told me that she wasn't going to be in my wedding. I wanted her to be part of the wedding more than anything. I wanted her to share in my happiness and realize that she wasn't losing me. Caitlin never seemed to understand how she could share me. I was happy, why wasn't she? Couldn't she be happy for me? After all the time I had spent running her here and there, and living for her, couldn't she for once be happy for me?

Caitlin and I moved into Phil's house a few weeks before the wedding. I had Caitlin help me decorate and arrange the house with our furniture. I hoped to get her enthused about living in our new home. I tried everything to make it comfortable for Caitlin. Maybe I tried too hard. We fought, but I thought it was a phase that would eventually pass.

When we were together, like going to the mall, we still had a good time. I helped her pick out clothes. While she was in the dressing room, I ran back and forth for her. I never minded helping her. In fact, I enjoyed it. It's something that moms do and don't think twice about. I didn't think things would change.

Summer came. Caitlin was scheduled to spend a one-week vacation with her father. Just before she left, I found out that she was going to a party where no parents would be in the house. She had tried lying about it, but I found out. She left mad.

The day she was due back home, she didn't show. I called her father's house. She told me that she wasn't coming back. How could things change so drastically?

I was crushed. I tried calling her to ask her out to lunch. She only laughed at me and said, "What for?"

Still, I knew my daughter missed me. She was putting up this big front. I thought that in no time, she'd come back.

School was starting in a few days. Caitlin called to ask for her school stuff, clothes, backpack, books, etc. I was okay with giving her those things as long as I could keep the rest of her belongings. I wasn't ready to give her everything.

She came for her school things, and I couldn't even go outside. I watched her load up from a bedroom window. She had this big smirk on her face as she was loading. She felt proud of herself for leaving her mom.

The following week was Caitlin's sixteenth birthday. I had been waiting for this day. I had taken my previous engagement ring, which had three diamond chips, and turned the chips into pierced earrings. A perfect sixteenth-birthday gift.

When her birthday came, I couldn't bring myself to give the earrings to her. It wasn't the same. Instead, I sent sixteen pink sweetheart roses to her at school. I never heard an acknowledgment from her. This hurt me terribly.

I had a hard time on her birthday. I just wanted to get through the day. My husband realized how I felt. He took the day off from work to be with me. If it weren't for him, it would have been pretty depressing.

The day came when I had to pack up the rest of my daughter's belongings. I sobbed. As I was packing, I looked at so many things she had saved: old achievement certificates (one dated back to fourth grade), swim-meet ribbons, yearbooks, cards, letters. I took my time. I cherished each item, remembering how close we had been. I didn't know when I'd be a part of her life again. I packed all of her dresses except her costume from ballet in kindergarten. I needed to keep that. I was afraid she'd think it was a waste. She might have tossed it. I carried all of the boxes and bags downstairs and out to the garage. I carried down the pictures and posters she had collected in her bedroom, beginning when she was two years old. These things were so familiar to me. Now they were leaving. I had a hard time looking at these things without crying. I just wanted this day over with.

Caitlin came later that day with her father. A couple of friends helped her load up the van. Two of the boxes didn't fit. Her father made her leave them at the curb. I would have found a way to fit those boxes in.

After Caitlin and her dad were safely down the road, my husband and I went out to the curb. We brought the boxes back into the house. They were filled with all her current magazines. I had been saving them for her over the summer. Another box contained all these lawn decorations she had been collecting: a skunk, a flamingo, a rabbit, and a few others. I never understood why she collected these things, but accumulating them just made her unique.

Now it's impossible for me to go into her room without the tears starting. Her bed, dresser, and bookcase are still there, but they are empty. No trace of Caitlin remains. I sit there and look around, remembering what it used to look like: her bulletin board over her bed and the many pictures of her friends lining the mirror on her dresser. Her closet doors are now bare. The posters gone. That room used to be the noisiest in the house, with the radio blaring and Caitlin on the phone trying to talk over the music. Now it's just so empty. I almost feel like moving so I don't have to look at that room.

With my daughter not here, I feel that a big part of me is missing. She made me who I am. I lived to be a parent. I miss being one.

I heard Caitlin now has her driving permit. I had been teaching her to drive on back roads. She has a job at Kmart. I wanted to be with her to share in her excitement of getting her first job. I don't even know what days she works, or how many hours, or how much money she makes. I don't know who her friends are (I'm sure they haven't changed that much), or who she might be dating, or what she's doing in her spare time. Those are things any parent naturally knows about her child . . . but not me. I've gone from knowing every part of Caitlin's life to knowing nothing. I'm left with an empty, helpless feeling.

I was the mom who was there for everything: swim practice, swim meets, lacrosse games, school dances, school functions, carpooling, birthday parties, making cookies, shopping for everything, knowing everything. I remember lying with her on her bedroom floor while she went through her yearbook, telling me every girl's name. I loved it. I was living my teenage years again. Now I'm back to being an adult overnight. ⟡

Finally, the ties between mother and daughter endure. Divorce, remarriage, and relocation threatened to tear Maryann Siebert and her daughter apart. Maryann refused.

BELATED APPLAUSE
by Maryann Siebert

And did you get what you wanted from this life, even so?
—RAYMOND CARVER

To be loved so much . . . Cleaning up one of the counters in the kitchen, the one with all of my diet books, scattered poems, torn recipes, and financial sheets, I've come across a recent photo of my daughter. Her face is so lovely, with that look of surprise as she glances over her shoulder, the pose so typical of her—not the deer-caught-in-the-headlights look or the come-hither look of my adolescence, but more of a "caught me, didn't you?" look. My eyes fill with tears, and the words "to be loved so much" envelop me.

William Blake, the Romantic poet, called moments like these "beams of love." On another day, I might have smiled at the picture and carefully put it away. Today I am filled with a visceral sense of love for my daughter. How I miss Emily and applaud her. She has charted her own path in life. She cares more for her work as an artist than for material comforts. She involves herself in human-rights issues. She carefully chose the right environment in which to blossom into full adulthood. I wonder, though, how did she develop such a consciousness of community and purpose so young?

This applause for my daughter did not always resound.

I'll never forget the day of my second marriage, a hot, brilliant day in August. Emily (by proxy because she was only fifteen) and her brother stood up as witnesses in our courthouse wedding. A very simple affair, but inclusive: the three most important people in my life, no one else. Or so I thought.

In the interim between that marriage ceremony and the reception, Emily stood outside our new official home. With arms akimbo, she fired a news flash over her shoulder: "I will not live here. You cannot make me." That began the turning point in my relationship with my daughter.

Allowing Emily to live with her father or her older brother in our hometown was not an option. Emily exploded in pain, became seriously depressed.

One night, during the first fall we were living in the new house, I heard her crying. On entering the bedroom, Emily sat up and sobbed, "Why can't we just go home?"

At that moment, I easily could have gone home. Our house in the neighboring county had not been sold yet. In response, I wrote a poem entitled "Trading Worlds." The first few lines read, "What ever made me think I could pick you up/like my favorite doll and carry you away/transport you whole."

My second marriage was anything but a lovefest, with a depressed, acting-out teenager trying to escape. In many ways, I felt like the mirror image of Emily. It wasn't just identification with her pain. I, too, was in pain, the pain of guilt and the pain of loss. I had lost my dream of a perfect family life. Like Emily, I had lost friends. I missed the easy access I had to my friends in my former community, whom I needed now more than ever. Few friends understood my motives. "Why did you do this so soon?" "What was the rush to remarry?" I never had the guts to say, "I did this for me. I just had to." In this, my *first selfish act*, as my therapist put it, I was so encased in my own need for protection—security from a male figure—that I shut out any perception of the needs my child had for a strong, self-reliant female to role model. I remember reassuring myself by saying, "This will be the grand experiment." Can you imagine such a flippant statement? I made it, thinking, "I can end this arrangement as easily as I have begun it." In those words, I disregarded the human factors of attachment, responsibility, and love.

I held firm. I became acutely conscious of the fact that how I reacted to this adversity would help show my daughter how to cope with her sorrow. I couldn't just "pack up my marbles" (though I was painfully aware of how I had done that to her) and go home, give up on the new marriage, and reject this man who loved me and us. For the first time in my life, I fought relentlessly for what I believed. I took a stand and did not waver. The stand wasn't for a perfect marriage with security or for a home with a vista of the New York skyline, as some were inclined to think, but for the integrity of the self.

I hung in there in the second marriage and, with determination and tunnel vision, did everything I could to help my daughter adjust to this far less than perfect world.

To complicate matters even more, in the bitter aftermath of the divorce, a friend told Emily's father that she was on drugs. My ex-husband and his fiancée told me together. At a local after-care program, Emily's father had stormed out of a family meeting because he felt attacked. All communication ceased. Emily didn't stay clean. She continued to use marijuana daily.

I had to take a stand, and that stand was "hard love," my own version of zero tolerance. I allowed no drug use or lying. It's amazing how many people—professionals included—wanted to dismiss my daughter's serious use of marijuana. Many said, "She'll get over it." Others, parental figures included, wanted to hide the drug use and blame others.

The roller-coaster ride continued until the summer, the summer of Emily's father's wedding. In lucid moments, Emily talked about the outrage she felt. She focused on her father's disrespectful treatment of her brother. Over and over, she asked, "Why isn't my brother in the wedding?" I knew she was saying, "Why am I not in my father's wedding? Dad, don't push me out." He relented and included them. During her father's wedding, both of my children played their roles well. Emily threw the rose petals, as she was expected to do. Her brother took charge of the floral arrangements, as he was expected to do. And Emily came home drunk that night, threw the wedding bouquet on the dining room table, and crashed on her bed.

Several days later, Emily climbed out of her bedroom window, leaving a note on her carefully made bed. She apologized to her brother and me. She wrote that she loved us but that she saw no other alternative but escape. She was running away with local Deadheads to join the summer tour of the Grateful Dead. This was the late eighties; the band was a pied piper for lost youth who traveled in carloads all over the country to hear them. Young yuppie business types as well as teenage suburban kids packed it in for marijuana and country cool, a laid-back life. Emily was barely sixteen. The world out there, through my mother-eyes, was filled with drugs, danger, and disease.

I called the police. As one sketched out the portrait of Emily to use in the countywide search, he tried to calm me down. "Lady," he told me, "if your kid has to run away with any group, she's picked a good one." Detectives found her before she left town.

The next day, with her father in France on his honeymoon, I made the decision with Emily to take her to an adolescent rehab facility. "We're buying time," my therapist comforted me. "Teaching her skills."

In fog and silence, I drove Emily to the Pennsylvania hills. My heart sank when we got to the center. Though at first it looked like a pleasant summer camp, on closer inspection, the place had the gray, dilapidated cast of a Norman Bates motel.

In the reception room, Emily begged me to allow her to come home. "I'll be good," she cried.

I looked outside the picture window at boys throwing lawn chairs at one another and said to the director, "My daughter does not belong here."

"Your daughter is on drugs," he replied. "She belongs here."

I turned my daughter over to strangers. Emily needed comfort and safety. I left her in the care of this highly recommended rehab. It turned out to be anything but safe.

I returned soon for a family weekend. All of us were there to support Emily on her twelve-step journey. The scenario again turned chaotic. Emily's father threw a chair at her brother and accused him of starting her on drugs. I accused his wife of blocking me out, and he accused me of disrespecting his wife. Familial screaming ensued. Emily, the sane one, tried to comfort everyone. Emily, the child who carried the family dysfunction, publicly voiced her love for all of us and her new acceptance of responsibility. She tried earnestly to lead us all toward reconciliation.

I sensed something was wrong with this facility. The cost was exorbitant, and the staff mediocre at best. Several days later, a scandal emerged. A female night attendee, who later confessed to supplying the young males with drugs and alcohol, was rumored to be soliciting the boys for oral sex. My daughter had to live with this utter confusion and with the knowledge that there was no safe place after all. In the end, Emily did not belong there.

That summer Emily spent in rehab, the next in a summer program at Carnegie Mellon for gifted art students, and the following summer in preparation for university that fall. Emily's recovery was not an unfaltering upward climb. The entanglements of the divorce and the real losses Emily suffered for my "second chance," and for her father's, complicated her growth.

Loss still rears its head. Loss, and the guilt over it, lives deep inside of me. Perhaps in Emily, too. Time cannot be regained. Paradise has vanished forever.

As we forge a new life, the ideal image of family is gone. Every holiday is a hassle. Who does what with whom? Who will be left alone without the children? To whom do you speak when a minor concern surfaces? With whom do you discuss the "doings"—not necessarily the crises—of the children? Where is the nest we humans want to believe waits just for us, that we mothers insist we should guard forever?

I'm a Catholic-school child of the fifties and a marginally rebellious girl of the sixties. I was raised on the *Lives of the Saints*, not by saints. My parents weren't ideal figures to me. Their warts were all too evident. Yet when I came home, my mother was always waiting.

I did what was expected of me—married early, had children, believed in the sacrament of marriage. With my unwavering acceptance, I would make marriage work, or so I thought. I didn't figure in my drive for education, for a career, for fulfillment outside of the home. I didn't add in a husband who would in time see me as the enemy. By the age of thirty-five, I was a full-fledged workaholic who found little peace outside of professional challenge. Emily rarely found me at home.

I ran away from a difficult marriage. The results could be an *Oprah* show on adult children of divorce. I hear the consequences in Emily's casual remark "I'm in no rush to marry." I'm stuck in a quagmire of guilt, trapped in the what-could-have-been. Within me is a constant struggle to accept myself for having created less than the best of nourishing homes. My Emily and I have been forced to accept a hard reality, a loving but hard reality devoid of many of the familial trappings.

Recently Emily sent me a book of poems by Marge Piercy. She underlined several lines that speak of a daughter's struggle for her mother's approval and her final joy at its conquest: "[W]ith these poems, finally I won my mother, the longest wooing of my life." I read these lines often. Sometimes I need only look at the miniature book of poems resting here on my desk to remember: We both came out of this whole, my daughter and me.

I could not have made it without witnessing her courage to face such a maddening world so young, and without recognizing the undivided love she has for both her father and me. ⋖⊃

legacies: from generation to generation

❧

*The biggest challenge for me is to make sure my daughter
has a different life growing up than I had. I will always be
here for my daughter. I will help her, as she is becoming a
woman, to feel proud and comfortable.*

—DEBBIE GAFFNEY

WHEN WOMEN SPOKE ABOUT THEIR OWN MOTHERS, I HEARD
an unexpected tone. The voices sang songs of forgiveness.

Few mothers of adolescent girls idealize their own mothers.
The women I contacted spoke openly about their mothers'
crimes and misdemeanors. Alcoholism. Abuse. Verbal tirades.
Emotional frigidity. Inept parenting. Overprotectiveness. All
had vowed to improve upon the emotional legacy handed down
to them from their own mothers. Yet their words held compassion. Over and over, they offered the same chorus: "I don't
blame my mother. She did her best. I love her."

As a psychologist, I'm used to a more strident attitude
toward mothers. For many in my profession, finding fault with
mothers is an obsession. I can't resist the temptation to illustrate
with a much-told joke: An elderly lady is bragging to her
friends, "Well. Let me tell you. My daughter loves me so much.
No daughter could love a mother more than mine. Every week,
she goes to her psychologist. She spends a hundred and twenty-
five dollars! Every week, I tell you. And what does she do? My
daughter, she talks the whole time all about *me!*"

Our daughters' adolescence often brings us compassion for
our own mothers. As they distance from us, we get a new perspective on the trials our mothers endured.

An envelope arrived in my mailbox with a return-address
sticker glued on the back flap. This is no ordinary address
sticker, no plain white rectangle with black lettering in Times

Roman font. This sticker pictures a pink-and-green-striped hatbox with a turquoise lid. A shoe, reminiscent of forties fashion, stands on that lid. This particular shoe isn't content to be sensible, laced-up black leather. This shoe, with its spiked heel and pointed toe and trim of neon green, finds fun in recollecting the style of our mothers' generation. All in all, this address sticker says a lot about its sender. Inside the envelope was a permission form. Catherine agreed to allow me to quote her.

I had interviewed Catherine a few weeks earlier. She had chimed in on the subject of mothers. The sound of her voice had rung with a combination of admiration, disbelief, and humor, a mix only a grown-up daughter can feel for a mom.

e

THROUGH ROSE-COLORED GLASSES
A Conversation with Catherine

"My mom's delusional. Having seven kids lobotomized her. We ask her about our adolescence. Her voice goes all high-pitched and dreamy. She says, 'You were all good all the time.'

"Discipline? Forget it. I was a whoopee!/I'm outta here/later, baby kind of teenager. I could have been playing in traffic for all my mom knew.

"My sister Anita got pregnant at nineteen. I got pregnant at twenty. But my mom keeps saying, 'No. No problems. You were good girls.' Mom's really sweet. Really sweet. As for advice, she's a total loss. And a fund of knowledge she's not.

"Shelley, my daughter, asks me about my adolescence. I say, 'Let's ask Grandma.' Shelley looks at me like I'm a fool and says, 'Grandma? Grandma won't remember.'"

Catherine had been blessed. Her mother's rosy-eyed myopia felt like naive affirmation, not neglect. Catherine looks back at her mother's optimistic delusions with mischievous delight.

Bonnie Riggs's mother also seemed out of touch. But for Bonnie, her mother's emotional absence felt like neglect. She contemplated that legacy of inattention with sorrow, fearing she had not learned how to nurture her own daughters.

MOTHERING WITHOUT A MAP
Thoughts from Bonnie Riggs

"My mother was an extraordinary beauty. She was like a fairy princess. She had a garden—a beautiful, perfect garden. She created it as a place of escape—a place to hide, to be with herself. It was an obsession for her. When I was still little, I asked for a piece of it, for a small plot to grow my own flowers. We had a large yard, most of it bathed in sunshine. She inspected her territory, led me to an overgrown bush, and pointed to the moss-covered ground beneath it. This was the patch my mother was willing to relinquish. Only in this too acidic soil devoid of sunshine did she allow me to plant my own seeds. All the rest she needed for herself. Somehow, even as a child, I knew I couldn't grow on her ground. I knew she couldn't give me her space.

"I had such an unhappy childhood. There was no joy in my home. I raised my children without an external map. I had to find my mothering from within myself.

"Sometimes I fell into the same narcissistic place as my mother. I understand why she needed solitude. I've taken refuge in her kind of self-absorption. I understand why I withdrew from my own children. Still, when I think how I retreated, it hurts.

"Regrets visit me often. I look back at my own children's childhood. I feel sorrow for the times I passed that legacy of narcissism on to them. I was too self-absorbed to attend to them, to give them space in my life. I wasn't tuned in to them. I put my own needs first—my education, my profession, the development of my skills."

I listened to Bonnie's self-assessment with a combination of compassion and astonishment. Throughout Sara's late childhood and adolescence, she had been friends with Bonnie's daughters. Sara had spent weekend after weekend in Bonnie's home. She returned home telling tales of her adventures with Bonnie and her daughters.

Bonnie was one of the few moms—maybe the only mom—I knew who completely participated in her daughters' early-adolescent fun. Bonnie didn't drop the kids at the roller-skating rink and run off to do her own thing. Bonnie stayed and skated and laughed and played. Bonnie had been so active, young, and vibrant, hardly like a mom at all. I had envied how generously she gave up her own time to participate in her daughters' lives. Yet where I saw her motherly involvement, she saw herself falling short of her inner standards.

As I reflected on Bonnie's self-perception, I noticed I was shaking my head involuntarily. I had to tell her how my perception differed from hers. "Bonnie. That's just not the way I saw it. You were so engaged in their lives. Remember the roller skating?"

At the mention of the Saturday mall outings, she chuckled in acknowledgment: "I forgot about that."

Bonnie allowed herself to revel in that memory for only a moment.

Then the sadness returned. "My daughters don't live at home anymore. I let so many opportunities to fully focus on them slip away. Now they're gone, too far away. I miss them."

Bonnie's lament belongs to nearly every mom. We can't do everything right. We can't transform the imperfections passed on to us from our own mothers into a flawless legacy of love. We can learn from our mothers' mistakes. We can set standards to ensure that our daughters will not suffer to the same degree from the same shortcomings. We can live with standards that are humanly attainable. We can do our best. ◄∾

A ll of us inherit mixed emotional legacies, parts of which deserve to be thrown out like the proverbial bathwater, others to be passed on to our daughters like cherished family recipes. Mothers work to separate the emotionally nutritious from the psychologically poisonous. Sometimes we succeed. Sometimes we fall short. We try. In the process, we mature.

There's nothing like having adolescent daughters to teach us forgiveness for our own mothers.

In perfect penmanship, Char Hogan introduced herself: "Well, I have three adolescent daughters, and one more on the way. There's my first, age nineteen (almost), my second, seventeeen and a half, my third, twelve and a half, and my little one, age six. Four incredibly beautiful daughters. I am truly blessed. And there's more! My oldest daughter has made me a grandmother twice. She now has a four-month-old baby (girl) and a year-and-a-half-old (boy)."

In that short paragraph, Char established her credibility. This is a woman positioned to comment on the legacy of generations. Char can see the frailties of her mother through the compassionate eyes of a woman who's been humbled by experience. She issued a plea to all of us: "Let us come together to heal old wounds and misunderstandings, and in so doing, heal others around us. Let us be conduits of love and compassion. The world needs it."

ONLY HUMAN
by Char Hogan

My mother liked a nice clean house. No. She demanded a nice clean house. When the house was a mess, she would yell and scream at us in frustration and anxiety.

We were just kids. We didn't comprehend all of the complicated layers of her life. We couldn't understand her anxiety over whether she could properly feed us, clothe us, and have warm beds for us to sleep in at night. We couldn't appreciate her loneliness and sadness over broken promises and broken hearts. We had no idea how weary and downtrodden she must have felt, going to work in the factory day in and day out.

We saw only the outer layer. Our mother couldn't function in chaos, couldn't give love and affection to her children, and seemed angry most of the time.

Looking back through understanding adult eyes, I see a part of myself, a legacy of my mother, her mother before me, and on down. I would rather pick and choose the wonderful parts to inherit, yet I find myself struggling with the most difficult. The battle seems inescapable. But one good thing is that with these passed-down struggles come understanding, compassion, forgiveness. I love my mother. She gave me life. I honor and revere her.

It took me a long time to see the good parts of my mother. It was easy, looking at the negative aspects, to be blinded and miss good parts. Now it's clear to me. She indeed did love us, very much so.

My mother was suffering from an impoverished life as a single mom in the fifties and sixties. She didn't know how to do things differently. She did her best.

I've come to understand the seemingly vast chasm that exists between her childhood years and mine. In some ways we feel worlds apart, yet we share a thread of commonality. I know it because I see it in my daughters. It's in a facial expression or a certain stance; it's in a tone of voice or a mannerism; it's sometimes subtle and sometimes blatantly obvious. I am my mother's daughter.

Yet with time and determination, I'm changing and evolving. While I see myself acting like my mother, I also see myself doing and saying things she has never considered. I am breaking the patterns of lifetimes. I am creating a new and different legacy to pass on to my daughters, and hopefully they in turn will do the same. We're evolving slowly but surely.

When my mother wasn't being a single mom, she was involved with drunken losers who took their frustrations out on her and us kids. She went through five of them before striking gold. For the past twenty-five years, my mother has been married to a man who truly loves her and treats her like a queen. She deserves it after the long trail of tears she traversed earlier in her life. ✺

Char Hogan and Karen C. live half a coast away from each other, in entirely different types of communities. Char makes her home in rural New England, Karen in the suburbs. Yet just below the surface, they have much in common. Both grew up under the judgmental watch of mothers who didn't know how to make a home safe or comfortable for children. Both learned to forgive and to respect their mothers. And as their daughters reach womanhood, both believe an almost mystical power is carried on from one generation to the next.

✑

THE HOPE CHEST
Karen C.'s Story

"I was an only child, raised by my mother, who was an alcoholic. Growing up, I learned nothing about healthy relationships between mothers and daughters.

"All my childhood, I wanted so much to have a real relationship with her. I never did. I didn't think my mother loved me.

"I, too, am an alcoholic. It took a lot of searching myself, coming to grips with my own alcoholism and depression. I didn't want to carry my baggage over to my children. I admired my mother for being so tough, but I didn't want to be a mother like her. More than anything, I was so afraid my girls wouldn't know I loved them. I've now been in recovery twenty-four years. I made sure my daughters grew up in a safe, loving home.

"I was sober when I had my daughters. My girls grew up in AA meeting rooms. I was determined to have a normal relationship with them, whatever 'normal' was.

"I had been sober one and a half years when Shannon, my oldest, was born. I was so terrified of making mistakes with her. I gave her a lot of attention and was almost paranoid in my fears of messing up, not giving her what she needed or not being a good enough mother. I was constantly watching other mothers and comparing myself, sometimes in a not too healthy way, but I learned to define what kind of mother I wanted to be—always honest and available.

"But mostly, I learned to be a good mother from AA. The basic principles: unconditional love and forgiveness. The basic rule: Say you're sorry. My mother carried resentments forever. She was verbally abusive and never said she was sorry. I made a decision that whatever happened, I would always be honest with my daughters, say 'I'm sorry' when I was wrong, accept them for who they are, and be supportive."

Karen not only practiced unconditional love with her daughters, she forgave and accepted her mother. In a thoughtful voice, without a trace of self-righteousness, she excused her mother's shortcomings.

"I didn't blame my mother. From the time I was one year old until I was eight, my father was in the hospital with multiple sclerosis. She did the best she could—not much nurturing and some violence."

Karen's compassionate attitude gave her unexpected influence.

"Late in my mother's life, she started having car accidents. I was afraid she'd kill herself or someone else. I confronted her about getting sober. I took her to AA meetings and she did it. My mother got sober."

Karen paused. The fact of her mother's strength, her ability to choose late-life sobriety, sank in. Then Karen's voice saddened.

"After my mother got sober, she got sick. The diabetes set in. My mother was a double amputee. She never complained. She never felt sorry for herself. She always got through it. In rehab, everyone loved her. She always had a kind word for anyone who helped her. And she remained sober.

"But even toward the end, we never talked about anything. I'd tell her, 'I love you.' But my mother, she couldn't quite say it back. Like Dana, my youngest daughter: There's only a fifty-fifty chance she'll say it back. When I hugged my mother, she stood wooden like a board. Same with Dana. My youngest is a tough cookie, just like her grandma.

"As difficult as our relationship was, I did respect her strength as she faced her alcoholism and diabetes in the last stage of her life."

Karen had one last story to tell, a story about tradition, about the wishes her mother had passed on to her and the blessings she did want to continue from generation to generation.

"One of the most emotional moments in my relationship with Shannon, my oldest daughter, came when she was coming up on her twenty-first birthday and getting ready to move to college in Virginia. Shannon was the first one in our family to go away to school, and it was extremely emotional for me.

"About a year before, I had seen an advertisement for hope chests in a magazine and cut it out. I still have my mother's hope chest. I wanted to give Shannon a hope chest, too.

"A couple of weeks before her birthday, my husband and I went to a furniture store. Wouldn't you know? The exact same hope chest I had seen in the ad was on the floor.

"I knelt beside it and just started crying.

"My husband was more than a little embarrassed.

"We took Shannon's hope chest home. When we gave it to her, I just cried and we held each other. I felt like I was passing on something from my mother and myself for her to hold all her dreams in."   ⋘

Judy Pohl's mother recently died.
    As Judy and I talked, she contemplated her mother's continuing influence on her and on her daughters.

A PRESENCE BEYOND QUESTION
Thoughts from Judy Pohl

"My mother was a chain-smokin', liquor-drinkin', foul-mouthed, dirty old lady. My girls loved her. They want to be just like her."

While Judy's daughters simply adored their grandmother, Judy's relationship with her mom was more complex. Judy recalled the lessons she learned in her childhood home.

"I grew up in a house where nobody talked about serious stuff. My parents never argued, never talked about money or raising kids, nothing important. When I left home, I wasn't prepared. The first time my husband and I had a fight, I thought we'd get divorced. I thought it was all over. I learned we could fight, go on, and love each other. When we had our girls, I vowed to talk about everything.

"When my mother was dying, I was totally open. I didn't want my girls to be shut out.

"Near the end, my mom wanted me to be with her all the time. She said she wanted to talk to me. I tried to talk about important things, about our past, about her faith. She didn't really want to talk. It wasn't her way. She just wanted me to be with her. Just sit with her.

"I'd come home from the hospital crying. At the dinner table, I told the girls everything. I felt it would be a disservice not to let them be a part of her death.

"Near the end, Anna, my oldest, visited her grandmother in the hospital. I gave them space. They joked and laughed, watched dumb TV shows. They held hands and cuddled up.

"My mom chose her time. Her doctor told me, 'If she goes home and smokes, she'll die.' We went into her house and purged it of every cigarette. I told her, 'When you go home, there won't be any cigarettes.' She said, 'There damn well better be.' She went home and smoked. She smoked up to the end.

"After the funeral, we had this bizarre wake. I broke out the last of her vodka, shook it up with her really disgusting powdered Manhattan mix, and poured cocktails for everyone. Then I found one cigarette, lit it, and passed it around. We drank and puffed and held our glasses high and made a final toast: 'This one's for Grandma.'

"My mom was buried at Arlington Cemetery. Catherine, my nineteen-year-old, wanted to visit her grave. I left her alone for a while. I came back to see Catherine leaning up against Mom's gravestone, puffing on a cigarette. Then, as we turned to go, she put the smoking cigarette on the stone and said, 'That one's for you, Grandma.'

"I thought it was kinda sweet.

"My mom never talked about her faith. But I knew she believed. She'd do little things to let me know. She bought me a rosary. I feel my mom with me. I talk to her. I say, 'Mom, will you watch out for Catherine? She's being a little stupid.'" ∽

Days after Mary Bernstein's mother died and her youngest daughter went off to college, she talked about taking stock. "Yesterday I decided: It's time for me to assess my inner life. I sat down. I looked inside myself. I saw nothing. Nothing. I decided: I have no inner life. I got up and did the dishes."

Mary, an artist with two daughters, interprets life from an odd perspective. She comes up with funny, quirky insights, with just a touch of the dark side, in moments of deadly seriousness. I know. Mary and I share a history. I count her among my dearest friends.

THE ARCHIVIST
Thoughts from Mary Bernstein

By the summer of 2000, Mary's father had died. Her mother was dying. My husband and I were in London. On Monday, August 7, Mary wrote:

HI, GUYS,

I just returned from another run to Maine on a "These might be her last hours" call. Mom, "the bounce-back kid," was improved when I got there, but she is almost blind. She can hardly find the food on the tray, never mind have the strength to spear it and bring it to her mouth.

Time with her is a weird meditation. We move between sitting on the porch (she can see the sea and the clouds somehow) and endless hours of TV, from dirt biking to *The Golden Girls.*

My mom needs a night nurse now. I spent one night sleeping in the chair next to her. Several times she woke up, suddenly disoriented, and I lifted her onto the commode.

Time is taking on new meaning: Every moment is short and precious, but also hours hang heavy when I am with her. It ain't like in the movies, when the important things are said and then there's a dramatic exit.

I hope to be able to stay home now to see Laila off to college on August 18. I'll have to take it as it happens.

LOVE, MARY

Mary was home on the day her youngest daughter, Laila, left for the West Coast. A day later, Mary was back in Maine, and her mother died. Mary and her brother made the arrangements. Mary drove back to her husband, her elusive inner life, and her home. Weeks later, she found herself facing generations of junk, an opportunity to take another assessment of life's meaning.

"I had all this stuff. Stuff my mother had left behind. Stuff my older daughter, Carrie, had stored. Stuff Laila, the younger one, had abandoned. Stuff I had forgotten. All of it left over. All of it squeezing out my space. I had no room left. I had to go through boxes and boxes. They were stacked on the sun porch. I sat in the middle of it all, walled in by cardboard, light from the windows barely able to reach me.

"I opened a container of my mother's things. I found this album, this archive of my childhood. My mom had saved everything about me. I leafed through newspaper clippings and photographs and report cards—all these tiny memorials to me. My mother made this book to capture every moment of my life. Sitting with it all, I saw how she had focused on me, how she had been my archivist, how her life revolved around watching my life. Suddenly, I wondered: 'Do I have this responsibility now? Am I supposed to gather up all my daughters' memorabilia and make albums for it?'

"The evidence of my mother's adoring attention sent me off sifting for the inner meaning of its ongoing legacy. Did my mother's uncritical eye, her unconditional approval, weaken or strengthen me? Did it limit my growth or facilitate it? Did it make me a more expressive artist or a less skillful one?

"Of course, asking those questions about my mother made me ask the same questions about myself. I'm at the age now, with my daughters reaching the end of adolescence, that I feel this inescapable guilt.

"Like my own mother, I had been so singularly focused on Carrie. My first baby girl. I was riveted to her every movement. Felt her every pain. Rejoiced in her every accomplishment. It was hard to distinguish her experience from my own. When she reached high school, that's when I started to wonder. I had watched her so carefully, always expecting and finding her brilliance. Was it too much pressure? Will she always have to find someone to give her unconditional approval? Is that a strength or a weakness? Carrie is wonderful and talented and smart and successful. I wonder if it's because of me or despite me?

"And Laila. My second. I was relatively detached. I didn't hover as much so. My anxiety level was so much less. She had more space to evolve on her own. I was able to sit back and watch with amazement. By the time she was in high school, I marveled at how such a normal, happy, popular kid could have come from me. Laila was still living at home while my mom was dying. She gave me strength. I wonder if she benefited from my neglect. Or not?

"In the end, I'll probably just leave all my daughters' photos and clippings in a big box. I'm not sure I'm cut out to be their archivist. Maybe that's good? Maybe it's not? It's just me. My legacy will be different than my mom's."

Our conversation didn't end with a laugh, only with a hug. After all, I also have two daughters and all the same questions. ∞

part four

Transitions and Transformations

Sandy's long silver hair flows down her back, held by a simple band. She jokes: "My daughter's adolescence—my hair turned white."

I comment on its shining beauty and give her my impression. "You look like a Wise Woman."

She laughs a soft, knowing laugh, nods, and doesn't object to my observation. Then, in a lilting southern accent, she sums up the last eight years.

"I *am* a wiser person now. I'm stronger. I'm more compassionate. I don't judge. I know the meaning of unconditional love."

This truth—that the act of nurturing our adolescent daughters transforms us as much as them—permeates the pages of *Ophelia's Mom*. I heard the difference in tone between mothers whose daughters were in the early throes of adolescence and those who had come to the end of the passage.

Mothers with daughters who were twelve or thirteen were more likely to speak with determined confidence or with anxious fear. The self-assured women made predictions: "My daughter's prepared for adolescence. She has a strong foundation, values, and self-esteem." Motherly pride sprang from their contributions. They believed they could steer a daughter's course, avoiding the whirlpools and maneuvering around the treacherous turns. They expected their hard-earned parenting skills to deposit their daughters, mature and safe, on the other side of adolescence. The more panic-stricken trembled, feeling helpless to protect their daughters from an onslaught of the nightmares they'd heard so much about. However, while anticipating that daughters would be transformed from children into young women, these mothers seldom anticipated how their own lives would be transformed.

Mothers who had traveled to the other side, whose daughters were eighteen or nineteen, were generally humbled by the journey. They had traveled through a territory that didn't match any of the maps they'd been given. They guided our daughters, using as our highest values the North Star by which they navigated. Over and over, like a daily horoscope, the mothers I heard from delivered powerful messages to their daughters: "You're beautiful and strong." "You can do anything you want to do, be anything you want to be." "It's your compassion and open mind that bring meaning to your life." "The judgments of the world don't matter. Find an inner voice that bathes you in love." "You won't be able to mold yourself into this culture's image of perfection. You can only be perfectly yourself." In sending those messages again and again, we come face-to-face with the limits of our own power.

Our daughters control when they deposit our good wishes and values into their psyches and when they return them to sender. Still, by the time they leave adolescence, the sheer dogged repetition of our messages ensures they reach the mark. But the target they strike may not be the one we aimed at. As one mother pointed out with profound insight, "The messages rubbed off on *me*. I started hearing my own voice. I came through my daughters' adolescence ready to fly." Love boomerangs.

We generally come out the other side of our daughters' adolescence wiser, stripped of innocent arrogance, purged of unfounded apprehensions, and clothed more comfortably in our identities. It's often like being purified in a washing machine. We go through the agitation and spin cycles again and again before we come out clean.

holding on to values

⌒

From I WISH FOR YOU, MY DAUGHTER
by Marianne Peel Forman

I wish for you a place
that you can call your own,
like Alabama and its
    everlasting kudzu
that is unstoppable and
    determined,
like Berkeley,
all tie-dyed and overgrown
    with incense.

I wish you nights when you
    pull off the side of
a country road and dance in
    the headlights of
your car
with the radio shouting out
    your window
or just moving to the song in
    your head,
creating shadows that no one
    can see
because the spotlight is on
    you,
in you,
and the dance is of your own
    design.

I wish you the moments
    when
you learn to embrace those
    too-big feet,
the neck that goes on forever,
those legs that seem to never
    end,
and the bump on your nose
that marks your heredity,
your Lithuanian roots.

I wish you a life
in which you go where your
    spirit takes you,
feeding your restlessness
with dreams and songs,
refusing to let life pass you by,
letting your own yellow scarf
blow and blow
in the gentlest of desert
    breezes . . .

⌒

M others launch daughters into womanhood with the best
of good wishes, with high hopes that girls will love themselves without compromise and discover a world without pain. In
reality, our daughters head straight into confused and unsettling

times. Meryl Brownstein wrote to express a concern shared by mothers of our generation.

"I started reading *Ophelia Speaks,* but I couldn't get through it. I found it very disturbing. I wondered the whole time: What's wrong? What's going on? Like most mothers, I just want my kids to make it into adulthood confident and sane. I struggle with trying to inject values into my kids in a way that gives them freedom and confidence."

Growing up in the sixties, we thought we had paved the way to a better world. We assumed that our movements—the civil rights movement, the women's movement, the antiwar movement, the new age movement—laid a shining road to tolerance, equality, freedom, and spirituality.

Now, with our own daughters coming into womanhood, we turn around to find we left their path littered with sex, drugs, and rock and roll, mired in glitter, with values spattered in mud. With all the flashy distractions, sometimes we feel like we're towing them toward goodness with gossamer thread and beckoning them toward virtue with a penlight.

Basic respect is an old-fashioned value that mothers struggle to infuse in daughters. But in an age of ambiguity, respect for self, others, and spirit challenges our daughters' personal strength and taxes their tolerance.

Encouraging Self-respect

Patricia Raglin was determined to nurture a feminist. She succeeded. But even this success story has had its bittersweet moments.

BASEBALL RULES
by Patricia Raglin

My daughter, Melissa, loved playing baseball. She played girls mixed with boys from age seven until she turned thirteen. She then switched to girls' fast-pitch softball. She was tired of dealing with the men of baseball.

But while she played baseball, my daughter, Melissa Raglin of Boca Raton, stood up for herself and womankind.

Melissa was a precious gift. I had a hard time getting pregnant and ultimately went through all kinds of procedures until I actually conceived. I was extremely protective. I decided early: I was going to make her a more assertive and confident person than I had ever been.

The nursery school complained that even at age two, Melissa bullied the five-year-olds, jumped up to hit them. So it started early. I encouraged her to "go for it" or "do it!" All my life, I had been told "Girls don't act that way" and asked "Are we ladies?" You know, the regular junk that kept women in their place.

When I went to sign my son up for baseball, Melissa tagged along.

I had always loved baseball but never got to play. I had been a Junior Oriole in Baltimore. In the sixties, I even rode the bus alone from Towson, Maryland, to inner-city Baltimore to go to games.

Melissa was a different story. As soon as her brother was signed up for T-ball, she said, "What about me? I want to play baseball!" She was six years old. Luckily, the league gladly accepted girls. The coaches asked Melissa if she would like to play T-ball like her brother. She immediately said, "No! I want to play real baseball!"

That was the beginning. Her brother played a few years, but baseball bored him. Melissa kept playing. She loved it. She hated standing around in the field, so she made herself learn how to play catcher. She wanted to be busy for the whole game. She got to be quite good at it.

I really loved hanging back and listening to the mothers of the boys as the new teams formed each year. "Look, it's a girl!" "Why doesn't she play softball?" I smiled and just waited until the season began. It never took long for the other women to be proud of her, too.

Melissa was a good catcher. She could hit, too. My daughter was an asset to the team. I'm not saying she was the best player or anything. Her running was not great. She didn't throw as powerfully as some of the boys. But she did make herself part of the team.

It was the end of the season and during the playoffs when the whole fiasco broke out.

A coach for the opposing team stopped the game and pulled an old, dirty, boy's athletic cup out of his team's bat bag. This man ordered Melissa, "Put it on." He was insisting Melissa place a boy's athletic cup in her underpants.

I was horribly upset for my daughter. I was literally yelling at the umpire, outraged that they had embarrassed Melissa like that. Of course, Melissa refused to back down and obey their stupid rules. I backed her up. The men ejected her from the playoff game.

I spent all the next day trying to find out if the league could make her wear a boy's athletic cup. I tried to find out if other girls playing baseball were wearing such things. I came up with nothing. Melissa was crying, all upset. I asked her, "Melissa, do you want to play baseball? Do you want to give in and wear the cup? Do you want to fight this thing? Or do you want to quit? Whatever you decide, I will back you up."

Melissa decided to fight. Boy, was I proud! She wasn't a pushover! She was going to make a difference in the world.

Man, I would have crawled in a hole. When I was twelve, I would have let people walk all over me. This was great! I told her, "Then we'll fight. Get ready, girl. We are going to battle!"

I got the ball rolling by making contacts with NOW and a few friends in the media. I got my fifteen minutes in front of the camera. But mostly, it was great sitting back and letting Melissa lead the way. I was so excited that people were paying attention to my little girl. She was making a worldwide stand for women, and she was only twelve years old.

Melissa Raglin made headlines around the world. She managed to make a national youth-league association wake up and change their rules. But in the midst of all the clamor, she somehow lost herself.

Later, Melissa became extremely embarrassed. Now, at fifteen, she refuses to acknowledge her bravery. She is extremely hostile to the mention of it. I think she was ridiculed at school. I don't know by whom. Maybe a teacher. Maybe other girls. My Ophelia is still a strong individual, yet she's afraid to make waves. She's scared she'll be ridiculed again. Melissa forbids anyone to talk about the whole episode.

In this age of instant e-mail, the Internet, and media news, she doesn't quite realize how fantastic she really was. I can't help it. I am still quite proud. I wish I could have gotten her a college scholarship or a trophy for her stand.

I guess in a way, I am living my life over in my daughter's life. ⌒

Feminists who worked hard to claim their value sometimes find their daughters' attitudes escape comprehension. The personal is the political. Feminism meets Girl Power.

I couldn't help but eavesdrop. The woman at the next table had a point of view, and she wasn't speaking softly.

"Suddenly, my daughter is hot. Really hot. Her body curves in all the most enticing places. This child is proud of her cleavage. She's fourteen and she flaunts it. The other day, I walked down the street with her and I saw the boys drool. I hated it. I loathed those lusty eyes popping out of their pimply faces. I detested that she lured them.

"At her age, I was different. I brandished a copy of *The Feminine Mystique*, wore gray turtlenecks, sensible jeans, and a no-nonsense attitude: 'Boy: Don't you even *think* of checking me out.'

"I thought, 'Feminism is lost on my daughter.' She says, 'I'm a Girl Power girl.' I had no idea what that meant.

"Then one day, when she didn't see me, I spied its meaning. A boy dared to make a semilewd comment. She spun around, gave him the finger, stared him down, and put him in his place. He skulked away, totally embarrassed.

"I figured, 'Hey, maybe my daughter's not beyond hope.'"

Like Patricia Raglin and the anonymous woman at the corner table, Lynda Goldstein puffs up with pride at the mention of her daughter. Lynda is a New York State legislator. Her daughter, Mollie, is a political powerhouse, a Yalie on the rise. Lynda isn't shy about taking credit for her daughter's activism. After all, Mollie has been tagging along since she was six years old, handing out campaign literature with Daniel Patrick Moynihan and cheering on the floor of the Democratic convention.

Even with all this careful modeling, Lynda couldn't entirely protect Mollie from being belittled. Lynda spoke about one such violation.

THE LEGISLATOR AND HER DAUGHTER
Thoughts from Lynda Garner Goldstein

"I modeled the strong, politically active woman, but Mollie had to hold on to her own identity. She had to be strong. It wasn't always easy for her. There were assaults on her ego.

"Like sophomore year in high school: An English teacher told her, 'Mollie, why don't you lose the glasses? Get a crop top. Go tell that hunk over there that you want to have a good time for an hour.'

"Mollie was so upset. That comment did touch on her insecurities.

"I was outraged. I talked with the teacher. This was a woman teacher. She told me, 'I thought I was being a caring adult.' I was incredulous.

"Around the same time, another teacher offered another morsel of 'wisdom.' He said, 'Mollie, sometimes you just have to let the guy win.'"

Bolstering Tolerance

The ugly face of bigotry wears different makeup from one generation to the next.

During the days when Dr. Martin Luther King, Jr., still lived and Bull Connor spewed hate, heroes and villains were easy to identify. As an adolescent, I had no difficulty choosing a part to play. The call for a cast of thousands beckoned good-hearted people to the March on Washington and the march to Selma. I hopped on buses. A face in a crowd of thousands, I sat at the foot of the Lincoln Memorial and walked beside Alabama railroad tracks singing "We Shall Overcome." But times have changed. Ideals have been diluted by reality. Good hasn't overcome prejudice with strokes of an enlightened president's pen. Victims and villains, the righteous and the racists, no longer play stereotypical roles. Now scraping away at the facade of prejudice exposes mothers and daughters to disturbing complexity.

In 1966 I lived in Roxbury, Massachusetts. I was nineteen and the only white person on my block. People in the neighborhood looked out for me. My landlord, the other tenants, all assumed I was a well-intentioned white person. In 1985 Manju's friendship with Lorraine brought me back to that neighborhood.

Manju was thirteen and our family had just moved to Framingham, a town accurately described as a patch of Middle America located a few miles west of Boston. Months earlier, Manju had sat at the dining room table, drinking hot chocolate and playing Uno. Staring at her hand of cards, she made a considered decision.

"Mom, I'm going to be friends with Lorraine."

I had no idea who Lorraine was. I trusted that Manju had identified a potential friend at her new school. I was pleased.

She explained, "Lorraine's new, too. Kids pick on her."

Manju had befriended a scapegoated classmate before. I had never been able to understand why girls had been cruel to this child. Trying to unravel another mystery of girl social order, I asked, "Why don't kids like her?"

"Lorraine's black."

Manju had answered without a trace of hesitation. My heart caved in.

Lorraine spent most afternoons and many weekends at our house. Manju formed few other friendships.

Then summer came. Lorraine's mother had had enough. Too many prejudicial slogans had been slung in her daughter's face. She had moved away from the inner city, hoping to provide a safer environment and a better education. It hadn't worked. They were moving back to Roxbury.

As Lorraine hugged me good-bye, she asked, "Nina? Can Manju come to my birthday party?"

"Of course Manju can come. I'll drive her into town. It'll be a great chance for me to show Manju my old neighborhood."

The day of Lorraine's party was perfect for a summer drive. The car windows wide open, we sped through Boston's western suburbs toward the inner city. I found my way down Blue Hill Avenue to the corner of Geneva Avenue, past Jeremiah Burke High School. Finally I faced my old building, the site of my first apartment. The granite Victorian still stood, but all the pride had been stripped from its three stories. The windows were broken, the steps trashed. Across the street, the open field where children once played was strewn with garbage. At the end of the block, the Safeway, the only grocery store in the neighborhood, was boarded shut and decorated with graffiti.

We crawled back into the traffic on Blue Hill, then stopped for a red light. A gentleman in a neighboring car signaled for my attention. "Excuse me. You should close your windows. You're not safe here." I pulled away, mumbling, "But I used to live here." Manju studied my face and observed, "Mom, things have changed." We rolled up our windows. In this complex time, what does a privileged white mother say?

H urtful comments meant to belittle are inflicted on girls because of their gender, their religion, their race, and their sexual orientation. The cruelty of kids is sometimes pure bigotry. With good intentions, Jan Tramontano deposited her oldest daughter in a den of anti-Semitism. She talked about the results.

ESSENCE IN PREJUDICE
A Story from Jan Marin Tramontano

My husband and I wanted a school district better than the one in the city. We packed up our family and moved to this suburb.

But there was a drawback—it was a very Christian community with little diversity. I'm Jewish. My husband's not. We have a rich spiritual life, but it's always been family-focused. We've celebrated the holidays at home, never belonged to a synagogue. Still, the mere appearance of our Judaism made my daughter alien to her classmates.

Rachel was eleven years old when she came home from school one afternoon and asked me, "Why do Matt and Rickie call me names because I'm Jewish? What does 'jewin' down the price' mean, anyway?"

I took a deep breath, trying to find an acceptable answer to questions that enraged me. Every day brought another derogatory expression. These kids had no exposure to difference. They said cruel things to Rachel, things no one has ever said to me, not in my entire life. They called my daughter a kike.

In the face of this hateful taunting, Rachel gathered her strength. She said, "Listen, Mom. If I'm going to suffer from being Jewish, I should know what it means to be Jewish. I know you and Daddy have always told me I'm sort of both—Jewish and Catholic—and that I'll probably pick one as mine when I grow up. But I don't want to wait. I've already decided."

As I started to interrupt, she put her hand out as if to say "Just hear me out."

"No offense, but I don't really see how you can be both. You're either one or the other. They're not even close to being the same. I feel Jewish. I don't know what it means, but that's how I feel. The jerks at school seem to think I'm Jewish, so this is what I want to do. I want to learn all about it."

"Honey, what does that mean? You want to join a temple and go to Hebrew school?" I asked, trying to hide the surprise in my voice.

"Yup. I want to learn it all. Hebrew and everything. Oh. And I want to have a bat mitzvah, too. Just like my cousins."

And so she did.

With Rachel fully in charge, we went to a number of temples in our area, attended services. And it was Rachel who talked to the rabbis to see if they were friendly. At one temple, she turned to me and said, "This is it. It feels like home."

Rachel worked diligently, but it didn't seem hard for her because of her interest. She studied the language, learned Jewish history and prayers. She chose her own bat mitzvah date because she wanted the Torah chapter that told about the Ten Commandments.

On the day of her bat mitzvah, Rachel was radiant. She sang like an angel, as if she was always meant to be standing there. Both sides of the family, Jewish and Catholic alike, were smiling through tears, beaming with pride.

We've traveled a hard road between then and now. I recall her determination most acutely when we're at our lowest points. And I believe with all my heart that Rachel's wisdom, her knowledge of what path is right for her, will sustain her.

That's the kind of person she is, a girl who has had the strength to transform prejudice into self-knowledge. ✑

These stories barely scratch the surface of prejudice. Beneath the obvious bigotry—chauvinism, racism, anti-Semitism, and gay-bashing—mothers and daughters struggle to live compassionately and courageously, despite the accidents of birth that make some of us privileged and others of us oppressed.

Nurturing Humanity

I've always wanted my daughters, Manju and Sara, to indulge in bold self-assertions of their inner worth. And I've always hoped they'd shy away from overvaluing material possessions.

Still, I love clothes. I can certainly be faulted for my lifelong obsession with fashion at a bargain. So when Sara went through an adolescent growth spurt, she had no difficulty convincing me that she needed a whole new wardrobe.

I sensed an extravagant opportunity for mother/daughter bonding. I proposed an overnight expedition to the closest clothes mecca: Boston. I dug up a tattered coupon and booked a hotel in Harvard Square. Sara and I hopped in my mini Mazda and sped off, leaving the dead malls of western Massachusetts behind. Buzzing along the Mass Pike, we shared one overriding goal: to shop until we dropped. Visions of trendy shops and bargain-basement prices danced through our heads.

We deposited the car at our hotel and headed for Urban Outfitters. As we wove our way through the twenty-something hordes in the square, the sight of sleeping beggars intruded on our materialistic pursuit. We weren't deterred.

By evening, we had accumulated bagfuls of teenage fashions. As we trudged back to the hotel, Sara's burgeoning wardrobe in tow, the homeless people had come to life. We weren't prepared. We carried too many packages and no spare change.

At the hotel, we pulled one new treat after another out of Sara's shopping bags. We laid the fruits of her springtime spree on one double bed. We settled back, rested, and declared it a good haul.

But we did not sleep. We talked about our materialistic discomfort. What to do about beggars? Do we give? Will our coins go for alcohol? Drugs?

Next morning, we headed off on the subway to downtown Boston, Filene's Basement our destination. Before facing the highly competitive squish of women in search of discount designer goods, we took a tea and muffin break. While sitting at a sidewalk table, we noticed a man in a wheelchair positioned outside Au Bon Pain with a cup in his lap.

Suddenly, for the first time in my life, I knew what to do about a beggar. Sara and I walked over to the panhandler. I asked, "Would you like us to buy you breakfast?" My invitation transformed this man. His bent torso straightened, his dulled eyes twinkled, his limp head nodded with excitement. He hurriedly wheeled himself into the restaurant and up to the counter. In a voice ringing with pride, he ordered his meal: "Coffee. Blueberry muffin. Orange juice, fresh-squeezed." I paid. Sara took his tray. I pushed his wheelchair. He directed us to an outdoor table. This happy man settled into being just another customer sitting at an outdoor café on a warm spring morning. As Sara and I left, we turned to drink in the picture we had created. I thought, "Now, this. This is good."

It wasn't that Sara and I were so generous. I mean, really! Just to see the contrast between our financial privilege and the life of a handicapped beggar is appalling. And that's the point. That day we saw the discrepancy. For the first time in my life, I didn't avert my eyes in shame. I didn't let my own embarrassment obliterate the humanity of a street person. Instead, Sara and I looked straight at him. We spoke to him. We made human contact.

I don't remember one piece of clothing Sara bought that day.

I will never forget the joy we bought for the price of a coffee, a blueberry muffin, and orange juice, fresh-squeezed.

I trust the same is true for Sara.

Mothers find ways to fill their adolescent daughters with a spirit of generosity. Marianne Peel Forman, a wonderful poet who lives in the Midwest, wrote about her method.

STUFF
by Marianne Peel Forman

My daughters tell me
that we need to buy
a bigger house,
that we no longer have room
for all the stuff.
And yet our home

modest in square footage
for this Midwest place
is mansion in dimension
to over ninety percent of the
    homes
around the world.

Instead
of finding a real estate agent,
I take them to a shelter
early Saturday morning
to prepare and serve food
for the homeless,
for the people down on their luck,
for those who have all their stuff
in their pockets
or on their backs.

They are surprised
by the size of the kitchen
and the dozens of pans of chicken
they must baste, turn, and baste
    again.
Over a hundred will come
just before noon,
a veteran cook tells them.

The mashed potatoes
are real and lumpy
and my daughters stir in
extra butter
because they like the flavor
it leaves on their tongues at home.

Children come,
mostly,
and mothers
who balance them
on tired shoulders and hips.

Their part in the line
was to serve the dessert,
the cake they had cut
in perfect squares,
making certain that the frosting
was evenly distributed
among the single plates.

One man asked,
"Which flavor would you
    recommend,
young ladies?"
and both daughters pointed to
    the chocolate cake
rich with layers
and creamy with topping,
not dry like the yellow cake.
They offered this moistness to
    the man
and I watched the food pass from
    their small
hands
to his.

The ride home was unusually
    quiet
and still.
All of us
without telling each other
burrowed through our rooms,
our drawers,
our overflowing boxes
that afternoon.
Separating temporary pleasures
from lasting treasures.

I found boxes
outside of each room
that night,
boxes of possessions
to give away.
And, like fresh moist chocolate
    cake,
I tasted the knowing
   that my daughters
now possessed.

Instilling Spirituality

M others often hope daughters will find a transcendent strength. For many, religion provides a path to spirit. For others, spirit resides within.

Wendy Elliott was keen to talk about adding a spiritual dimension to her daughter's life through role-modeling and ritual. "I'm a practicing Buddhist. I can't stress enough how important I feel a spiritual foundation has been for Tara.

"Throughout my relationship with Tara, I've modeled a way of being that's given her strong tools. Since early on, I've taken two hours a day for myself to meditate and run. She learned, 'Mommy needs time for herself.' She's seen that a spiritual practice is a priority.

"For me, during difficult times, my imagination kept me alive. I've sent Tara to the Waldorf School. I make up rituals. For her twelfth birthday, we had a Goddess costume party. For All Souls Night, we put up pictures of all the people and animals in our family who have died. For her next birthday, we'll do a coming-of-age ritual. We're planning a canoe trip to an island with girl and women friends. In the evening, we'll have a women's circle around a fire. We'll encircle her, giving her thoughts of love and strength. Then we'll all leave her for a solo night on the island. The next morning, she'll swim from the island to shore."

Wendy feels certain her planned coming-of-age ritual will imbue her daughter with spirituality, enabling her to migrate through adolescence with strength.

The traditional bat mitzvah serves the same purpose in Judaism. I've known a good number of mothers who've guided daughters through bat mitzvah and coming-of-age ceremonies. Alicia Samuels created a rite of passage for her daughter, Nadine. Alicia gathered the most important women in Nadine's life in one room. Alicia described her creation.

"My mother and my sister came. Virginia, the woman who raised me, was there. A few close friends, my cousins, her godmother, all sat in the circle. Every one of us spoke to Nadine. I talked about how she started out in my circle, in my body, how we shared the same circle. I told her I felt like I was giving her to a larger circle. I cried. Nadine sat silent the entire time. She just took it all in.

"The next day we had this huge event outside this Victorian mansion, under a tent. People she chose gave talks about the teaching of world's major religious traditions. Nadine's dad led Sufi dancing. Nadine loves Sufi dancing. She performed a piano piece and gave a speech.

"I put it all together for Nadine, but after her ritual was over, I realized it was as much a coming-out for me as for her. I put out to my whole family and to my husband's family who I am by what I created for Nadine. Before Nadine's ceremony, these people didn't know what my values were and what was important to me. I didn't plan it that way, but that's what happened. I don't know how much spirituality I communicated to Nadine."

Few of us ever know how we've influenced a daughter's faith. Spirituality is such an internal matter. Whether we are Christian, Jewish, Muslim, Buddhist, Hindu, or subscribers to a personal faith, we can never clearly see our daughters' relationship to Spirit. Still, we get glimpses. I got one of those glimpses the night Margaret died.

When Margaret Left Her Body

The Gosselins—Margaret, Philip, Sathya, and Gabrielle—were our dearest family friends. Our extended family, really. Margaret, Philip, and baby Sathya had been at my side when Sara was born. My girls—Manju, then eight; Sara, just ten months old—and I sat with Margaret while she gave birth to Gabrielle.

Now, sixteen years later, at one-forty A.M., our family walked through the darkness, out our back gate, toward the Gosselins' house. Phil had called. Margaret had died an hour ago.

We found Sathya and Gabrielle in their living room. Sathya received our hugs. Manju sat close to Sathya, the young man she called her brother. Gabrielle, her body curled into the arm of the sofa, her head buried in her arms, couldn't look up to meet our eyes. Sara collapsed around her, enfolding her best friend in her arms. Michael and I walked upstairs with Philip. We walked into Margaret and Philip's bedroom, took our place next to Margaret's dead body, and meditated.

Gazing at the empty vessel that had once held the most vibrant woman I had ever known, I faced the gray pallor of Margaret's corpse.

Suddenly my mother-mind sprang into turmoil. Did I want my daughters to see death? I was cross-legged on the floor, suspended between the impulse to protect my children and the recognition of their maturity, when I heard the door open. Manju tiptoed by me and stroked my head. I reached up and clasped her fingers. She passed and sat next to her dad. Moments later, Sara stepped gently into the room and sat by my side. I placed my hand on her knee. She rested her palm over mine. Over the next minutes, I inspected my daughters' faces, looking for clues to their emotional experience. In Manju, now a woman, I saw strength. In Sara, still an adolescent, I saw serenity. I closed my eyes and heard Margaret's spirit laughing, bouncing around the room like a ball propelled by freedom.

We left the Gosselins as the sun was rising. Sitting in our kitchen, we talked. Manju felt gratitude—glad she had made it home from New York to spend just a bit of time with Margaret before the life was fully emptied from her body, and glad to be with Philip, Gabrielle, Sathya, Michael, and me. Sara felt at peace in the presence of the dead body. She had looked at it and known "It was just a thing. Margaret had gone somewhere else."

pushed into self-discovery

PRISONER OF LOVE
by Janis Greve

My daughter sits next to me
   on the couch,
painting my nails in reckless
   strokes,
not caring whether she stays
   within the lines
or how much she smudges.
I have made my choice from
   the crowd
of tall-hatted bottles, chosen
   a color
I could live with.
She has already painted her
   own nails
and now moves on to mine as
   if she were running
down the keys of a piano,
   playing scales,
fingers flying.
We are one continuous series,
a twenty-digit picket fence.
She's a stern mistress,
   lacquering up each

finger's face as if drowning it
   duly
with love, silencing its
   complaints
This is for your own good, her
   manner says.

This is so like her,
how she's taken my hands
   and changed them,
wrenched them into fresh
consideration
every time I grip a pan
or turn a page, thumbnails
   bobbing up
like small faces I didn't
   recognize, copper-
   colored with tiny
teddy-bear decals.

Our daughters paint us with their strokes and remake us into new selves.

We lovingly prod them toward maturity, hoping to mold them into women of character. Then throughout their adolescence, they push and spin us in circles until we stand up straight.

By the time they leave home, the tables have turned. Our daughters have changed us as much as we've changed them.

S orting out her daughter's stuff, Connie Petersen found her own values. Connie discovered her own most closely held values in her daughter's messy room.

"SAVE! THANK YOU!"
by Connie J. Petersen

Katie's room is always a mess. Why does it bother me so much? She leaves her shoes out in front of the closet—black furry slippers resembling gigantic bear paws, brown Doc Marten sandals, Steve Madden clunky-heeled monsters, gym shoes known simply as Skechers, and Oxy canvas sneakers that look like clown shoes—as if they couldn't fit inside the space just two feet away where they could be out of sight, let alone out of the way. Her desk is cluttered with pictures and cards and notes and ribbon and paper, so much that you can't find an inch of clean space. And the floor! Green and silver pom-poms, a white bra, blue glitter nail polish, a dollar bill, the high school yearbook, a handwritten note about a baby-sitting job (God only knows if she found that reminder), a pair of scissors, strips of construction paper, the blue laundry basket full of clean clothes. I tripped over books and bags and other piles when I attempted to find the remote control to the CD player she'd forgotten to turn off before she left for school.

I sigh a lot when I enter her room, wondering how she is like this when her mom is so neat and holier-than-thou, in that department at least. My bed is always made unless I am sleeping in it. Books are stacked neatly on my reading table. Dirty clothes are in the hamper, clean ones hung in my closet or folded tidily in the drawers of the dresser. My husband is orderly about his surroundings (especially the garage). We all think that Katie generally takes after him. Even her two brothers, PJ and Joey, occupy rooms that stay reasonably neat. So where does she pick up this bad habit?

As I frowned at the mess and vowed to "discuss" this with her the minute she got off the school bus that afternoon, I noticed one little penciled note on the first shelf above her desk. In her handwriting, it said, "Save. Thank you!" For the cleaning lady, I supposed. And on top of the note lay three little leaves from her grandma and grandpa's trees.

When my parents died, our friends back in Northbrook gave us trees in memory of them. The young trees were planted across the street from our house there, on the golf course, by the seventh tee. My dad's tree was first, planted so I could see it from my bedroom window, and Katie could see it from hers, too. When Mom was still alive, one evening she and I rode a golf cart to see my dad's new tree, and she said to me, "So where are you going to put mine?" Then we clipped a couple of leaves from his tree for her to press in the family Bible. Four years later, hers was planted just across the cart path from his. They are young honey locusts that grow above small granite plaques with my mom and dad's names on them. And on a regular basis we went to those trees to talk to them, Grandma and Grandpa, to pray, really.

At Christmastime we always put a pine wreath with a red velvet bow at the base of each tree. Against the fresh white snow, the wreaths made the bare little trees look stately and warm. Every Christmas day our whole family went over to the trees together. We even took the dog, Bailey, so he could run up and down the hills of the golf course. We went to the trees often, but the ritual was particularly important on special days like Christmas.

On the first anniversary of my mother's death, I experienced healing from planting flowers around her tree. I lugged three pink petunias (high tolerance for dry, hot weather), a small shovel, and a full watering can over to the golf course in midday. Under the May sunshine, I felt Mom's spirit approving my determination as the golfers who passed by simply looked at the lady digging, planting, weeding, and crying. Then they hit their balls and went on. The trees looked spry with their tender, green, featherlike leaves. They stood erect and obedient in the warm Illinois springtime. No matter what the season, those trees were always there for us. Growing and changing.

Then there was the day we moved. The day we knew that we wouldn't have the trees across from our house. The day we'd have to say good-bye to our trees, Grandma and Grandpa, and move across the country. Oh, of course the trees would be there. And of course they'd grow. And of course we'd see them again when we visited. And besides, they were only trees, anyway. But it was a heavy moment, as if we were saying good-bye to my mom and dad forever.

Jim, my husband, took our car on the cross-country trip. Right before Joey, Katie, PJ, Bailey, and I left for O'Hare, we decided to pay one final visit to the trees. It was an unseasonably warm November morning. We said good-bye to Grandma and Grandpa and told them we'd be moving to

Seattle, but they'd always be in our hearts. Always. Then we snipped a few leaves from the branches to keep in our Bibles or journals or wherever. We'd put them in a special place, to remember. We tearfully walked away, each of us with honey locust leaves in our hands.

Mine are in my journal beside my writings about the move. But Katie's are on her desk where she can see them, and where they reminded me that of all the occasionally bothersome things about family members—messy rooms, bad habits—there is goodness. Katie is truly more giving than I am. When she was in first grade, she prayed every night, "God bless all the people I know and all the people I *don't* know!" And now this high school sophomore has tied to the headboard of her bed a nylon designer cosmetic bag where she tucks favorite sayings and blessings and goals in her life. Inside this special silver pouch is a note she has written:

> Here lie my beliefs, my treasured memories, loved ones, quotes I have been given, and a glimpse of my heart. I can go anywhere I choose. Just watch me.
>
> —Katie Petersen

Amid the spiral notebooks, polish remover, phone directories, and candy wrappers, I was blessed to find what matters. Being clean is *not* next to godliness. But being loving is.

"Save!" I say to myself. Save every last bit of it. Even the piles of dirty laundry. (Well, okay, maybe just the clean pile.)

And "Thank you," I say to God's work through my daughter. ∽

Sometimes adolescence wreaks havoc on daughters' souls. In the midst of straightening our daughters' tangled emotional lives, we sort out our own meaning and values.

As Laurie Hannah exhausted every effort to help her daughter, a new sense of self unexpectedly awakened.

IN A MOTHER'S TEARS
Thoughts from Laurie Hannah

As a mother, my intuition told me that something just wasn't right. Deborah, my fourteen-year-old daughter, had changed into someone I hardly knew.

Then, this past August, she was diagnosed with bipolar disorder. Also known as manic depression, this mental illness is characterized by drastic mood swings.

When I was first told the diagnosis, I was somewhat relieved. There was a reason for the extreme and bizarre behavior I was witnessing. I began a crusade to educate myself, joining parent advocacy groups, going to conferences, reading books, collecting information, networking with other parents, networking with the school, and going to counseling. I immediately went on family medical leave, working a reduced schedule so I could closely monitor Deborah until she stabilized.

I tried to push all of this new knowledge on Deborah. I expected her to react positively to my assistance. She didn't; she felt controlled and smothered, and lashed out even more. Since August, my life has become an emotional roller coaster.

As a mother, I felt if I tried hard enough, I could "save" Deborah from this awful illness. I figured I could "fix" everything. Her life would be "normal." My daughter wouldn't have to suffer. But Deborah is in denial and won't accept any of my help. I want so desperately to protect her.

Yet I am slowly realizing that Deborah must want to be helped— nothing can be pushed on her. I am constantly fighting the urge to push my ideas on her; after all, "Mother knows best." Instead, I try to be subtle with her. Then I retreat to my bedroom and cry. I struggle between elation (when she's in a good mood), anger (when she won't speak to me), and hate (when she's swearing at me). My heart aches for Deborah, and each tear I cry represents my love for her. Still, I have to learn: I can throw my energy in, but I can't take ownership of her illness.

At thirty-seven, I've been through tragedy. When I was being sexually abused and was trapped in a violent marriage, I felt "poor me." Only after these traumatic periods were over was I able to see the lessons inside the crisis. This time it's different. I see the lessons during the crisis, while it's happening. With Deborah, I'm right in the middle of it, and yet I can feel my own growth.

Before Deborah's diagnosis, I had been in a funk—unsettled, feeling something had to change, but I didn't know what. I had made a list of all the factors contributing to my funk.

And I prayed for guidance.

Then Deborah was diagnosed.

I asked myself, "Is the diagnosis an answer? Is this how the Lord answered my prayer?"

I went back to my personal process. I took out my list.

~ I need more time with my girls
~ I need a flexible work schedule
~ I need to care for Deborah and explore new options for myself
~ I need to be more at peace with myself

Everything I needed to do for Deborah, I needed to do for myself. My list was validated.

I went to a career counselor at a nearby college. It's amazing. The Lord has put certain people in my path. She's one of them.

Throughout my life, I've worked in business and gotten jobs. I've done well, but I always felt something was missing. Then I'd leave. I've tried to figure out the source of my dissatisfaction. I've done test after test. Every test told me I was doing what I'm good at.

This counselor suggested I take a values test, to look at whether my work is compatible with my values. The results showed I care most about helping others and making a difference in the world. I care least about advancement and making money. It was a revelation to me. My whole life, I have never had work that's been aligned with my true values.

I decided to make a change, to do work I have passion for. I looked at my life. I've loved working as a personal trainer, and I compete in women's bodybuilding. I love everything to do with health and fitness. I set my goals:

~ To increase my knowledge of health and the body
~ To learn to help people holistically

This long-term direction has laid to rest a big concern of mine. I don't have to continue in the business field.

If my daughter hadn't been diagnosed, I wouldn't have reassessed my life so quickly. I increased my prayers. The Lord is answering them. I've been getting directions every day.

No pain. No gain. I feel like I finally understand. Pain is the price for growth—to be a better person, mother, and wife.

Now, in November, the medication is slowly helping to improve Deborah's condition and she receives weekly counseling. I've never prayed so much. It's out of my hands. ~

Like Laurie, Sandra Goldman found herself transformed by her daughter's adolescence. When Sandra's daughter turned into an embarrassment, Sandra was forced to rediscover her own lost independent spirit.

METAMORPHOSIS
A Story from Sandra Goldman

"My daughter used to be nerdy.

"In eighth grade, Maggie received the award for most outstanding student.

"I took pride in her accomplishments. I had absolutely loved being a mother. The early years were a joy and a delight. I stayed home until Maggie started school. In elementary school, teachers showered me with praise, telling me my daughter was intelligent, creative, loving, adorable. She received all these awards: most outstanding math student, most outstanding language-arts student, most outstanding artist.

"Maggie had no interest in winning those honors. I don't think she even unwrapped the boxes with her prizes inside. She wasn't competitive. She boycotted the ceremonies. She didn't want to be there. And she certainly didn't want her parents sitting in the audience beaming with satisfaction. Still, quite honestly, I was proud of my parenting.

"But all my pride and joy came to an abrupt halt.

"Right after Maggie's crowning school achievement, she went off to an art-history program for gifted and talented high school students. At the end of the summer, my husband and I picked her up.

"We arrived on campus. All the kids were walking across a quad. We wanted to get a glimpse of her, but we didn't want to intrude on her world. We were hiding behind a bush, peering out between the branches, watching the students walk toward us. I noticed this strange-looking girl. Her hair was blue. She wore baggy pants, cut off above the knee. On her head sat a clown hat. On her feet, combat boots.

"I said to my husband, 'I think that's Maggie.'

"He said, 'No . . . It can't be.'

"Of course it was Maggie.

"At the beginning of the summer, we had crossed the state line with our nerdy girl. At the end of the summer, we crossed the same state line with a transmuted adolescent, a girl with attitude. She sat in the backseat, refusing to talk and wearing headphones. I could hear these violent noises coming from her Walkman. I'd never heard those sounds before. I had no idea about the lyrics. We had always listened to classical music at our house.

Two months earlier, I had left with the town's most self-effacing outstand-ing student. I returned with the town's most visible nonconformist.

"This new look was the first in a series. After blue hair came shaved head. After shaved head came a self-inflicted bull-ring through her nose.

"For a while, she successfully hid the nose ring from me. Somehow she pushed it up inside her nose when she was at home. Then one day, I was walking through the mall. Just walking through the mall. I see Maggie, my daughter. She has a bull-ring in her nose.

"Okay. Next: She negotiates removing the bull-ring for a pierced eyebrow. I take her to a sanitary place.

"We had many colors of hair before she settled into her current style—dreadlocks. I have to say I find dreadlocks disgusting. They're matted, dirty hair. Dreadlocks are never washed. To keep them in, she puts this wax in them. They smell gross. Hers are pink.

"We live in this conservative town. With the advent of blue hair, Maggie became a misfit. I've noticed the discomfort of other parents. They stopped wanting their kids around her. I'd call to offer a ride. Moth-ers would say, 'Thanks, but she already has one.' I'd try to arrange for her to get together with old friends. The kids were always 'busy.'

"When Maggie started working at Barnes & Noble, in the café, these parents would come in to check her out. She told me, 'Parents of kids I played with in elementary school come in, order their coffee, sit down, and stare at me.'

"I can't entirely blame them. Sometimes even I look at her and think, 'This is what I produced?'

"Maggie has a reputation in this town. Like the other day: Her little sister met a girl at some school activity. As soon as the girl heard her last name, she nearly jumped up and down with excitement. She screeched, 'Oh my God. Maggie's your sister! She's my hero!' Around here, Maggie's famous. She painted a mural of hope. It was featured in a centerfold article in the local newspaper and won a national arts award. But her accomplishments don't matter to the other parents. Look at her. Those parents don't want to hear their thirteen-year-olds swooning with admi-ration for this grunge of mine.

"Maggie tells me, 'Mom, this place isn't good for you, either. It's poi-soned you and you don't even know it.' She's right.

"I went through a change when we moved to upper-middle-class suburbia. I adopted the mentality. I did all the soccer-mom activities. I lost myself and she lost me. I got sucked into the 'my kid is better than your kid' elitist structure.

"Maggie's taught me: I can't take in what people see. I have to hold on to my internal values.

"Still, I have to confess, I'm glad Maggie and I have different last names. (She has her dad's surname. I kept my maiden name.) I have a professional reputation to maintain. I run the youth programs for the city. Can you imagine? If people automatically knew she was my daughter?

"At graduation last spring: I'm sitting in the audience. I watch the graduating class. Every other kid has on a black cap and gown, no embellishments. Maggie has her robe hanging off her shoulders, gown open. She's wearing combat boots.

"A teacher stands up in front of the entire auditorium to give a speech about Maggie before giving her this award. The teacher is saying wonderful things about my daughter, talking about her talent, her values, and leadership. My parents are sitting next to me. Tears of pride are flowing down their cheeks. I'm just holding my breath, thinking 'Please. Maggie. Zip up your gown and don't say a word.'

"Maggie stands up, walks toward the podium. Her gown's flapping open. Then just as she arrives at the stage, she zips it closed. She walks up to the teacher, hugs her, says a courteous 'Thank you,' and walks off.

"I took a deep breath and rejoiced, 'Thank God.'

"My husband asks, 'Why can't we have a normal kid?' Then he answers his own question. 'We raised our daughter to have a mind of her own, and now she does.'

"Maggie's in New York now. In the city she's finding like-minded souls to link to. She fits in there.

"Before she left, she came home with a poster for a meditation class. She handed it to me and said, 'Mom, you have to go to this class. It's made for you. You have to meet this woman. She's just like you.'

"I travel across the state line to take this class. I get out of this town.

"My daughter left home and sent me to an environment where I feel like I belong, where I affirm my values, where I feel normal, where I can feel proud that I raised an eccentric soul who's going to do great things.

"And me? I'm getting more spiritual. I comfort myself by leaving both Maggie and myself to the cosmos. I tell myself that everything will turn out as it should. I'm getting back into activities that fill me up and make me happy." ∞

Throwing mothers into turmoil, pinning us down until we yell, "I give up. I promise. I'll be better"—perhaps that's the work of adolescent daughters. It's certainly the effect.

Judy Pohl has four daughters. Every one has left her stamp on Judy. Number one was the first to tear her apart and open her up to greater tolerance.

KICKING AND SCREAMING
A Story from Judy Pohl

"Anna, my oldest, talked to me about everything. The heaviest conversations were in the car.

"I remember sitting in a parking garage at the mall, and she's asking me about sex. 'How far should I go? What should I do?' She's being very technical about body parts.

"I got embarrassed, felt awkward. I mean: What's the line between my business and her life? I answered her questions as honestly as I could.

"She promised me she wouldn't have sex until after high school graduation. And she didn't. But one month after graduation, she did.

"She always said to me, 'I'll tell you anything.' Sometimes I didn't want to know. I'd put up my hand and say 'TMI'—too much information.

"That's the kind of relationship we had.

"Anna went off to college and got serious about a guy. Next thing I knew, it cooled off, but they stayed friends, good friends. I'd ask about their relationship. She'd just say, 'It's complicated.'

"Anna and Joe got an apartment together in Boston. Now they were roommates. I asked about sex. She said, 'We're not doing *that*.' They really were just roommates.

"One weekend, I took the train to Boston. I'm sitting with Anna in her kitchen. We're chatting, just talking. Somehow we start talking about homosexuality. For some reason, I have no idea why, I ask, 'Are you gay?'

"Anna says, 'Yes.'

"I don't know what I said next. I can't remember. I thought, 'Oh. My God.'

"I was heavy into Christian fundamentalism at the time. I worried, 'What will God think?'

"The rest of the conversation went foggy.

"The next day, I left to go back home. I had eight hours alone on a train to stew in my grief, doubts, fantasies, and questions. I had imagined a big wedding. Now there'd be no wedding. I had imagined grandchildren. Now there'd be no grandchildren.

"I had thought homosexuality was an unforgivable sin. I worried. I imagined Anna's lifestyle—wild parties, many partners, AIDS. Questions circled around my mind: 'Who do I tell?' 'What do I say?' I arrived home.

"I'm not the type to keep things to myself. I told my husband. He thinks Anna isn't really gay. He thinks it's a feminist way of identifying, that it's a phase.

"I think she really is gay. She says, 'I'm lesbian, Mom.' I don't know why I'm more comfortable with the word 'gay' than 'lesbian.' It's easier for me to say.

"Now it's a year and a half later, and I'm at peace.

"I was going through changes of my own. Fundamentalism was too narrow for me. Fundamentalism says you can't be saved if you're not Christian. I'd think, 'What about people who live out in the bush? Should people who never even heard of Jesus suffer?' Then, with my own daughter being gay, I'd ask myself, 'Who's to say that love between two people, any two people, is wrong?' I read the Bible. Those passages they quoted in church didn't read quite the way they said. I didn't see the scriptures damning gays. I listened to Anna. I became less and less concerned about the rules.

"Who the hell am I to say there's only one way to love, only one way to salvation? I do think promiscuity is wrong. So does Anna.

"Actually, I think Anna taking up with alternative religions put more tension into our relationship than her being gay.

"Faith is important to me. As soon as she went to college, she dropped her faith like a hot potato. That was okay. Lots of kids bag church as soon as they leave home. I didn't mind that much.

"But then she comes home Thanksgiving Day. I'm chopping and mixing and cooking and baking. She walks into the kitchen and announces she's into Wiccan. I'm standing over this pot of steaming mashed potatoes, thinking, 'Why is my daughter telling me she's a witch? She knows my whole life is religion and family.'

"I learned to be more open about her religion, too. She loves all these potions. I have this skin condition. My hands get these little white blisters all over them and they itch like hell. Nothing has ever helped. Anna tells me she'll send me a cure. She boils herbs for days and comes up with this remedy. She sends it to me. I use it. It works. Her brew is the only thing that helps.

"Anna and I have a really good relationship. She always tests the waters. I go in kicking and screaming. She tells me she's proud of me." ☙

Q uestions of purpose and meaning begin visiting mothers when daughters enter adolescence. One roof shelters two women—daughter and mother—both searching for new identities. But for mothers, the journey is often delayed by the emotional demands of living with a teenager. Finally, when daughters leave, we have the space to focus on ourselves.

Before her daughters were born, the next anonymous mom lived on idealism. The civil rights movement, the antiwar movement, the prochoice movement, the new age movement, the environmental movement: Spiritual concerns consumed her youth. Then she got married, settled down in a small town, and had two daughters. Life changed. She spoke, reviewing those changes.

℮

SEARCHING FOR A NEW SELF
Thoughts from an Anonymous Mom

"I devoted my entire life to making the world a better place. I had worked with marginalized people stricken by poverty. I've always been interest in freedom and nonfreedom. The ways this culture gives some freedom and robs from others.

"When I had my daughters, my life changed. It had to. My idealism got lost in a million details. I made certain they ate, and got dressed, and brushed their teeth, and caught the bus, and got to school on time, and had friends to play with, and felt good about themselves, and loved themselves. From the ridiculous to the sublime, I gave them all my psychic energy. I did everything in my power to make them comfortable with themselves.

"Then my older daughter went to college and my younger decided to go to a private residential school. For twenty years, I had stayed in the same little rural community, keeping their lives stable. I woke up one day and realized I didn't have to stay there anymore. I could do anything I wanted, go any place I pleased.

"I thought, 'it's time for my daughters to take off, and it's time for me to take off.' I decided to put my ideals at the center of my life again. On a whim, I applied for this job on the other side of the country. I got it. I have the most incredible job I've ever had. I work as a program director of a foundation. My new work gives me the possibility of making a difference in the world in a way that has always been meaningful to me. All day, I meet with people, figuring out how best to spend money to make the world a better place.

"Now I have the maturity to do this work. I got that maturity from raising two adolescent girls. This opportunity opened to me because something had opened inside of me. In the process of trying to make my daughters comfortable with themselves, I became comfortable with myself.

"I remember this profound moment. I was sitting with my older daughter and her therapist. This therapist said, 'You can't accept imperfection in others if you can't accept imperfection in yourself.'

"The therapist sent that message to my daughter, but I heard it. I realized that to really have compassion for others, I needed compassion for myself. I demand less from others. I've settled into a mature self-acceptance.

"I'm flying. This is the most creative time in my life. I see my daughters blooming, and I'm blooming, too." ∞

Tara Bell recalled a similar day, the day she recognized her impending independence.

"I had just celebrated my fiftieth birthday. My job was ending at the end of the school year. My daughter was a senior in high school. She'd be leaving for college soon."

With all those changes pressing in on her, Tara stuffed her journal in her backpack and headed out for a hike. She walked through fields, along a river, up a craggy mountain, and settled on a ledge overlooking a valley. Sitting with inspirational beauty spread before her, she took out her journal and wrote:

> My next step is independence in a way I've never known. This is my time. How will I use it?
>
> My first thought was, "Who will I become?"
>
> The answer came on the next breath: who I really am.

Life doesn't deal out just one identity crisis per lifetime. Certainly the adolescent coming-of-age stands center stage. But off in the wings, mothers grapple with a parallel transformation.

As our adolescent girls try on new personalities, as they learn to be themselves, we face who we have become. Challenged by our daughters' experimentation, we rediscover lost fragments of ourselves and explore new expressions of our identity. As our girls challenge us to love and let go, we're thrust into a search for meaning and purpose.

Into the Limelight

on to a new stage

DURING A DAUGHTER'S ADOLESCENCE, A MOTHER FINDS comfort in the platitude "This too shall pass."

As final grace notes, Gail Parker, Stephanie Palladino, and Roberta Jones offer reassuring warmth. They write about the moment they realized, "All has turned out well." In the end, the adolescent tug-of-war between mother and daughter is replaced by a comfortable intimacy.

SURVIVOR
by Gail Parker

"Mom, *Survivor* is on."

My older daughter—recently graduated from college and living at home for a short time before she starts her career—brings tropical wine coolers into the family room and we settle in to watch the latest episode of the summer's hottest TV show. We've both gotten hooked, so this has become our Wednesday-night ritual.

We chatter practically the whole time the show is on. We check out the contestants' bathing suits and tans and tattoos and try to figure out who's going to get axed this week—who we *wish* would get axed—and analyze the contestants' strengths and weaknesses. We laugh or shriek and moan at some of the crazy things they have to do on this show to "survive," and wonder whether or not we'd be able to.

Suddenly it dawns on me: "Hey, we're having fun."

For a moment, time stands still as I savor the feeling, and in that moment I realize I've come to yet another milestone in my life. I am at peace with my daughter. She is no longer struggling to break free from her parents' control; she is free of it. She is no longer trying on different personas to see which one fits; she has found herself. She is no longer an adolescent, tossed about by confusing emotions; she is a young adult, steady and sure in the knowledge of where she's going. She's nervous and excited about all the big changes ahead, to be sure, but she is handling them with grace and aplomb. And I am at her side, proud and delighted.

Of course, it wasn't always so. Her balmy elementary school years left me completely unprepared for the turbulent middle school and high school years. We weathered the usual difficulties—the slammed doors ("Slam that door one more time and we're taking it off the hinges!"), the hissy fits, the selfish demands ("Take me and my friends to the mall, but don't say anything—and don't wear *that*"). But for some reason, there was more. The slick double life, the questionable friends, the dark, difficult days of choices poorly made. Mistakes on her part and on my part. Anger, resentment, hurt.

But then the college years came, giving us breathing space, and along with it, a new perspective. Slowly, almost imperceptibly, things began to change. My daughter left and came back, both literally and figuratively.

And now here we are, mother and daughter—*friends*—sitting in the family room together, watching the contestants of a game show called *Survivor*. Would we be able to do what it takes to win? Looks like we already have. ❧

SWEET EMBRACE
by Stephanie B. Palladino

I still remember the cool caress of the thrashing waves across my body, and the simple joy of bobbing up and down in their mighty grip. It was a Sunday in early September, not yet officially autumn. You were home for three weeks before returning to school. You stood by the shore's edge, your slender arms folded across each other, your ankles barely covered by the foam of the ebbing waves. I kept calling your name, but the sound of my voice was surely muffled by the roar of the ocean's song. Each time I completed my ride on the crest of a crashing wave, I'd look in your direction and wave my arm in a "come on in" sweeping motion. I so much wanted you to join us—to share the pleasure we had so recently discovered playing in this familiar sea.

What were you thinking as you watched us from land? Your mother, your father, your two younger sisters, all swallowed again and again by the pull of the white, foamy monster. Our heads disappeared beneath the surface and reappeared minutes later. We gesticulated back and forth to one another as we rocked across waves. Had you ever seen us so giddy?

As I surfaced above the water's pull once more, I glanced over to the shoreline, but strangers stood where you had been. I spotted you swimming in my direction. With each stroke, you locked your gaze on mine. One by one, each of us swam over to meet you. For a few sweet moments, your giggles and shrieks mixed with ours as we all frolicked together in the ocean's wet embrace. ∽

MAINTAINING FORM
by Roberta Jones

Rigidly prepared, like a diving
    board
maintaining its form,
I wait for you
as you painstakingly finish your
    climb
up the ladder,
both of us anticipating your dive.

I remember your first dive,
when I bribed you to let go
with promises of Barbie clothes.
I held you then,
as you brought up your courage,
and leapt off me into the pool.

Over the years, we've tested each
    other.
You've learned
I can hold up under your dives,
and I've learned
you always return after your swim.

Now, as you walk out to
the very end of me,
your toes hanging over my edge,
we're so practiced,

I flex slightly with the weight of
    this act,
but I won't buckle.

Before you dive,
you tell me another version of
    your five-year plan,
releasing the scent of freedom
lying dormant in my cells.
I want to go with you,
but I know I can't.

I shudder when you kick off,
and I can't suppress a groan.
But I quickly spring back
as I catch your splash.
Then I watch you swim away
and allow myself to fall apart
just for a while.

And though it may be a long
    time
before you come back,
I know you're not done
and I must remain where you
    left me,
maintaining my form.

ON TO A NEW STAGE ~ 285

Years later, you come back in the
    night
and I feel you unfasten the screws
that bind me to my post.
You take me to the edge of the sea,
where you leash an endless cord
through holes left by the screws.

I feel the pull of the moonlight
    on the tide
as you hold me in the water

while securing the cord to the pier.
You tell me this cord will keep me
tethered.
You can reel me in when you
    need me,
but I can also swim my own
    journey.

resources for mothers
of adolescent girls

These are a few possible places to look for support. These organizations may or may not suit your needs. Please use your judgment when considering each possibility.

Al-Anon Family Group Headquarters, Inc.
1600 Corporate Landing Parkway
Virginia Beach, VA 23454-5617
For meeting information in the United States and Canada,
call (888) 4AL-ANON
www.al-anon.org

BECAUSE I LOVE YOU
The Parent Support Group
PO Box 2062
Winnetka, CA 91396-2062
(310) 659-5289
www.becauseiloveyou.com

Families Anonymous, Inc.
PO Box 3475
Culver City, CA 90231-3475
famanon@FamiliesAnonymous.org

Mental Health Information Center
(800) 969-NMHA
TTY Line (800) 433-5959
www.nmha.org

National Mental Health Association
1021 Prince Street
Alexandria, VA 22314-2971
(703) 684-7722

Pachamama and Girls' Day
Ideas for Staying Close
PO Box 421
Leverett, MA 01054
Pachamama2@aol.com

PFLAG
Parents, Families, and Friends of Lesbians and Gays
1726 M Street, NW, Suite 400
Washington, DC 20036
(202) 467-8180
info@pflag.org

ToughLove
PO Box 1069
Doylestown, PA 18901
(215) 348-7090
toughlove.org

WEBSITES

www.strugglingteens.com

www.focusas.com (focus on adolescent services)

www.opheliasmother.com

www.opheliasmom.com

about the author

NINA SHANDLER, ED.D., is a licensed psychologist and author whose professional concerns have mirrored those of the baby-boom generation.

Nina received her doctorate from the University of Massachusetts. She has counseled women, children, and families in private practice, clinics, and schools. Throughout her professional life, she has presented workshops and lectures to parents, couples, and teachers. Her psychological articles and case studies have appeared in *The Family Therapy Networker, Teaching Tolerance*, the *Communiqué, Best Practices in School Psychology*, and the *Networker Case Study Book.*

Nina's *Estrogen: The Natural Way* (Villard, 1997) brought her considerable name recognition among women in midlife. Her writing career began twenty-five years earlier when she joined forces with her husband, Michael, to write *The Marriage and Family Book, Yoga for Pregnancy and Birth, Ways of Being Together,* and *The Complete Guide and Cookbook for Raising Your Child as a Vegetarian,* all published by Schocken Books.

Nina and Michael, organizational consultants, live in Amherst, Massachusetts. Their younger daughter, Sara, is now a junior at Wesleyan University in Middletown, Connecticut. Their older daughter, Manju, lives in New York City, where she is an artist, puppet-maker, and costume designer. Manju's credits include mask-making for the Broadway version of *The Lion King.*